Deep Smarts

How to Cultivate and Transfer

Enduring Business Wisdom

Dorothy Leonard

Walter Swap

HARVARD BUSINESS SCHOOL PRESS

Boston, Massachusetts

No part of this publication may be reproduced, stored in, or introduced into a retrieval system, or transmitted, in any form or by any means (electronic, me-chanical, photocopying, recording, or otherwise), without the prior permission of the publisher. Requests for permission should be directed to permissions@hbsp.harvard.edu, or mailed to Permissions, Harvard Business School Publish-ing, 60 Harvard Way, Boston, Massachusetts 02163.

Library of Congress Cataloging-in-Publication Data
Leonard-Barton, Dorothy.
  Deep smarts : how to cultivate and transfer enduring business wisdom / by Dorothy Leonard and Walter Swap.
    p. cm.
  Includes bibliographical references.
  ISBN 1-59139-528-3
  1. Mentoring in business. 2. Executive coaching. I. Swap, Walter C. II. Title.
  HF5385.L46 2004
  658.3'124—dc22

                                                          2004006928

The paper used in this publication meets the requirements of the American Na-tional Standard for Permanence of Paper for Publications and Documents in Li-braries and Archives Z39.48-1992.

*To the more than two hundred managers,
entrepreneurs, coaches, scientists, and consultants
whom we interviewed (many of them more than once)
in the course of writing this book. And especially to
Fred Gibbons, whose generously shared Rolodex
launched us on this journey.*

CONTENTS

WHY DEEP SMARTS? We did not choose the title of this book lightly. The term describes a *special form of experience-based expertise* that we believe is critical for managers to understand and appreciate—for their own benefit as well as that of their organizations. Two influences drove us to that conclusion: our prior work on innovation and creativity, and three years researching and writing about coaches attempting to transfer their wisdom to less experienced managers. In our earlier research on knowledge assets (*Wellsprings of Knowledge; When Sparks Fly*), we encountered individuals with deep smarts, but we did not single them out for special attention. However, that earlier work sensitized us to the significance of experience, expertise, and tacit knowledge in creating the huge gap between those with true business wisdom and those with mere competence.

All innovative undertakings morph, be they books, paintings, managerial initiatives, or children. Those of us charged with developing them should not delude ourselves that we can tightly control their progress. In our case, it was not intellectual curiosity alone that led us to explore side paths. We were running through an environment enlivened by economic earthquakes and the resulting chasms that suddenly appeared in our paths. When we started out in early 2000, new Internet companies were as thick as hiving bees, and our focus was on understanding how various wise "graybeards" were helping young entrepreneurs learn to manage new companies. The question driving us seemed straightforward: How do the older, more experienced folks transfer their knowledge? That is, how do coaches teach?

But wait! Reality was not so simple. When we looked around, we found that some of the coaches had peach fuzz instead of gray beards. And some of the gurus were not calmly dispensing wisdom, but were themselves milling around in confusion, wondering if their old rules still applied in the New Economy. Then the bubble burst. Some advice was vindicated; some was shown to be dead wrong. Failed entrepreneurs sheepishly returned to school. Gray hair and profitability were back in style. In less than two years, we had observed a truncated life cycle in knowledge—the birth and death of what was considered true and wise—and an experiment in how quickly intelligent, motivated people can learn. We had seen the value and limits of firsthand experience. Most important, from our front-row seats at the grand experiment taking place, we had witnessed the enormous difference between essential business wisdom and its counterfeits.

Our original question grew arms, amoeba-like. We needed to reexamine common assumptions about expertise and dig deeper into the very nature of practical wisdom itself. What constitutes expertise? How is it grown and nurtured? How do we know it when we see it? When is experience an essential guide? Can experience-based knowledge actually be transferred? In the face of huge uncertainty about what is true, what can managers do? And if some kinds of experience-based knowledge are so much more valuable than others, what do managers need to understand in order to exploit the potential benefits of business wisdom?

From our interviews, our firsthand observations of coaches and their protégés, we knew that the best coaches had gone beyond telling the novices "how it's done." These experts were not just attempting to *transfer* what they knew, but to coach their protégés to develop equivalent knowledge. Indeed, directly transferring wisdom was an impossibility because the coaches' deep smarts were the result of years of experience. Reflecting on our earlier research in large companies convinced us that deep smarts are tremendously important not just to coaches operating in the microecology of start-up companies, but to managers in mature organizations as well. Back to the field we went, to examine the role of expert coaching and learning inside such organizations. A huge amount of what we had learned in entrepreneurial situations applied. In mature organizations, as in start-ups, we found that deep smarts constituted more than technical expertise, but encompassed beliefs and assumptions underlying both decision making and coaching. But now we had a runaway book! Too much material to cover.

Fortunately for you, we had reviewers, to whose deep smarts we listened—*most* of the time. (You may recognize the spots in the book where we didn't!)

HBSP editor Jacque Murphy kept patiently reminding us that no matter how much fun we had telling the reader about our colorful adventures in Silicon Valley and India and Singapore, managers wanted the essential, actionable message distilled for them. Barbara Feinberg was a wonderful intellectual helpmate—for example, rescuing us from the pit of despair one frigid and memorable December day with a swift application of her own deep smarts. In two hours she solved a knotty structural problem that had bedeviled us for four months.

Research associate Brian DeLacey was our intellectual companion throughout this marathon. He ran alongside us for three years, enthusiastically contributing ideas, contacts, and voluminous background materials. He took primary responsibility for the study of six of the incubators and the start-ups they supported, as well as a number of the in-depth Harvard Business School cases we have drawn upon. The footnotes acknowledging his help seem paltry when weighed against his contributions. Fred Gibbons, highly respected denizen of Silicon Valley, opened his Rolodex to us and spent his social capital lavishly on our behalf. Kanwal Rekhi introduced us to the vibrant Indus community. One of his referrals, B. V. Jagadeesh, was extremely generous to us in India—both professionally and personally. The HBS research centers were instrumental in our research: Chris Darwall (then director in California) started us on the journey with the specific suggestion that we look at the role of mentor capitalists in promoting start-ups—and helped us find them; Camille Tang Yeh (executive director, Asia) provided essential help before, during, and after our research sojourns in Hong Kong and Singapore. And four anonymous reviewers provided encouraging and thoughtful commentary on our draft book.

A number of others contributed to the research: Mimi Shields, Andrew McLean, Allison Nicole, Liz Kind, Fred Young, and Michael Restivo all were involved to some degree in interviews, data analysis, or case writing. David Crosswhite and Harry Dent got us in the door at Best Buy and shared their experiences at Whirlpool. Kathy Farren, whose ability to juggle numerous details and logistics is exceeded only by her cheerful attitude, kept us as organized as anyone could. Jan Simmons pulled us over the finish line when we couldn't stand to look at the manuscript one more time. And Michelle Barton not only cheered us on when we faltered but helped us decide among several alternative paths at a critical juncture. The Harvard Business School Division of Research and Tufts University both generously supported our explorations; we could not have conducted this work without their financial investment and allowance of time devoted to research.

It is traditional for authors to thank their spouses at this point, and to mention their saintlike forbearance in the face of long hours of absence and devotion to the keyboard instead of to family occasions. We can't do that, because we are wedded to each other as well as to this endeavor. Instead, each of us thanks the other for patience and good humor during this 24/7/365 collaboration. We think it must be a bit like space travel. Close quarters and shared oxygen require attention to courtesy and ironing out small differences of opinion lest they grow. But that is true of marriage in general. And we are enormously grateful for having each other along on the trip—a partner to share the bumps and triumphs.

Winchester, Massachusetts
May 13, 2004

Deep Smarts

ONE

The Importance of Cultivating and Transferring Deep Smarts

DEEP SMARTS are the engine of your organization. You cannot progress without them, and you will manage more effectively if you understand what they are, how they are built and cultivated, and the ways they can be transferred. Throughout your organization are people whose intuition, judgment, and knowledge, both explicit and tacit, are stored in their heads and—depending on the task—in their hands. Their knowledge is essential. They are, relative to others, expert. These are the people with deep smarts, and it is not an exaggeration to say that they form the basis of your organizational viability.

There are many reasons for us to be concerned about identifying, nurturing, and transferring deep smarts. We face change of all kinds, at an unprecedented rate—and the nature of that change grows more unpredictable daily as technology expands options and global events complicate decision making. We need leaders with high levels of judgment, experience, and capability, as we have seen how profoundly even a few individuals lacking such abilities can influence the course of our lives and the lives of our organizations. We also know that in the coming decade, because of demographic shifts, the so-called developed nations are about to face a large short-fall of leaders and managers. We need to grow new ones, at *all* organizational levels, as expeditiously as we can. But we need people with deep smarts, not just high IQs.

More than forty years ago, Peter Drucker wrote: "It is only in respect to knowledge that a business can be distinct, can therefore produce something that has a value in the market place."[1] But not all knowledge is created equal. The knowledge that provides a distinctive advantage, both for organizations and for managers as individuals, is what we term *deep smarts*.

Deep smarts are a potent form of expertise based on first-hand life experiences, providing insights drawn from tacit knowledge, and shaped by beliefs and social forces. Deep smarts are as close as we get to wisdom. They are based on know-how more than know-what—the ability to comprehend complex, interactive relationships and make swift, expert decisions based on that system level comprehension but also the ability, when necessary, to dive into component parts of that system and understand the details. Deep smarts cannot be attained through formal education alone—but they can be deliberately nourished and grown and, with dedication, transferred or recreated.[2]

We cannot afford to leave the accumulation of deep smarts to chance and random experience. Rather, we need to be purposeful in our approach. Many current management practices, particularly the ways we try to transfer deep smarts, are ineffective. We unintentionally stunt the growth of this brand of expertise when we fail to differentiate between the kinds of knowledge that can be transmitted as fast brain food and those that need marinating and slow cooking.

What Do Deep Smarts Look Like?

We know we are in the presence of deep smarts when we see an expert quickly size up a complex situation and come to a rapid decision—one that proves to be not just good, but wise. After we have seen someone do this a few times, we think of him or her as "really smart"—but we don't mean just their native intelligence, although they often have that in abundance. We mean that we trust their judgment, that when many opinions are on the table, theirs have more weight with us. When we ask them a question, we have the sense that some powerful computer in their brains is rapidly sorting through relevant firsthand experiences, pieces of process knowledge, and evidence shaped by personal beliefs and interaction with other smart people to come up with a nuanced answer. So people with deep smarts have a different kind of expertise than those who deal exclusively with abstract problems (e.g., a theoretical mathematician). People with deep smarts address practical, real-life, and often urgent issues, and management is a field that requires this kind of expertise. Deep smarts are not infallible, of course. Even the most experienced expert can mislead or be misled—and we do talk about such hazards in this book. But this kind of special expertise is vital to organizational well-being. Let us look briefly at a couple of situations that show deep smarts at work—without suggesting that these vignettes demonstrate all the aspects of deep smarts in depth. (That's what the rest of the book is about.)

Deep Smarts in the Boardroom

*I*N EARLY 1997, *Intuit reached a critical crossroads in its life. Best known for its financial planning product, Quicken, the company had just sold off its bill-paying operations. As the* board met to consider a new strategic direction, there was little dissent about the strategy itself—but a lot about how to finance it. Because of a shortfall in revenue, the sentiment around the boardroom table was that the company could not meet its earnings commitment either for that quarter or for the foreseeable future. Board members were further resigned to an inevitable drop in stock price when the earnings were announced, from the current $22 to somewhere between $13 and $15 a share. However, they believed that it would be worthwhile to continue to miss earnings and invest in the new strategy.

Drawing on years of experience with a variety of companies and resulting deep smarts, then-CEO Bill Campbell argued passionately against this fatalistic viewpoint. Wall Street analysts, he argued, had already discounted the slower growth and the resulting decline in the top line. Lower revenues would not hurt the stock price. But deliberately deciding midway through the quarter to miss earnings was contrary to all good management practices. Perhaps even more important, he pointed out, if the stock dropped, employee options would be worthless, and some critical individuals might well leave the company. Such defections could hurt the company even more than the financial blow per se. It was pure bullshit that they could not spend money on new initiatives and still make the bottom line! He knew how to cut costs—and where to start.

Campbell's smarts prevailed. Not only could he detail where he would change operations, but he also understood the big picture, the financial environment. He could foresee Wall Street's reactions as well as those of his employees. Finally, he was savvy about how to influence his board members. The next few months were to prove him right. Management cut expenses, hit their quarterly financial targets, and the stock stayed steady. The course set out that day was successful for Intuit, and Campbell's promise to employees that the stock would double within a year was fulfilled.

Deep smarts like these not only enable those who possess them to act with conviction but also to convince others to follow their lead.

Now consider another person who has to make decisions based on inadequate information and experience-based intuition for a living.

Deep Smarts in Venture Capital

V INOD KHOSLA *has been described as "perhaps the best VC [venture capitalist] on the planet."*[3] *He has helped create more than forty companies, including several that brought him billions in personal wealth. What deep smarts enable him to see opportunities where others don't? In November 1995, Pradeep Sindhu approached Khosla with a "typically techie" idea: use algorithms to reduce the cost of memory and increase the speed of computing. Good idea? Not if one simply extrapolated from existing current markets. Cisco Systems was already well entrenched, selling to corporations; telecommunication carriers were uninterested in high-end routers as they had plenty of computing power for any needs they could foresee. Here is where Khosla's deep smarts came into play. From his experience as a cofounder of Sun Microsystems (and his work with start-ups thereafter), he knew that you can't look at customers' current solution sets to figure out what they will need next. Sun owed its existence to the inability of contemporary computer companies to look beyond their current customers' demands. Digital Equipment Corporation, for one, had passed up the opportunity to license from Stanford University the technology underlying distributed computing—and their loss was Sun's gain. Khosla believed that you need to look for changes in the assumptions underlying current businesses and technology: "Value creation points occur during transitions." So Khosla's reaction to Sindhu's proposition was: Forget corporations as customers. This technology isn't enough of a differentiator. But what if the Internet really took off? What if the* public *started sending huge quantities of data around? Then there would be a need for different services (i.e., he foresaw the exponential growth of companies like AOL). Such services would require a different type of router, and* that *was an interesting application. "It's not a quantitative analysis, but a qualitative run through the model," he explains. From these insights was born Juniper Networks.*

These two examples are drawn from leaders at the top of organizations. But deep smarts can be found at any level—and may lie unrecognized until those possessing them have departed. Nor are managers the only ones with such smarts. There are dramatic instances of individuals who lead in knowledge but who may not possess formal, hierarchical power. Consider the contribution of the scientist in the following anecdote.

Deep Smarts in Product Development

*I*N THE EARLY 1980S, *two companies producing tactical missiles were competing for a U.S. government contract that would net the winner billions of dollars over the thirty to forty years of expected weapons production. After each competitor had fired six working prototypes, it was clear that neither company had an edge; both missile designs fell short of the required performance. At this point, in one of the companies, a scientist with deep smarts intervened. Although he was not a member of the project team, he had more than twenty years' experience developing missiles and had heard about the difficulties encountered in the test. Calling together the primary project participants in an auditorium, he proceeded to awe them over several hours with a proposal for detailed changes that he had worked out by himself, in one week of concentrated effort. Methodically, and without notes, he walked them through the redesign, from the weapon point to its aft, explaining all the interdependent software, wiring, and hardware changes that would be required to win the competition. The implications were immense. The redesigned missile would require as many as four hundred people working up to a year and a half to get it ready for production. But his changes* *were supported and the company won the contract. More than twenty years later, it is still reaping the harvest sown by a man with deep smarts about the entire missile as a system.*

Applying Deep Smarts to Organizational Knowledge Gaps

The process of specifically building and transferring deep smarts aims to address knowledge gaps in the organization. A *knowledge gap* is, quite simply, the difference between what someone knows (and knows that she knows) and what she needs to know in order to accomplish some task with competence, if not expertise. Knowledge gaps may be chasms or cracks. They exist anytime and anywhere in our organization (or our private lives) when background —education, upbringing, life experiences—is insufficient for making wise decisions or taking effective action.

Consider the following examples of knowledge gaps that require the cultivation and transfer of deep smarts.

- The Jet Propulsion Laboratory (JPL) needed to pass along the understanding of why Mars Pathfinder missions conducted under the mantra of "better, faster, cheaper" succeeded or failed—but 40 percent of their experienced managers were about to retire. With them would go years of experience, judgment, and intuition. In fact, a number of managers believed that many JPL failures could be traced to a knowledge gap among inexperienced project managers—and some of those younger managers agreed with the assessment.

- Brad Anderson, CEO of the highly regarded retailer Best Buy, decided that the sustained success of his company depended upon building an internal, employee-based capability to innovate continuously. He didn't want a new department, segregated from the rest of the company, but an innovation process that would permeate the organization and guide strategy. However, although his employees were extremely bright, hard-working, and terrific at delivering on set goals, innovation had never been made part of their job description. Exhortation would not change the DNA of the organization. Anderson needed to have some deep smarts about the innovation process transferred into the firm.

- Venture capitalists Beckie Robertson and Sam Colella needed to "grow" a smart young entrepreneur, Benjamin Wayne, into a CEO who could take over start-up Collabrys and grow it quickly, before it was overwhelmed by the competition. Despite his youth, Wayne had a fair amount of relevant experience, but the company was formed to take advantage of the Internet—and both the technology and the market were evolving at a fast pace. The venture capitalist coaches had a lot of deep smarts about forming and growing companies; they had next to none about this new technology.

Three different situations; three different problems. But what all have in common is the need for deep smarts—to cultivate them and transfer them from relative experts, acting as knowledge coaches, to people with less experience so as to fill a knowledge gap.

Deep Smarts and Climbing the Ladder of Expertise

Of course, the world is not divided between the two extremes of novices and experts.[4] The cognitive territory between the two is occupied by intermediate levels of expertise. Whether to label a coach an "expert" or a "journeyman," or a start-up entrepreneur a "novice" or "apprentice," is usually a subjective decision. (See figure 1-1.) Unlike chess, for example, where international grand masters can almost always be expected to defeat lesser-ranked players, management employs no such comparative ratings of skill. Venture capitalists, coaches, and entrepreneurs are judged on the basis of the extent

FIGURE 1-1

Ladder of Expertise (Deep Smarts)

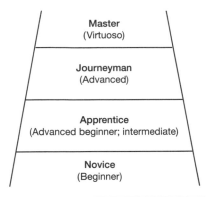

and depth of their experience successfully working in, leading, and assisting companies. Managers in large organizations are usually judged by a consistently profitable bottom line in the divisions they lead or by the number of innovations that succeed in the marketplace. Thus the assessment of whether or not someone is an expert in management depends largely on operational results, which are assumed to indicate some level of expertise.

However, it is useful to draw an analogy between the acquisition of deep smarts and the progression from novice to expert in some domain. Not only are we thus enabled to talk about stages of knowledge along the way, but we also have a way to characterize individuals who have accumulated knowledge, but whose performance falls short of expert. Attaining true deep smarts takes time as well as effort, and it would be misleading to assume that knowledge gaps between the extremes (novice and expert) can always be filled. All of us at some times in our lives assume the role of novice, and if we persevere in accumulating experience and knowledge, we may also have the privilege of taking the master's role. Most of us spend our professional and personal lives moving up the ladder of expertise. Figure 1-1 shows the ladder as open at the top. Even virtuosos can continue to learn, and those individuals with deep smarts who are open to new knowledge are the most valuable to our organizations.

Whom Is This Book For?

As may be obvious by now, this book is written principally for *general managers* who believe that investments in organizational learning and in people will grow the bottom line—and who recognize that developing the next generation of leaders is a critical part of their job. Such managers will read this book to deepen their own sophistication and managerial intuition about leadership. They will use this understanding to assess development strategies, succession planning, and potential losses of critical knowledge. They may also find reason herein to change some of their assumptions about—and reactions to—the behavior of those they manage. However, the book addresses *functional managers* as well—particularly those who have responsibility for developing, guarding, and leveraging the knowledge that provides the distinctive organizational advantage about which Drucker spoke. Their functional homes may be in human resources, research, or operations. Finally, we have found that the book has implications for the *individual* reader who may find guidance for developing his or her own career.

As discussed in more detail in the following sections, the ideas and observations in the book are synthesized from a number of sources. We are writing to the practitioner, the man or woman dedicating life energy and thought to leading others, so we draw heavily on our own field-based research in organizations—both large and small—for practical examples. In particular, we spent more than two years studying how novice managers in start-up companies attempted to absorb the deep smarts of their chosen coaches, and we followed the efforts of managers in several established and mature organizations to transfer deep smarts. From these in-depth studies grew the concept of deep smarts itself and the recognition that deep smarts can be deliberately built and transferred to the advantage of both organizations and individuals. But we have also drawn on the research of others in fields such as cognitive psychology, educational psychology, and social psychology to deepen our own understanding of the behaviors we observed. From this journey of discovery, we came to believe that understanding deep smarts is no more optional for today's sophisticated manager than is the ability to read a balance sheet.

Preview of the Book: Cultivating and Transferring Essential Business Wisdom

Figure 1-2 serves as a guide to both the book's content and its organization. First consider the two axes, starting with the horizontal: Internal (Self) and External (Other People). Deep smarts are formed and influenced internally by who we are—our personal background, education, and upbringing (left side of the figure). But they are also built and shaped by external sources: other people who coach us directly and people whom we admire and emulate (right side of the figure). As suggested by the vertical axis (Acquiring and Shaping), deep smarts build through two generic processes. The first is knowledge acquisition through personal or vicarious experience—that is, a buildup of knowledge, based on our own experience-based expertise or that of others, that can be used to quickly assess situations and make decisions, including the use of networks to solve problems.

FIGURE 1-2

The Role of Knowledge in Cultivating and Transferring Deep Smarts

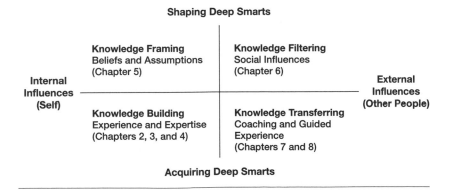

The second process, shaping, is less obvious and conscious—but no less powerful a part of deep smarts. As we will see in this book, deep smarts are, at least in part, socially constructed forms of expertise, so they include one's own convictions about what is real and true as well as whatever beliefs and assumptions we accept from admired or powerful others.

Each of the quadrants of figure 1-2 represents the interaction of the two axes and focuses on a topic important to understand in depth. The book begins with the lower left quadrant and proceeds clockwise—from knowledge building to knowledge framing and filtering, and then to knowledge transferring. Chapters 2 through 8 conclude with two forms of summary: Implications for Managers and a "Keep in Mind" list.

The following sections preview the major themes addressed in each chapter.

Building Deep Smarts

Chapters 2, 3, and 4 (lower left quadrant in the diagram) lay the foundation for the rest of the book. We hope that reading these chapters will encourage managers to think more deeply about the enabling or limiting nature of experience and the gap between a novice and an expert. Such heightened understanding will enable managers to leverage the connection between deep smarts and organizational performance.

- *Chapter 2: Experience matters—a lot.* This may seem obvious, but we have found that we have a different appreciation for this fact now that we understand *how* experience affects the brain and builds deep smarts. We address the role of experience and of learning-by-doing in creating an experience repertoire. We also discuss the capabilities and limits of simulations in building deep smarts.

- *Chapter 3: Experts are truly different.* People with deep smarts are experts—and they have capabilities that individuals further down the ladder of expertise don't have. What we think of as intuition is really swift pattern recognition, based on experience. Experts aren't just possessed of *more* knowledge; they are able to use their knowledge differently than the rest of us. We include know-who as a form of knowledge that builds deep smarts. And we look at the ways that expertise can mislead as well as benefit.

- *Chapter 4: Deep smarts can be assembled.* No one person or small group can hope to provide all the deep smarts that are necessary to deal with a complex project. And time constraints limit the ability to grow the expertise that may be needed. We discuss various ways in which deep smarts may be assembled, including the use of personal and professional networks.

Knowledge Shaping—Framing and Filtering

In chapters 5 and 6 (top two quadrants of figure 1-2), we address the "softer" side of expertise: the beliefs, assumptions, and social influences that contribute to deep smarts—for better and for worse. Even if we don't totally accept someone else's version of the truth, our decisions and actions are often influenced by others' convictions and beliefs. In order to understand and leverage deep smarts, then, we have to consider all the major sources of knowledge and influence that build and shape this kind of practical wisdom. Novices (and people lower in an organizational hierarchy or newly arrived in a group) are particularly vulnerable to such influences. However, our research showed that even highly experienced "experts" are far from immune. Part of what makes it so important for managers to understand deep smarts is that we don't tend to face these influences head-on. That is, we know that perception is often reality, that one person's truth is another's myth and that beliefs and social influences can affect the way knowledge is imported, evaluated, and diffused in our organizations. But we don't often challenge our own organizational and personal assumptions, or take social influences into account when we make decisions about how to develop our future leaders.

- *Chapter 5: Belief is knowledge—and vice versa.* Deep smarts
  are influenced heavily by personal, disciplinary, organizational, and cultural belief systems to a perhaps surprising
  degree. Knowledge is almost never objective, but particularly in social situations such as management, what we
  "know" is extensively shaped by our underlying assumptions about the world.

- *Chapter 6: We think for ourselves more rarely than we
  imagine.* People (and organizations) whom we admire
  very powerfully influence what we take to be truth. Moreover, we develop some of our deep smarts by imitating
  role models—many of whom are never aware of our emulation. However, therein may lie a problem, as without
  direct and extensive knowledge transfer, we rarely acquire
  enough of the deep smarts we admire to achieve the same
  level of success as our models.

Transferring Deep Smarts

Chapters 7 and 8 (lower right quadrant of figure 1-2) address
the question: How can deep smarts best be transferred? By the time
the reader reaches these two chapters, she will know that the answer depends on the sophistication of the transfer methods employed
—as well as on the relative depth of the smarts. We emphasize the
role of the expert (including expert managers) as knowledge coaches
in this segment for a number of reasons, primarily because deep
smarts cannot be easily hired or swiftly replicated. We draw a distinction between the usual concept of a mentor in an organization
and a knowledge coach. While some of the specific coaches we refer
to in this book also served as personal mentors, we find that in many
situations, mentors are not expected to transfer skills or know-
how. Rather, mentors help individuals hack their way through the corporate jungles and understand the organizational norms and politics. Here we are concerned with the way that coaches help build deep
smarts—in part by transferring as much of their own knowledge as

they can to their protégés and peers, but more importantly, by guiding the experiences of the protégés so they may create their own deep smarts.

- *Chapter 7: Knowledge coaches can speed learning.* Knowledge coaches have a complex but potentially valuable role in organizational learning. They can be drawn from the ranks of apprentices or journeymen as well as from those of the masters—although the smarts transferred will necessarily be more fragmentary than if the coaches have reached mastery. We discuss matchmaking between coach and protégé, some of the pitfalls of the psychological contract between the two, and the ways that people just one step ahead on the ladder of expertise can teach. We also lay out four modes of knowledge transfer used by coaches, ranging from very directive teaching to more self-directed learning.

- *Chapter 8: Guided experience is the most powerful transfer method.* We focus on the best use of knowledge coaches— to build deep smarts in their protégés by guiding them through various kinds of experience. In particular, we look at the way that guided practice, guided observation, guided problem solving, and guided experimentation grow capabilities similar to those the coaches have—including the tacit dimensions of their knowledge. The last three techniques are particularly powerful for encouraging skills in innovating.

The Challenge of Cultivating Deep Smarts

Chapter 9 draws together the themes of the book. In this concluding chapter, we examine the implications of cultivating and transferring deep smarts for managers both as leaders and as individuals—and the challenges to doing so. We suggest ways that managers may wish to apply the insights in the book to their development of future leaders, and to their own careers.

Research for the Book

The past few years have taken the two of us on a journey to understand what constitutes deep smarts and why they are important to us all—but especially to those who are charged with helping organizations learn efficiently and effectively. In order to understand how to cultivate and transfer deep smarts, we trained our sights on novices (first rung of the ladder shown in figure 1-1) who were being coached by individuals further up the ladder. In their inexperience, such novices provided a foretaste of the problems that leaders in today's organizations might well face when the forecast of an imminent dearth of experienced leaders comes to pass. Because deep smarts constitute practice-based wisdom, our research was conducted in the field, in different-sized organizations, over several years. We started with a study of a particular cohort of novice managers.

In the years 2000–2001, a group of entrepreneurs unwittingly took part in a global experiment to learn complex new management behaviors—in a hurry. The experiment was to start a new business based on a poorly understood technology, in unexplored markets, and in the face of extreme competition. Capital was no problem; it was abundant. Deep smarts were scarce. The participants weren't all total novices, and those who were didn't always realize that they were. Their coaches were not all experts—and those who weren't didn't always realize that they weren't! But the entrepreneurs generated a stream of start-ups that were the equivalent of laboratory fruit flies—companies hatching at historically unprecedented rates of speed. The entrepreneurs presided over their success or, far more likely, demise at equally rapid rates. It was an unusual opportunity to see relatively inexperienced managers trying to innovate and operate, to learn while doing at a frenetic pace, and to observe relative experts attempting to transfer their own practice-based smarts. Of course, we are speaking of the Internet boom.

We were in California's Silicon Valley and in Boston, Massachusetts, during 2000, when Internet companies were birthing in cubicles, garages, boardrooms, and dorm rooms. We interviewed the entrepreneurs and their coaches, followed two companies in great detail from their inception, and wrote detailed cases on four of the companies. To Hong Kong, Singapore, India, and China we followed the tentacles of ready money, wild ambition, and encouragement from the investment world that spawned start-ups there, often with the assistance of coaches in the United States. And when the boom turned to bust in 2001, we went back to the thirty-five companies and reinterviewed both the entrepreneurs and the coaches we had studied earlier. The swift birth and death cycle of these companies and the rapid rise and fall of what passed as business wisdom provided an unusual opportunity to analyze, close-up and personal, the nature of true deep smarts versus purported ones, and to observe the difficulties of building and transferring this practice-based wisdom. (See the appendix for a brief but more comprehensive description of this initial study.)

The coaches in this entrepreneurship study were of three types: (1) venture capitalists, working for a firm managing investment funds; (2) mentor capitalists,[5] that is, wealthy individuals (in our study, always cashed-out entrepreneurs) who had experience in starting up companies and had invested money and their own coaching efforts in start-ups; and (3) the managers in incubators—organizations that provided space, funding, and/or other forms of help to entrepreneurs of nascent companies. In the period of time we studied, hundreds of these incubators sprang up—start-ups in their own right—to nurture new companies and provide alternative funding sources. All three types of coaches were engaged in similar knowledge transfer endeavors.

As we were drawing this study of start-ups to a close, we embarked on several case studies in large established organizations to check our observations in a different setting. In organizations such as the World Bank, Best Buy, Whirlpool, and the Jet Propulsion Laboratory, the impetus for managers to develop and transfer deep smarts from coaches to relative novices is different from in start-ups—but the management issues are quite similar.

The preponderance of examples in the book are drawn from situations involving innovation. There are a number of reasons for this.

First, managing innovation involves a complex set of knowledge-based skills; thus innovation projects offer a rich context for both creating and transferring deep smarts. Second, we are aware of the dual demands on managers today: Keep daily operations going and improve them at the same time. Fly the plane and redesign it in midair. Almost every organization we can think of today is wrestling with the same dilemma: how to "make the numbers" with current operations and simultaneously innovate. How to preserve and pass along hard-won knowledge about what works. And how to forge a culture that actively embraces knowledge transfer and learning. Tomorrow's leaders, coming up through the ranks today, are unlikely to escape this innovation dilemma, and their coaches will have to help them prepare for continuous change and learning. Third, we authors can bring our own constantly evolving smarts to bear on innovation. We have spent years studying and writing about creativity and the implementation of new technologies, setting up new businesses, and promoting organizational change initiatives.

When we started the research for this book, we had management issues in mind exclusively; however, as we researched and wrote, we found ourselves remarking on how useful it might have been in our own careers had we better understood the nature of deep smarts. Therefore, we believe there are implications here for individuals in their personal lives as well as in their professional work, managing the development of personnel, and we address some of those implications for individual career development in chapter 9. We are all experts; we are all novices. We all confront knowledge gaps; we could all be, and use, coaches. We could all wring more from experience and learn more effectively by ourselves and from others.

TWO

Building Deep Smarts
Through Experience

T HE SINGLE MOST IMPORTANT THEME of this book is
that people learn—create and recreate knowledge—through
experience. "Of course," you say. But if it's so obvious, why don't
we *manage* as if we believed it? Part of the answer is that the statement is deceptively simple. There are all kinds of experiences—real
and simulated, guided and unguided, planned and random, broad
and deep. In this chapter, we aim to persuade you that you will
manage others, coach subordinates or peers, and shape your own
career better if you understand these distinctions and the connection between experience and developing deep smarts. Figure 2-1
highlights this quadrant of our knowledge diagram.

FIGURE 2-1

Deep Smarts and Knowledge Building

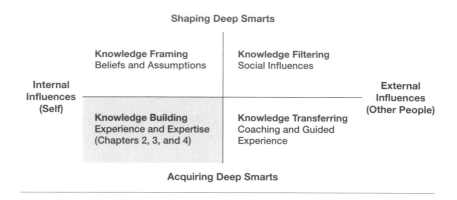

Experience—When Does It Matter?

What is the most critical question you want to ask the surgeon who is going to operate on you? You've sat in the waiting room and you've seen the diplomas on the wall. Maybe you've had time to step close enough to see how long ago the degree was granted. If it was three years ago, do you think, "Good—this person has the latest knowledge"? Or do you want to ask, "How many times have you done this before . . . successfully?" Surgeons learn through practice. On us, the patients. Despite increasingly sophisticated simulations, medical school students have to learn through direct experience how to locate a vein, insert a needle, and draw blood; what questions to ask to distinguish a heart attack from heartburn; and when to prescribe a medication with possible serious side effects.[1]

And what happens when those deep smarts based on vast experience suddenly vanish? Several years ago, a leading expert in fitting specialty contact lenses for people with cornea diseases died suddenly, before she had fully trained a protégé to take over her practice. Dr. Eleanor Mobilia's career spanned fifty years. She had conducted decades of research on contact lenses and had fitted thousands of patients. The protégé, Dr. Janet Rand, reflected on the difficulties of recreating Dr. Mobilia's deep smarts:

There are a lot of different scenarios for the shape of the cornea due to how the eye heals. They're like snowflakes. Everyone heals differently, so it's a very inexact science. Dr. Mobilia had fit thousands of eyes of each shape and she knew the type of lenses that would best be tolerated. I'm sure she had a plan for how to fit patients with really irregular corneal transplants. But most of her knowledge there was lost. After she passed away, I had a transplant patient with an eye that was so flat the lenses would just fall off. Nothing I tried worked. . . . I'm sure [Dr. Mobilia] knew by looking at some patients, this is impossible and not to even try fitting them until they had further surgery.[2]

So we know there are times when experience matters, and we even have a pretty good idea of what kinds of experience we hope a person has accumulated. But do we have a similar appreciation for the importance of experience in designing our own careers, in managing the careers of others, or in building and retaining deep smarts within our organizations?

By 2002, almost 40 percent of the science and engineering workforce at the Jet Propulsion Laboratory (JPL) was eligible for retirement. By 2006, half of the entire workforce of NASA (National Aeronautics and Space Administration) will be. These birthplaces of so many space missions, including the Pathfinder missions to Mars and the space shuttle program, could lose decades of experience. But does it matter? Do you see it as "new blood" replacing "deadwood"? Veteran project manager John Casini sees some advantages: "It's not all bad that people retire. . . . People need to move out of the top positions in order to allow in younger people with newer thoughts, better thinking, more innovation. . . ." On the other hand, his equally experienced colleague Joe Yuen doesn't "see any benefit from having experienced people going out the door—none at all." Much depends, of course, on the criticality of the experience lost. Michael Hecht, a principal technologist at JPL and by his own admission one of the inexperienced project managers who was bounced into this new management position out of necessity, sums up the issue bluntly: "The worst thing about having inexperienced people running projects is that it only takes one mistake to lose a mission."[3]

The loss of experience through retirements is widespread. As cities and states struggle to balance budgets, enticing longtime employees to retire is a common solution—but one that has unintended consequences. Referring to three brothers retiring with a total of 121 years of service in Boston city government, one observer noted, "They play critical roles, and they basically have the years of institutional memory that the city has relied on to make critical decisions in running the city, whether it's collective bargaining or something else."[4] The forced "retirement" of legislators in some states as a result of term limits certainly infuses new blood into deliberative bodies, but also wipes out the hard-earned knowledge of negotiation and compromise with political colleagues. The result can be legislative gridlock.

We all face knowledge gaps as we plan our careers and manage our organizations, even if the consequences of filling those gaps are not as dire as a lost space mission or an ineffective government. In this chapter we will examine the critical role of experience in developing deep smarts.

- How does experience build knowledge? Should experience be *designed* to build certain kinds of knowledge?

- How do we know what past experience is important for the future?

- When is broad experience more important and when is depth critical?

- Are there good substitutes for direct experience?

Understanding How Experience Builds Deep Smarts

As we will discuss in detail in chapter 3, the ability to see patterns in a sea of information is a hallmark of deep smarts.[5] At the heart of building this pattern-recognition ability is experience. In this section we discuss how experience builds deep smarts and the resulting ability to recognize patterns. But all experiences are not created equal. Individuals and managers in organizations frequently allow experiences to accumulate randomly or reactively. It is possible, however, to think purposefully or strategically about building a repertoire of experiences.

Experience Repertoires

Consider an accumulation of experiences as forming a distribution. Throughout a person's life and career, he experiences a variety of situations, some quite frequently, others more rarely. The situations will rarely be identical, but over time the person samples tasks with enough common characteristics that he begins to build a repertoire, a menu of experiences that apply to particular situations. An experienced management coach recalls: "I've done a wide variety of things in business—everything from fighting the government and unions to setting up IPOs [initial public offerings] to doing acquisitions, divestitures, ramp-ups. Having lived through all that is very valuable."[6]

Some of this repertoire of experiences may grow haphazardly, as a response to changes in the environment. But much is built up deliberately, either designed by the individual or dictated by professional training. In either case, the emphasis may be on developing depth of experience within a narrow range or on attempting to cover a broad range with correspondingly less depth. The surgeon who removes your gallbladder may vaguely recall enough from her days in medical school to theorize about why your left foot is bothering you, but you are unlikely to ask her about these problems because she has deliberately shaped her practice around understanding your plumbing more than your structural support system. On the other hand, you rely upon your primary-care physician to speculate broadly enough about the pain in your side to send you to one specialist after another to track down the source, be it muscular or organ-related. The surgeon has elected to develop deep smarts within one experience distribution—a particular kind of surgery—and will have few experiences outside that specialty. The primary-care physician has a different kind of deep smarts as a result of accumulating many experiences across a wide variety of medical specialties. For him, expertise resides in diagnosis, an ability to handle a large number of relatively common complaints, and managing an extended network of specialists.

Within any experience repertoire, some experiences occur frequently and others are rare. If the repertoire is represented by the usual bell-shaped curve of a normal distribution,[7] the frequent, common events constitute the tall middle segment and the rare situations are in the "tails." (See figure 2-2.) Even beginners in a given career—management, medicine, landscaping—will encounter the common events often and will soon become familiar with those situations. As they encounter less common situations and practice their responses, they expand their experience repertoires, enhance their pattern-recognition skills, develop competence, and move up the ladder of expertise.

We do not always require direct experience to build an experience repertoire. Building deep smarts often starts with capturing and codifying other people's prior experience. Managers learn from accounts of "best practices," or perhaps vicariously from autobiographies recounting the trials and (more often) triumphs of industry leaders; chess players pore over classic games of past masters. Some fields are better than others at documenting and assembling experience-based wisdom. And some professions are better at paying attention to the tails of experience distributions—the rare events. In medicine, researchers publish unusual cases and discoveries so

FIGURE 2-2

Distribution of Experiences

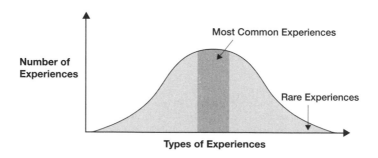

that they become codified in a gradual accretion of knowledge. In this volume, however, we are most interested in the knowledge that is *least* likely to be captured and codified in publications and archives. The knowledge embodied in people and their brains—and built up through years of experience—is simultaneously the hardest to manage and the most important to us as individuals and as managers.

How does one best build a repertoire broad enough to encompass rare events and system wide effects, but deep enough to allow the swift application of judgment that deep smarts permit? As we shall discuss in chapter 7, in frequently occurring situations, rules of thumb, best practices, and other forms of codified guidance can be very useful in communicating the lessons of experience. But what about those situations in the "tails"?[8] For managers, the discovery of a major shortfall in funds that could indicate fraud by a trusted employee? For physicians, the rare drug interaction or the fatal disease masquerading as a common ailment? For the commercial pilot, a landing gear failure, or smoke pouring into the cabin? The rare event may be totally unimportant—or critical.

One of the reasons so many Internet start-ups failed was that their founders had so little entrepreneurial or managerial experience to match their technological deep smarts. Moreover, what experience they did have was gained with only one end of the distribution of possible financial situations—an up market. Growth was the common environment and money was abundant. (See figure 2-3.)

FIGURE 2-3

Experience Repertoire of Entrepreneurs During Boom Times

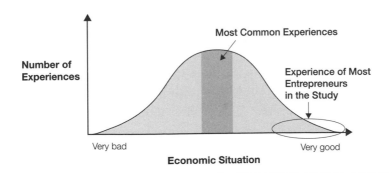

After the Internet bubble burst, these start-ups suddenly faced a new situation: scarcity of money. Having never lived through straitened economic times, the novice managers reached into their experience repertoires for something to apply to the new situation, and found—nothing! Experienced coach Audrey MacLean "told everybody that it's a nuclear winter and that start-ups need to turn themselves into small furry animals that don't need much to eat and won't freeze to death." Easier said than done, if you've never faced a nuclear winter before. These entrepreneurs were smart. They knew a lot about technology and perhaps more than anyone about the Internet and its potential. But deep smarts in one area don't make experts in another—an insight that escaped even some of the most savvy and experienced coaches. Reflecting on what she had learned about coaching young entrepreneurs during 2000 and 2001, venture capitalist Heidi Roizen admitted: "My biggest mistake was believing that somehow people with no experience, because they understood the new economy, were going to be masters at controlling costs and managing operations."

Most of the venture capitalists and mentor capitalists in our study had lived through times of scarcity as well as plenty. Their experience repertoires were extensive and they recognized a pattern when they saw it. Many tried in vain to transfer their experience with lean times to their protégés. Stan Meresman tells of countless board meetings in which he raised the necessity of drastically cutting costs. The inexperienced entrepreneurs were devastated and would tend to blurt out something like: "We wouldn't be able to do that unless we take out 25 percent of our people and not do this new project." Right! But they still didn't really understand. Meresman sent them off to cope with this new reality, knowing that they would come back having cut too little. He would have to go through all the reasoning again and show them how their tiny 5 percent cutback still didn't get them to cash flow positive. Such minor tinkering with the budget only gave them another quarter or two before they went "off the cliff." In contrast, the experienced entrepreneurs "got it, did it, ran with it; you came to the next board meeting and it was already implemented."

Douglas Kay, president of Mondo Media, was the kind of experienced entrepreneur Meresman was speaking of. Mondo Media is a San Francisco company that creates animated content, such as minishows, for the Web, then syndicates the content to a network of affiliates. As the market for online content began to collapse in 2000, Kay recalls his coach telling him, "If you're going to make a change, make it as dramatic as possible so that you don't have to do it again." The coach remembers telling Kay, "Don't put time into looking for additional money, don't put time into thinking that there's a great acquisition partner out there if you just could find them. Put time into figuring out how to make sure the money that you have is going to last as long as it can, so you can reinvent your business." Kay and the rest of Mondo's management team took the coach's advice to heart. Between our first interview with Kay in 2000 and our second in 2001, Mondo's payroll was reduced from 120 to 50. The drastic action helped ensure the company's future. Among the scores of Internet content producers, Mondo Media was one of the few left standing and, in fact, it attracted more than $17 million in third-round venture funding in early 2001. Kay didn't necessarily have experience with "nuclear winter," but he did understand the concept of reduced resources—so hearing the message once was enough for him to take action.

Learning by Doing

Experience defines us professionally—especially in those fields in which practice is more critical than "book learning." Management is such a field, as is medicine. No matter how prestigious her medical school, we are more interested in how many times our physician has successfully performed the exact procedure we are about to undergo than whether she got an A in biochemistry.

In an article about his own personal learning to be a surgeon, Atul Gawande writes:

> *Surgeons . . . adhere to a curious egalitarianism. They believe in practice, not talent. People often assume that you have to have*

great hands to become a surgeon, but it's not true. . . . To be sure, talent helps. . . . Nonetheless, attending surgeons say that what's most important to them is finding people who are conscientious, industrious, and boneheaded enough to keep at practicing this one difficult thing day and night for years on end. . . . And it works. . . . Indeed, the most important talent may be the talent for practice itself . . . a person's willingness *to engage in sustained training.*[9]

It is this willingness to practice (despite the fact that experts enjoy practicing no more than the rest of us) that distinguishes those who go on to become master surgeons, cellists, marksmen, award-winning salespeople, or CEOs. Only by such practice do surgeons master the intricate dance between the impulses of the brain and those of the hand, or salespeople the connection between body language and a sale. No amount of reading can substitute for building up the tacit dimensions of knowledge. For instance, there are no practical ways of calibrating the amount of pressure to apply when inserting a catheter. The physician learns by inserting many catheters. The salesperson learns to close deals by making lots of sales. In a television interview, the three-year-old Tiger Woods was asked how he had become such a good golfer. " 'Practice,' " the boy said, though the word came out 'pwactice.' "[10] It may have taken another ten years or so for Woods to develop deep smarts about playing golf, but he has never stopped practicing every shot to further burnish his game.

Practice means doing something more than once, but mindless repetition can consolidate bad habits. Recent work shows that "false memories"—that is, "recall" of fictitious events that someone has repeatedly suggested have actually occurred—are processed identically to true memories in the brain,[11] indicating that what we "know" to be true can be utterly false, just practiced a lot. *Deliberate practice* goes beyond rote repetition to "doing one's homework" mindfully and with reflection, generally with the help of feedback to guide one's progress.[12] We will explore this in more depth in chapter 8.

Learning from Entrepreneurial Experience

One of the great advantages to conducting a study of how novice entrepreneurs learned during 2000–2001 was that the market provided an agonizing, acute intervention in the learning process. The abrupt shift from tropical to arctic financial climate whipsawed hapless novice managers from one extreme tail of the experience distribution of financial environments to the other. The entrepreneurs learned that they had to manage very differently—and the coaches learned that their prior experience was more applicable than they had thought. (See figure 2-4.) The fortuitous timing of our study of entrepreneurs and coaches therefore provided an in-depth example of how and what people learn from direct experience.

We asked each of the entrepreneurs in the study to rate themselves on the ladder of expertise (ranging from novice to master, as described in chapter 1) a year ago and at present. There was a change from 2.07 (slightly above "apprentice") to 2.94 (slightly below "journeyman"). On average, the entrepreneurs also saw themselves as more self-sufficient than they were a year earlier: Reliance on "my own knowledge, experience, and education" increased from 42.5 percent to 52.9 percent, indicating that they believed they had learned from their managerial experiences of the

FIGURE 2-4

Coaches' and Entrepreneurs' Experience Distributions

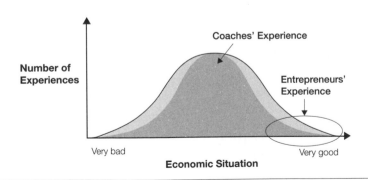

past year. Of course, these are self-ratings and retrospective ones at that; but they do suggest progress on the road to deep smarts. (See the appendix for a full description of these questionnaire items.)

But what *kinds* of smarts did the novice entrepreneurs say they learned between 2000 and 2001? Much depended upon how reflective they were about the experience they were going through. Some were already abstracting their experience into rules of thumb— guidelines for the next time they undertook company building. A few examples follow.

- *Hire and fire to cultivate and retain deep smarts.* Unimobile's Vishaal Gupta voiced a lesson that many managers never learn and then wonder why their company is not more innovative: "One thing I realize very clearly now is that you always need to hire people who are better than you. . . . You need to have the right team." And Beth Cross put very succinctly what we have heard many highly experienced general managers say: "You never let people go too early; you always let them go too late."

- *Protect your intellectual property.* One CEO of a start-up noted: "The things that survive are technology and patents and basic value that you're building into the company. . . . [If I were to start over] I would say: 'We need to secure intellectual property protection.' "

- *Spend to invest, not to impress.* Cambridge Incubator's Tim Rowe observed, "If I were to build this incubator again I wouldn't have these desks, I wouldn't have these armchairs. That money is better in the bank or spent growing the business."

- *Trust yourself—but be willing to listen to others as well.* Inexperienced managers have to learn trade-offs between being carried away with their own intelligence and being paralyzed by lack of self-confidence. Before being humbled by a crumbling environment for telecoms, an entrepreneur in a telecommunications start-up recalled thinking, " 'I am invincible; I can do anything.' I believed I knew everything." Over time, he learned to listen to his coaches.

Mondo Media president Douglas Kay had the opposite problem at the outset; if he were to return to his beginnings, he says he would "trust my instincts more. I'm trained as an engineer—very analytical and process-oriented. I've learned to make decisions on less data, be comfortable making the call on 60 percent data instead of trying to get to 90 percent." And Semprio founder Paul Hardy summed up the way that he learned to tread a middle ground between the two extremes of over- and under-confidence: "What I have learned is a balance between listening and trusting myself and my own experiences—and times when I say I really have to listen to these guys, they do bring some great experience. . . . I have had to reduce my amount of 'control freak,' learn to listen, but learn when to draw a hard line."

For those novices managing a start-up for the first time, the "lessons learned" were subject to the caveat that learning from a sample of one is hazardous. However, at least this one experience, which was enriched (a form of enrichment few would want to repeat) when the market soured, started them on the road to building a whole distribution of experiences. Ash Munshi, who had started two companies and was on his third in 2002, remarked:

> *I consider each one of these companies as a data point of experimentation for me personally. . . . My primary goal is to become better at what I do, set a target for myself, enjoy the experience of getting there, but learn something so that the next time I can do it better. So I think about this whole [entrepreneuring] process as iterative refinement.*

Most of the entrepreneurs were so focused on their immediate problems that they could not take this fairly objective view of their own learning process. Only the most reflective among us can recognize at the time that a difficult lesson learned is a valuable contribution to an experience repertoire. But viewing any of life's failures in this light provides a foundation for progress.

Building Receptors in the Brain

Neuroscientists have known for some time that experience alters the structure of the brain, encoding the new information in specific structures and thereby modifying those structures.[13] The result? Direct experience is more effective in locking in memories that can be retrieved later, and hence is more useful than is vicarious learning.[14]

In order for someone to capture complex, experience-based knowledge, the person's brain has to contain receptors—neural structures that are the physical representations of frameworks, domain knowledge, or prior experiences—to which the current inputs can be connected. Without these receptors, the new messages and information cannot be incorporated into the brain structures, and remain relatively incomprehensible or meaningless.[15] Recent studies using functional magnetic resonance imaging (fMRI), for example, have found that as people become more "expert" in recognizing novel three-dimensional facelike objects, there is increased activation of a region of the brain (the fusiform gyrus) associated with recognition of faces. That region is the neurological receptor center for facial recognition.[16] Neuroscientists who study the specialized functions of the brain note that specific areas link our perceptions to long-term memory. For instance, when someone at a party smiles at us, the image of his or her face will be received and processed in the fusiform gyrus. This region in turn connects to long-term memory in the prefrontal cortex, and we then smile in recognition of a friend, or frown in suspicion at an antagonist.

What happens if we perceive something, but there is nothing in our memory to link it to—nothing that helps us make sense of what we see or experience? To someone who is not a "gamer"—someone who plays a lot of electronic games—the following question is almost unintelligible: "What three-dimensional avatar would you like in the next MUD you enter?" Gamers have had the experience of representing themselves in cyberspace as some three-dimensional object (an avatar) while playing in a multiuser domain (MUD). Even when the terms are explained, however, a nongamer will not know what criteria to use in selecting an avatar, or what it is like to enter an environment shaped by other users. Someone who has not played such games or, more basically, considers them alien territory, lacks the receptors to process the query intelligently. We all have these blank spots in our brains—gaps in our experience that make it difficult for us to process a totally new experience. *In fact, information does not become knowledge until it connects with something we already know.* This is what is meant by the popular comment that some information "went over my head."

This peculiarity of our brains means that coaches and learners have to consciously *build* receptors, and be aware when they are missing—when there is nothing in the learner's memory to which a new experience, topic, or concept can be tied. As we will see in the following chapters, receptors are created in a number of different ways. New experiences—serendipitous or planned, real or simulated—can challenge the mind and thus begin to grow the receptors for further experience. Frameworks, overviews, and rules of thumb provided by someone more experienced all provide a mental architecture to which experience can be related. The box "Building Receptors at GE Healthcare" provides an example of how even a seemingly simple decision can fail if the team lacks appropriate receptors.

Building Receptors at GE Healthcare

WHEN GE Healthcare set up a new operation overseas, it appointed an experienced manager to be a "pitcher" and someone in the new plant as the "catcher." From long experience, veteran GE Healthcare "pitcher" Ron Speagle knew that having a ready, willing receptor for knowledge about a changed process helps ensure that local employees understand both *why* and *how* processes are to be designed or changed. Speagle recalled a simple example of helping a team in China understand the importance of what GE calls "critical-to-quality" (CTQ) factors. When he arrived at the Chinese plant, he found planning under way to free up space for expanded

continued

production by relocating raw materials from the manufacturing facility to a warehouse. The local team was ready to sign the lease and start moving materials, but had not applied a formal CTQ process. From his experience, Speagle could see numerous potential problems with the chosen site. Speagle notes, "This was a good team, but their different experience caused them to overlook the importance of the total material flow process and how its quality was essential for manufacturing and shipping." For this team, there were no receptors to initiate a CTQ process or evaluate a "total material flow process." They needed to be taught to "catch" what Speagle was pitching. Simply vetoing the chosen site would transfer little knowledge. Instead, Speagle helped the team develop a CTQ list for evaluating sites. The critical factors included such issues as proximity to the manufacturing plant, easy access for large trucks, road conditions between facilities, and basic amenities for employees. List in hand, the team members went to visit the selected site. They could see that it met few of the criteria and immediately disqualified it. However, thanks to the exercise of applying the CTQ framework, the team now had a basic understanding about siting facilities and a new set of receptors on which to build experience.

Learning Through Simulations

One way to ensure that people widen the range of experiences through which they learn is to construct a set of *simulated* experiences.[17] Simulations can range from simple role-playing scenarios, to engaging case studies that relate to one's work, to full-immersion, multisensory, virtual reality war games. While direct engagement with real situations and real people is the "gold standard" for experiential learning, simulations offer a number of attractive benefits. First, simulations can be a highly efficient means of creating receptors, enabling the person to make better sense of later real experiences. Second, simulations can help develop certain skills more efficiently than real experiences. Third, simulations allow practice with rare and/or dangerous events that may be difficult or impossible to create in the real world (e.g., a jumbo jet spiraling out of control), thus filling out the learner's experience distribution. Fourth, simulations allow users to take risks and learn through failure without causing real consequences.

Sense-Making Receptors

Simulations help the learner to develop or build upon the receptors necessary for the acquisition of more complex knowledge. Rather than relying on haphazard, unguided (albeit real-world) experience, simulations focus attention on specific knowledge gaps and thus enable one to target unfilled areas of an experience distribution. Simulations can also literally be "rewound" and replayed for any number of learners. Thus, receptors can be developed and experience repertoires broadened to the extent that the simulation designers have resources and the learners have time to engage. The famous case method of education, originally imported from law to business at Harvard, is an example of transfer of expertise through intense simulation. For the two years of their business education, the M.B.A. students make decisions about business situations drawn from real life. The assumption is that by practicing being a manager (and building on receptors developed by the students over an average of four years of business experience prior to matriculation), the graduates will develop many more receptors and enhanced pattern-recognition abilities.

Several years ago, an M.B.A. student from a military background told of preparing for his role as a peacekeeper in Haiti. A diligent learner, he first went to the site of the Center for Army Lessons Learned and scanned the hard-earned, experience-based advice offered for people in his position. Then he took part in a simulation of a bread riot. "I made all the same mistakes everyone else did," he said ruefully. "But then I went back to the list of what to do and not do—and it made a lot more sense to me." The simulated experience had helped to create the receptors that were necessary for accurate pattern recognition and effective decision making.

Prior to embarking on a six-month program designed to enhance their innovation skills, internal teams at Whirlpool and Best Buy took part in a three- to five-day "boot camp" set up by their Strategos company coaches, in which the emotional and cognitive turmoil the Best Buy employees would surely experience over their multimonth innovation journey was compressed into a few hours. The purpose of first simulating the long journey ahead was to open their minds to new ideas, that is, to create new receptors: start rethinking the organization through the experience of a customer; start questioning assumptions not only about the company but about societal trends; start dealing with the discomfort of a messy process with no immediate output in view; get a foretaste of potentially difficult team dynamics. Some of the exercises the group went through were deliberately designed to create a bit of frustration so that the team members could learn to deal with the emotion—as, for example, when they were constructing a jigsaw puzzle and a confederate had a missing piece in his pocket. These shared experiences helped later in the real-world exercises, not only because participants had a better idea of what they were trying to accomplish, but also because they were more emotionally prepared for a tough job.[18]

Skill-Building Receptors

Various simulations, including commercially produced electronic games, are widely used by the U.S. armed forces to develop skills based on the receptors developed in basic training. According to the chief scientist for the army's Simulation, Training and Instrumentation Command, the Iraq War of 2003 was "the first war of the 21st century, the first war with 21st-century training systems, and the first war where everyone [was] trained on simulators."[19] Many battlefield simulations are developed by gaming companies such as Electronic Arts and Quicksilver. The University of Southern California directs the Institute for Creative Technologies (ICT), which in turn employs gaming companies, directors, special-effects experts, and screenwriters to develop highly realistic games such as Full Spectrum Command. In case you were wondering if the army takes the Hollywood collaboration seriously, in 1999 ICT was awarded a five-year, $45 million contract to develop simulations. In 2002 the grant was raised to $100 million.[20]

Sometimes the receptors are already well in place, the result of the current generation of action/adventure gamers. In the following example, soldiers developed receptors in childhood, added to them in basic training, and thus were well prepared to absorb new knowledge from simulations:

> *Major Brent Cummings, an instructor at Fort Benning, said the*
> *Full Spectrum Command game is effective because army trainees*
> *enjoy computer games. "The students I'm getting, they're guys.*
> *They already play these games," he said. "[Class] is usually from*
> *8 A.M. to 5 P.M. But the guy, if he's having fun with the simulation,*
> *he takes it home and plays all night." . . . Players pick weapons for*
> *each unit, direct platoons to their targets, and build attack plans.*
> *Only then does the animated portion of the game begin and users*
> *can watch their troops follow orders. With help from a massive*
> *dose of artificial intelligence, the game's virtual soldiers defend*
> *themselves when attacked and don't shoot innocent bystanders.*[21]

Practice with Rare Events

Simulations can be constructed to stretch the range of experiences normally encountered in real life. Unusual or rare events that lie at the extremes of the distribution of experiences can be simulated, and as such rare situations are encountered in the real world, they can be added to future simulations. The military routinely accumulates such experiences. Military engagements are a lot like chess games in that they often begin in familiar ways, but soon spin off into something unique. How does one develop pattern-recognition skills when there are so many different possible patterns? The Joint Warfighting Center at Fort Monroe, Virginia, is dedicated to sharing lessons learned from warfare among the different branches of the armed forces. Because each branch has different but related war experiences, sharing these through simulations can expand experience repertoires, including rare—but potentially critical—events.

Failing Safely

Simulations enable learners to fail in a safe environment and to learn from those failures. (Aren't you glad that your surgeon at least practiced on a cadaver and perhaps a high-tech dummy before removing your gallbladder?)

Computerized business simulations are designed to allow budding managers to learn from failure safely. Simulearn's "Virtual Leader" sets up a group of five animated characters with artificial intelligence, personalities, points of view, allies, and agendas. The learner joins this group as its leader, challenged with having them work together toward a common business goal. For example, the learner must fund a new call center initiative, but part of the budget must come from another department. If the learner doesn't understand the relationships, agendas, and individuals in the group, or how to read their body language, he may fail in the task. If the new leader's approach is failing, some of the simulated group members are programmed to start playing with their pens, stop talking, fold their arms, or push away from the table. If the learner reads the situation correctly, he immediately knows that the meeting is deteriorating and the business goal is in danger of not being achieved. Mike Ulven, senior national account executive for Coca-Cola, says the simulation "helps you appreciate the diversity of thought in complex sales situations. . . . This [simulation] is about behavior change. You practice what you have learned in a game environment to the point that it becomes a part of your own behavior."[22]

Limitations of Learning from Experience— Simulated or Direct

Both simulations and direct experience share some limitations. First, it makes little sense to immerse someone in a simulation or a real experience without *some* basic receptors to appreciate the information being conveyed in the simulation. The generation of soldiers raised on shoot-em-up electronic games can respond more easily to complex military simulations. Soldiers lacking those receptors would need initial training to prepare them. Similarly, a business case study would have limited value for someone who does not already possess a certain amount of domain knowledge. Both simulations and direct experience create receptors, it is true—but learning is more efficient in both cases if there are some receptors in place.

Second, as is true with almost all learning experiences, people must be motivated to learn. Motivation can be enhanced when the simulation is made highly realistic. And if performance in the simulation may predict future highly consequential behavior for the participant or others, motivation runs high. Consider a simulation that is both realistic and consequential. The army captains going through the Full Spectrum Command simulation know that they will be facing the real thing in the (perhaps immediate) future—and that their learning will likely spell life or death for the soldiers under their command. An army colonel described the advantages of simulation for *National Defense Magazine*:

> *[The simulation] was specifically designed to make trainees "think through" the challenges associated with urban combat, said Col. Paul E. Melody, the Army's director of combined arms and tactics directorate at the Infantry School, in Fort Benning, Ga. . . . The simulation, he explained, is a useful tool for a captain seeking to learn how to "build a plan to fight the enemy." The trainee "enters his plan in the computer," said Melody. The computer, assisted by the instructor, plays the role of "an asymmetric threat," such as a terrorist organization. What makes the training valuable, he said, is that "the captain only sees what he would see if he were in combat, as he moves into a building. It lets him experience the command-and-control challenges of fighting in this kind of terrain." . . . [T]he captain leads a force of three rifle companies—with about 140 troops each. Rob Sears, an ICT producer, said that engineers were instructed to create a game that would "get into the thought process" of crafting war tactics.*[23]

Third, both simulations and direct experience are of limited use without performance feedback. In electronic games, this feedback is provided by the game itself in the form of "hits," penalties, and scores. But in those simulations where it is not always clear what the "right" answer is, such as a business case study, the guidance of an expert is needed to enable learning. In real life, feedback is absolutely critical, as we all know. And wise managers learn how to deliver both carrot and stick—not just stick.

Fourth, because they cannot anticipate all possible scenarios, even the most carefully designed simulations do not guarantee success when encountering the real thing. A few days into the 2003 war with Iraq, Lt. General William Wallace, commander of V Corps, said, "The enemy we're fighting is a bit different than the one we war-gamed against, because of these paramilitary forces. . . . We knew they were here, but we did not know how they would fight."[24]

Finally, extensive experience with simulations can have unintended consequences—both positive and negative. For example, frequent players of realistic, violent video games such as Counter Strike develop enhanced visual abilities such as keeping track of multiple objects that change rapidly.[25] Other research indicates that frequent players of violent video games such as Mortal Kombat may develop more aggressive tendencies in real life.[26]

Experience and Leadership

Top managers are responsible for developing the leaders who will follow them. And leaders, we have argued, need a broad base of experience in order to develop deep smarts. Leaders cannot be *trained* into being. Attending leadership training classes, reading books, even talking with experienced leaders—none of these can substitute for experience, especially (as we will see in chapter 8) when that experience is thoughtfully guided by a coach. The need for developing managers is about to become acute in the United States. By 2008, the oldest baby boomers will be sixty-two; replacement needs for all employers during the 2003–2008 period are projected to be about 25 percent greater than in 1993–1998, and some occupations will be especially hard-hit, including management and education.[27]

Smart people sometimes underestimate the value and importance of experience. They know they are quick to learn; they probably *enjoy* the challenge of learning something without a lot of prior knowledge transfer. And all of us can point to instances when experience has misled. But experience shapes who we are. Experience influences the way our brain processes information and determines what possibilities and options for action we can imagine.

Diverse experiences expand our worldview and give us multiple perspectives on a given problem. Therefore, it is to the advantage of any organization to encourage its members to expand their experience repertoires, to rotate through different functions, gain international experience, seek out education that may not precisely fit the current job description. We know several young people whose lives were changed by a fairly casual (but astute) suggestion about possible alternative actions: "One more year in this product development job and then you should move into marketing." "Yes, the job offered is only a lateral move, rather than a promotion, but you would learn a lot about doing business in Asia." The more diverse the experiences, the broader the experience repertoire. A general manager profits from a variety of positions in an organization, for example—sales *and* operations; staff *and* line. In-depth experience with disparate elements of an entire system, be it technical, organizational, or societal, enhances the ability to anticipate and understand interdependencies—an ability at the heart of deep smarts. And if organizational leaders do not guide members to deliberately construct an experience repertoire, individuals can do so for themselves, as we shall discuss further in chapter 9.

One of the reasons that a repertoire is important is that one can "learn" from an inadequate or nonrepresentative experience— and base subsequent decisions on a shaky foundation. No matter how reflective we are, going through a process only once is rarely sufficient. We are always in danger of thinking we've figured out the path to success—or the route to failure—from one experience, not realizing the particular set of circumstances that makes it dangerous to generalize. (See "The Dangers of 'Learning' from One Experience.")

The Dangers of "Learning" from One Experience

IN 1997, NASA's new leader Daniel Goldin moved NASA away from producing billion-dollar missions that required a decade to develop, build, and launch (e.g., the Hubble telescope) and toward less expensive and more innovative projects that were produced on a faster timetable. Nicknamed "Faster, Better, Cheaper" or "FBC," the reforms were intended to unleash dormant creativity and reduce aversion to risk. Instead of creating missions every four to five years, at a cost of billions, the spacecraft would be launched toward Mars every twenty-six months, at relatively low cost. The $260 million Mars Pathfinder spacecraft, with its Sojourner rover, successfully explored the surface of Mars. The team members responsible for this first great success had been deliberately chosen for their energy and intelligence but—aside from team leader Anthony Spear—not for their experience. Spear had an expert advisory group and, in addition, as a senior manager recalled, "Spear had his finger very closely on the whole process." Unaware of how much Spear had invisibly guided the process, the youthful team members thought that they understood exactly how to manage projects. A senior manager commented that it "took a while to recover" from that belief. As project leaders from Pathfinder made their way into management positions on other projects, their mistaken belief in their own project management expertise resulted in an inability to consistently repeat Pathfinder's success. Between 1992 and January 1, 2000, NASA attempted sixteen missions. Of these, six failed—four of them in 1999. The junior project leaders had not built up enough experience.

In the following chapter, we explore the role of experience in creating differences between experts and novices. In subsequent chapters, we look at why *guided* experience is superior to experience alone, and at the ways that coaches can best help new managers learn from experience.

Implications for Managers

Experience is the basis for deep smarts. Life is lived in only one direction, so we have only one opportunity to wring the most from a given situation, although of course we may revisit it mentally to learn more from what happened. Moreover, we can't plan our life experiences with any certainty. (Life would be a lot less interesting if we could!) But at the individual, group, and even organizational level, it is useful to think deliberately in terms of experience repertoires.

If our experience repertoire is limited relative to those with whom we compare ourselves, and narrow compared to the situations we face, we have an obvious disadvantage. Increasingly, organizations are using competency maps to think deeply about what specific training individuals need in order to develop the organization's overall capability. In large businesses such as IBM or Intel, these maps are then systematically matched to programs of study within the corporate university that will help individuals and managers fill their knowledge gaps. While many of the courses cover technical skills, most corporate universities also offer such complex, hard-to-teach subjects as leadership and project management.

Programs of study in these "softer" subjects are valuable for creating receptors for future experience—especially if the students have little prior direct experience with the subject being taught. Deep smarts are built on a scaffolding of frameworks, concepts, and mental models that are acquired through experience, education, or observation. Without such receptors, information remains just that—information (or even just data), but not knowledge, and certainly not deep smarts. Therefore, coaches and other managers need to cultivate their own awareness and sensitivity to the level of receptors individuals have in order to benefit from experience.

Simulations are underutilized as surrogate experiences—but we don't mean just expensive computerized immersions into virtual reality. Working through simple cases, scenarios, and examples helps create deeper receptors and a taste of real experience. Of course, the usefulness of such simulations depends upon the deep smarts of their creators and designers, but they could be used much more than they are to complement direct experience.

However, if, as we argue here, *practical, real-world experience* (especially with different elements of a system) is the critical ingredient that differentiates deep smarts from other kinds of expertise, it is just as important to map out the jobs and situations that will fill the knowledge gaps in an individual's desired experience repertoire as it is to identify needed formal training. Training programs cannot substitute for direct experience. On the other hand, experience without some guidance is ad hoc and inefficient. The key to developing deep smarts, as we will explore at length in chapter 8, is to combine experience with guidance.

Keep in Mind

- Over time, individuals and organizations develop experience repertoires, gradually filling out a distribution that includes common and rare experiences.

- People who have experience at only one extreme of an experience distribution (such as a very favorable or unfavorable economic climate) do not have the smarts to operate under other conditions—and especially not under conditions at the opposite extreme.

- Willingness to engage in deliberate practice—repeated practice that is thoughtful, mindful, and accompanied by feedback—is crucial in developing deep smarts.

- In order to accept new knowledge, a person must have appropriate mental receptors. That is, the person must be psychologically open to the new experience and have sufficient prior mental scaffolding to make it into knowledge—not just information.

- Simulations can effectively augment personal, direct experience with the real world. Simulations help develop receptors for new knowledge, build skills, and enable learners to practice with rare events, thus building up an experience repertoire in a cost-effective, purposeful way. Simulations allow the learner to fail in an environment where there are no real consequences.

- A necessary but not sufficient requirement for leaders is to develop a broad, diverse experience repertoire, preferably with direction from a skilled coach, so as to enable system level understanding.

- The most powerful way of creating experience is through guided experience (see chapter 8).

THREE

Expertise

Developing and Expressing Deep Smarts

IN CHAPTERS 1 and 2 we developed the central concept of this book: Deep smarts are a special brand of expertise that consists of highly developed complex skills and system level knowledge developed through practical experience, including simulated. In this chapter, we draw on two bodies of research—general work on expertise and our own studies of decision-making capabilities of managers and their more experienced coaches—to illuminate deep smarts. While deep smarts and expertise are not equivalent, research on the latter is relevant and helps us understand how experts differ from novices (and apprentices and journeymen), how they are able to exercise their deep smarts, and how even experts have limitations.

The Ten-Year Rule

What is required to attain deep smarts? As suggested in the previous chapter, one thing that all experts have done more than novices or even highly competent learners is to practice. Although the sheer amount of practice and experience is not a powerful predictor of expertise (indeed, we can lock in bad habits through practice), *deliberate practice*—the combination of an extended period of concentrated effort with self-reflection (and, as we shall see in chapter 8, guidance and feedback from a coach)—has been shown to build expertise in a wide variety of domains, including competitive sports, music, and chess.[1] But how *much* deliberate practice is necessary to become an expert in a complex area of study? This depends to some extent, of course, on one's native talent. But even an acknowledged chess prodigy such as Bobby Fischer needed nine years of intensive study and competition to become an international grand master.

So where does that leave the rest of us, the nonprodigies of the world? Most evidence suggests that it takes at least ten years of concentrated study and practice to become expert (as opposed to merely competent).[2] The Ten-Year Rule places some inescapable limitations on the development of expertise in management or any other knowledge-based, complex domain, limitations that are frequently ignored or minimized by those trying to accelerate the process. For example, in 2000, when there were more ideas for companies than people to develop them, one of the coaches in our study said, "There aren't enough CEOs in Silicon Valley; we have to *grow* them." He was certainly correct that experienced CEOs were in short supply, but if the intent of this observation was to argue for developing a stable of new CEOs prepared to take over the multitude of hatchling companies over the next couple of years, then it reflected a basic misunderstanding of the nature of expertise. Because the deep smarts needed to manage a system as complicated as a company are highly complex, they are subject to the Ten-Year Rule. CEOs *couldn't* be grown fast enough to head up all the companies that needed them.

Sometimes experience-based knowledge applies to a related domain, thus truncating the ten-year learning period. For example, an experienced manager from oil exploration was asked to take over the internal knowledge management program for his company. He found that he achieved expertise faster in his new domain than he had in his first. He attributed that achievement to three transferable skills: First, he himself had learned how to learn better; second, he knew how to use his personal network to help him in the learning process; and third, what he had learned about motivating people, building teams, and ferreting out the reasons for resistance to change were all managerial skills applicable in his new situation.

In sports, music performance, and other largely physical domains, the performance of experts is usually obvious: Nobody would mistake the concert pianist at Lincoln Center or the professional basketball player driving to the hoop with their merely competent counterparts. But are differences between experts and novices as obvious in *cognitive* realms, where managers play out their careers? Can we easily identify the Tiger Woods of superior conceptualizing, the David Beckham of planning, the Luciano Pavarotti of decision making? We turn now to some of those distinguishing abilities.

The Differences Between Experts and Novices

Experts behave differently from novices in a number of ways. In the following sections, we discuss some of those differences. While in most cases it would certainly be preferable to be guided by an expert rather than a novice, the advice of experts does not come risk free. Later in this chapter, we will consider some of the dangers associated with having a high level of expertise.

Experts Recognize Bear Traps

Experts simply know *more*, to begin with. Their extensive experience repertoires give them the basis for their wisdom. As one coach, Rich Zalisk, observed: "When you do something once or twice you can't help being a product of that specific experience, and you remember it vividly. But when you see something ten or fifteen times, you tend to pattern-recognize, step back a little, and say, 'You know, I've seen this situation ten times before, and eight out of ten times here is what is going to happen.' " In the following example, you can see coaches Fred Gibbons and Bill Krause warning their protégés away from some tempting bait.

Knowledge Coaching at Active Photo

*I*T IS THE *second board meeting of the three young (mid-twenties!) founders of ActivePhoto with two of their investors/ advisors: Fred Gibbons and Bill Krause. Both are experienced coaches and entrepreneurs (Gibbons the founder and former CEO of Software Publishing and Krause the former CEO of 3Com). In the first board meeting a month earlier, the two coaches helped their protégés with many administrative details such as setting board meeting agendas, structuring stock options, and setting salary ranges.*

Today, they spend most of the time discussing which customers to pursue. ActivePhoto has been approached by another start-up, BestOffer.com, that wants to use AP's technology. The advisors see unnecessary risks in such a customer base: "Why chase someone who may die on the vine?" asks Gibbons. Cofounder Sebastian Turullols suggests an advantage to dealing with other start-ups: "But if we get in early and they take off?" Gibbons: "Why should you be in the venture capital business?" Krause chimes in: "They can't pay." The team pushes back: "They can pay; they are funded." Gibbons: "If they are a paying customer and they can use our product as is, off the shelf, no customization, okay. But if they want us to share their risk, no. We already have application risk. We don't want to add business risk."

This, it turns out, is excellent advice. The more closely the start-ups in our thirty-five-company sample were tied to Internet dot-coms as customers, the more likely they were to die an early death.[3] Gibbons and Krause possessed neither extensive knowledge of the Internet nor prescience about the impending dot-com implosion. Indeed, at the time they gave this advice, money was still flooding into Silicon Valley and the media were still touting the New Economy. But they did have years of experience managing cash flow in their own companies and in companies they had advised as board members or coaches. And they had lived in the business climate long enough to anticipate monetary flash floods and to recognize the frequency of start-up failure. The result was that these coaches had deep smarts in management processes and also, more critical to the survival of ActivePhoto, in business judgment. Their reasoning was simple: Choose customers who are likely to be able to pay *next* year (not just this year).[4] Whereas the novice managers focused on the near-term benefits of an alliance, the advisors were thinking of the larger economic system within which they operated.

Experts Make Decisions Swiftly

Experts are not simply novices with a lot more knowledge. Their expertise enables them to make quick decisions. In 2002, Shane Dyer decided that he was not well equipped to take ActivePhoto further, and the three founders sought a CEO. Tom Riley, an active advisor and investor in the company since its inception, first headed up the search and then, at the urging of another prime investor and coach, took the job himself. One of his first challenges was to pare down the list of eight potential deals and activities under consideration. For someone of his experience, it was much easier than it had been for twenty-six-year old Dyer. As Riley recalled:

When you have limited resources, it's very hard to choose what to do. So the immediate normal tendency is to wait until the picture gets clearer—not really charge ahead on any one of them, not eliminate any of them—just keep juggling them all. . . . But for me, it's as if I've got the special glasses that you put on and all of a sudden you say, "My God, number four, that's a home run, we have

to be doing something on that right now. And number two, call
them up and tell them you are not going to respond. . . ." It's al-
most like those drawings that just look like dots, but if you look
at it in a certain way, all of a sudden you can see the pictures form-
ing. [The three inexperienced founders] were just seeing the dots.

Riley immediately eliminated one possible partner, an event photography company that essentially wanted an engineering contract
house—not a long-term arrangement. "It was not a strategic priority; it was some short-term dollars and a real waste of time." But
further down the list was the camera company, Ricoh, which was
launching a new high-resolution camera that could combine a photograph with voice and written notes. At the time, Ricoh was unable to send the picture to the Web, but ActivePhoto cofounder
Sebastian Turullols had solved their problem and figured out how
to send photos to the local server. Riley recalled:

We had a software fix to a major weakness in this huge product
and Ricoh was asking if we would help them with their customers,
if they could participate in trade shows, be our software partner
to help launch it into new markets. . . . I thought, "They need us,
they need us for everything. . . . Why did we wait for this? Why
didn't you tell me this when I first walked in?" This was like a
little gold nugget sitting on the pathway and we were walking
right past it.

In contrast to the young CEO, who wanted to keep options
open, Riley's analysis of the situation was swift and decisive. He
was able to recognize immediately the dangers inherent in one customer relationship and the possibilities of the other. Ricoh, in fact,
became a crucial partner for ActivePhoto.

As this example suggests, expert managers are able to access
their vast archive of knowledge and select a small number of high-
quality responses—quickly. In many fields requiring deep smarts,
experts do not have to review basic factual information or struggle

with distinctions between relevant and irrelevant information, because their knowledge is more abstract and contextualized. In the field of medicine, for example, experts encode information about patients at such an abstract level that they can rapidly make diagnoses without having to consciously review and interpret basic facts.[5] Expert physicists organize problems around abstract, general laws and consider possible solutions at the same time they frame the problem, while students invoke rules of thumb—formulas—that in turn suggest specific calculations.[6] Expert firefighter commanders can quickly size up complex situations, even unusual ones, and react swiftly.[7] In short, experts are able to determine quickly what facts are relevant in a particular context, allowing them to focus their attention on just the information that is currently pertinent.[8] This combination of pattern recognition, abstraction, and focusing on only the relevant dimensions of the problem results in a highly efficient, fluent decision process in complex tasks—a process that is largely tacit.

Experts Recognize Context

Not long ago, one of us arrived at De Gaulle Airport in Paris. The taxi driver was unfamiliar with the location of the hotel and used his GPS to navigate a tortuous, albeit "direct" route through busy Paris streets. On a return trip a few days later, an experienced driver headed immediately out to an expressway, thus tacking on a few kilometers, but halving the travel time. The first driver was slaved to his GPS, which used the "rule" of taking the "shortest" route. The second driver used his deep smarts about Parisian travel routes to take into account traffic lights and likely congestion to arrive at a superior solution. Like a real expert, the second taxi driver *conditionalized* his knowledge.

Experts integrate the experience-based patterns they have built up with information about the context, resulting in a superior choice of action because it is contingent on variations in the situation. Coaches of start-up companies often urge their charges to

"Focus, focus, focus." However, the more expert the coach in our study, the more likely he or she was to realize when exceptions must be made, when such general rules didn't fit the situation. When, for example, would focusing exclusively on one particular market be premature? The expert manager recognizes the context, the pattern that directs the application of the rule—or suggests exceptions. The deeper the knowledge, the more the individual is able to take context into account.

One of coach Fern Mandelbaum's protégé entrepreneurs in Silicon Valley asked her advice about setting a valuation on his company. The higher the valuation, the more the entrepreneur's (and investors') stock would be worth, so he naturally wanted to set his sights high. However, he was focusing more on the money than the smarts that might accompany it. Although they could almost certainly get at least a $25 million valuation, Mandelbaum knew that the people she thought would be the best advisors were unlikely to accept higher than $20–$22 million. She explained to the entrepreneur:

> "There are certain people we want to get in this round—people who can really make a difference for us—that have a very clear sense of what valuation feels right. I could get a $75 million valuation, but that's dumb money, it's not strategic money." So I went through this whole example and [the entrepreneur] said, "You're right. We should be at twenty."

The entrepreneur's instinct was to grab as much money as possible—and run! But Mandelbaum placed the decision in a richer context. She knew that start-ups require the deep smarts of board members and investors as much as their money.

Experts Extrapolate

Experts not only can decide what to do in the current context, but they can also extrapolate—generate and evaluate hypothetical alternatives. Some of these solutions might have been tried in the past. ("The last time I encountered something like this, I tried X and that worked pretty well.") At other times, the match between the present and past might be imperfect. ("This reminds me a little of a personnel problem I had last year. . . .") Or there might not have been a solution associated with the situation in the past. But because the understanding is relatively abstract, and not tied to a specific instance, the expert can anticipate the consequences of various options arising from the data. For example, a chess player recognizes the significance of a position, even one not previously encountered; realizes there are numerous directions the game could go; anticipates the consequences of each of these different lines; then makes the "best" choice. At the highest levels of mastery, this process is largely unconscious.[9]

The coaches in our study were able to draw on their experience repertoires (see chapter 2) to foresee possible repercussions from actions in the present. One of the entrepreneurs, Sanjeev Malaney, recalled working with his coach, Rich Zalisk, to make difficult decisions, such as the rate at which the company could grow:

> *We grew from $9.6 million to $14.5 million in 1996, primarily with a single product. In 1997 we started to focus on diversifying the product line into new applications and new markets. As we started to do that, we recognized we might slow the growth down temporarily, but it was well worth taking the risk. Rich said, "We can milk this cow for awhile but unless we invest in something new we are going to mortgage our future." Rich was better able to look forward than I could have. I normally made decisions when I felt the pain. Rich was able to see ahead. He had seen enough business cases that he could predict that if we didn't take a specific action, we would be in deep trouble in the future.*

Several of the coaches in our study were able to anticipate slumps in local economies based on the downturn in the United States. K. O. Chia, an experienced coach and venture capitalist in Hong Kong, provided a "heads up" to entrepreneur Alex Chan. As Chan recounted:

Early this year [2001], K. O. was just back from the States and he asked me about our business outlook, and I told him that we still had a strong outlook. I told him, "I know in the U.S. things are very bad, but it doesn't seem to affect Asia that much because we still see business in Singapore and China growing. In Hong Kong we still have a strong backlog." But K. O. was telling me that we have to be careful, because if the U.S. economy is bad it will affect Asia. Asian manufacturers will hold down their expenses, and the telcos will be affected. We hadn't seen that happen yet. But he warned me again, and in April or May we started to see things really happen like he predicted. Fortunately, we had taken his advice and had become a bit more conservative.

Experts Make Fine Distinctions

Expert musicians can hear small differences in intonation or harmony that are indistinguishable to the untrained ear. An expert philatelist can instantly notice subtle distinctions among varieties of the same postage stamp, or between forgeries and authentic specimens, that make the difference between a worthless stamp and one worth a small fortune. Expert antique dealers, such as those featured on *Antiques Road Show*, make similar distinctions, to the delight or chagrin of the owner of the family treasure. There are even experts in detecting emotions in others. There are forty-three muscles in the human face, and most of them seem to have the sole function of expressing emotions. Psychologist Paul Ekman is an expert in distinguishing emotional states (e.g., disgust from anger), and the FBI, the CIA, and police forces have used his deep smarts to help uncover potential criminals and terrorists.[10] This ability to make fine distinctions is another aspect of deep smarts.

One of the highly experienced coaches we interviewed noted key differences between the qualities desired in a CEO (chief executive officer) versus a COO (chief operating officer). A CEO, he said, is an outward-facing person—charismatic but not necessarily liked, quick to grasp the big picture with the fewest number of data points and come up with an appropriate strategy. The COO is more focused inside the firm, and is known for being methodical, caring, patient, and a good teacher. Such distinctions, the coach maintained, are why COOs are not necessarily the logical choice to become CEOs. Failure to recognize the difference in the two roles can result in promoting the wrong person.

Experts Know What They Don't Know and When Rules Don't Apply

Experts have a better chance of recognizing gaps in their knowledge than do novices, who may have little idea of what is even included in the particular knowledge domain. Experts also are more likely to know when they are encountering an unusual situation. They may even be more cautious than novices in assuming that their own experience applies in a particular context. Experienced entrepreneur Robert Maxfield says that advisors to a company cannot just apply a set of rules. In fact, directors should be wary of giving explicit directives based on their own experience, "because no two situations are ever exactly the same. . . . There is just no way unless you're *doing* it to understand the whole context for a company at any given time." Maxfield continues:

> *My style is to simply say, "Let me throw out something that might resonate with this particular context. It seems to me it does, but you guys are closer to it than I am. Let me tell you a story about XYZ." And then I'll give the context: "Here was the situation and we decided to do thus-and-so for these reasons. And here's what happened. To the extent this seems applicable to our situation here, you might want to weigh it with all the other factors under consideration."*

As we will discuss later in this chapter, not all experts are this aware of their own limitations. However, if we are the experts, we should be cautious about the bounds of our rules of thumb; if we are the novices, we should push for access to the deep smarts that underlie the rules.

How Experts Do What They Do

Clearly, deep smarts are of great value. Experts not only need less information than novices, but they can also adjust to different contexts, extrapolate to future possible situations, make fine distinctions that are invisible to novices, and abstract their experience into rules that often apply—but recognize when those rules should *not* be applied as well. How do they do it? What connections and pathways lie in their brains that novices don't possess?

Pattern Recognition and Intuition

As we discussed in the previous chapter, deep smarts are based on wide experience, resulting in an extensive experience repertoire and system level comprehension. Armed with this broad-based knowledge, the expert becomes increasingly aware of, and sensitive to, meaningful patterns in a sea of information ("I've seen something very much like this before"). When knowledge is fragmented, it takes deep smarts to aggregate it, make sense of it, see the relevant pattern, and act on it. The skilled primary-care physician may aggregate all the different specialists' reports to make a diagnosis; the veteran general gathers intelligence from the whole field of battle; the experienced general manager looks at the whole system of an organization. In contrast, novices focus on rules of thumb that can be readily memorized: ("When faced with situation X, do Y").[11] Such rules ignore variations across situations. Research on chess players, for example, shows that after very brief visual exposure, experts could reconstruct meaningful middle-game positions much faster and more accurately than less skilled players could. Simon and Chase estimated that chess experts retain more than ten thousand patterns in their heads, which then serve to guide appropriate moves.[12] Later research raised this number to between a hundred thousand and more than a million.[13] Chess novices, on the other hand, rely on rules of thumb such as "control the center" and "castle as soon as possible." Merely competent individuals reason their way through a situation, calling upon prior experience, but they are not able to make judgments quickly and "intuitively" as do experts.[14]

Fred Luconi, an "angel" investor in many companies, describes well the pattern-recognition process as applied to management:

> *You have these models that you carry around. . . . You have hired, promoted and fired hundreds of people in your life, you have seen the way it looks during the interview, you have seen the way people do and don't tell you certain things in the referencing process, you have seen how people are either political or nonpolitical. . . . After awhile, you say about a given situation: "that's going to be one of these." . . . You can project what's going to happen. You have to have lived through all of those to have a gut sense of which things have a chance of succeeding, which are going to be difficult and which are impossible. If you don't have [a mental] model, you don't have a framework to react instinctively. You have to be careful to make sure your models are up to date and they are still relevant. But the more you see, the more it's the same. There are differences, clearly—that's what makes it interesting. . . . But there are an awful lot of [familiar] dynamics going on.[15]*

Despite the claims of young entrepreneurs during the Internet bubble that the New Economy rendered old contexts irrelevant, Luconi saw familiar patterns of behavior from his experience in start-ups and general management situations. Many of the rules of thumb he had developed over the years still applied, even if the market into which the entrepreneurs were entering was new and different—because his deepest smarts were built around management basics.

What many people think of as a flash of intuition, and what managers are prone to describe as "gut feel," is often extremely fast and unconscious pattern matching.[16] Children do not experience such flashes of intuition, because they lack the extensive patterns that can lead to unconscious matching with current experience. But experts have reservoirs of patterns accumulated over many years. They usually do not sort through those patterns consciously, nor are they always able to articulate their reasoning.[17] Instead, the recognition of a familiar, holistic system and the search for a relevant pattern proceed so swiftly and efficiently that only those patterns that are appropriate to the situation emerge into consciousness.[18] One of the challenges for anyone, but particularly nonexperts, is knowing whether a given pattern holds for the particular situation at hand. Fred Luconi knew that the entrepreneurs he was coaching faced some quite common start-up experiences with which he was deeply familiar, but they wanted to believe that their entire business situation was new and different—out on the tails of the distribution of entrepreneurial experience.

Tacit Dimensions of Knowledge

Knowledge has been defined as "information that is relevant, actionable, and based at least partially on experience."[19] If one accepts that definition, then all knowledge, we argue, has some tacit dimensions—some aspects of knowing that are not readily articulated. As expertise deepens and knowledge is represented increasingly abstractly, the tacit dimensions of knowledge become more dominant. Pattern recognition and the intuitions that spring, often suddenly, from accumulations of experience are frequently tacit in nature. In 2002, the founder of a Web-based Chinese start-up recalled a conversation with her very experienced coach, Koh Boon Hwee:

> Boon Hwee went to the U.S. in February [2000]. He had a feeling that the bubble was about to burst, although at that time the market was still running up like crazy. When he came back, he said, "I tell you, this market is about to come back down again." So we knew we needed to execute as fast as we could. We negotiated with the venture capitalists. They lowered our valuation—we took it. They put a tough clause [into the contract]—we took it. Our goal was to close as soon as possible. We closed our round on March 23; the money was in the bank on March 28. And the market has crashed ever since.

While Boon Hwee may never have seen the exact situation before, somehow he picked up on signs that the great cyberspace rush was about to come to a halt—and the overall pattern suggested disaster ahead.

Now consider another example, this time of an expert firefighter confronting an unusual fire. Gary Klein recounts this incident in *Sources of Power*:

> *It is a simple house fire in a one-story house in a residential neighborhood. The fire is in the back, in the kitchen area. The lieutenant leads his hose crew into the building, to the back, to spray water on the fire, but the fire just roars back at them.*
>
> *"Odd," he thinks. The water should have more of an impact. They try dousing it again, and get the same results. They retreat a few steps to regroup.*
>
> *Then the lieutenant starts to feel as if something is not right. He doesn't have any clues; he just doesn't feel right about being in that house, so he orders his men out of the building. . . .*
>
> *As soon as his men leave the building, the floor where they had been standing collapses. Had they still been inside, they would have plunged into the fire below.*[20]

In Gary Klein's study of expert decision making from which this example is drawn, the lieutenant attributed the close escape to "ESP," or a "sixth sense." Boon Hwee "had a feeling" about the market's imminent demise, despite the continuing run-up. Tacit knowing can be embodied in physical skills and expressed in the deft interplay of muscles, nerves, and reflexes. Embodied in cognitive skills, tacit knowledge may be expressed in insight, intuition, and decisions based on gut feel. The coordination and motor skills required to skillfully perform a complex piece of music or head a soccer ball past a goalie are largely tacit, as are the cognitive skills required to recognize when a young manager has what it takes to become a successful CEO.

Because of their largely tacit nature, the insights or intuitive leaps that inform expert decisions are difficult to trace back to the specific patterns that inspired them. After persistent questioning and analysis, it became clear that the fire lieutenant in the earlier example had actually recognized a number of key aspects of the fire that led him to the decision to evacuate his team quickly. For example, the room was hotter than he would have expected from a small fire, and the fire was very quiet. He unconsciously deduced that there must be an unsuspected basement beneath the living room, and that was where the main fire was; he then "intuited" that his men were in danger.[21] It is likely that similarly persistent questioning would have revealed the patterns that Koh Boon Hwee observed in the United States that led to his "feeling" that the bubble was about to burst and that his protégé's company should get its financing as soon as possible.

The Limits of Expertise— and Deep Smarts

Although the term "expert" implies high credibility, one cannot always depend on an expert's advice. Much depends on that individual's range of experiences, personality, and operational environment. Expert advice may be limited in at least three ways. First, experts may tacitly know more than they can reliably explain. Second, the stage of knowledge in a particular domain may be so primitive that no one really has deep enough smarts to advise. And finally, experts can be subject to false knowing: ignorance, overconfidence, and failure to examine assumptions. While we celebrate the value of expertise, therefore, we also must be cautious about accepting without question expert knowledge as truth.

Inability to Access Tacit Knowledge

Even if we believe that we have achieved a degree of pattern-recognition ability, we may be unable to abstract rules accurately from those patterns; and when we do try to focus on the true origins of our deep smarts, we may mislead instead of enlighten.

Much of the knowledge we learn from experience is unconsciously gained, since we do not normally pay much attention to *how* we learn. Cognitive scientists who have studied "implicit learning" have consistently found that people acquire knowledge without conscious awareness, and consequently know more than they are able to communicate or even realize. As Reber has written, "Knowledge acquired from implicit learning procedures is knowledge that, in some raw fashion, is always ahead of the capability of its possessor to explicate it."[22] In fact, forcing individuals to describe what they thought they understood about implicitly learned processes often worsens their performance compared to when they are allowed to simply use their tacit knowledge without explicit explanation.[23] Pushed to explain the reasoning behind a decision, an expert—like the fire lieutenant—may with great effort be able to offer a plausible set of linked clues making up the pattern. However, when the pattern is deeply buried in the subconscious, attempts to retrieve and articulate it may be fruitless, misleading, or —had the fire lieutenant taken the time to discover the reasons for his decision before acting—disastrous.

Psychological research has also revealed that all people (not just experts), when pressed to explain their choices or decisions based on unconscious reasoning, will give explanations that are clearly unrelated to their actual behavior. For example, customers asked to choose among brands of hosiery overwhelmingly preferred those placed to the right of the other selections. But asked *why* they chose the brand they did, they never indicated the real reason—physical placement. Instead they cited price, color, or other attributes.[24]

So developing expertise implicitly limits what can be explicitly transferred. Directives or suggestions may be expressed as intuitions and insights and may accurately reflect the expert's knowledge. However, as discussed in chapters 7 and 8, directives are of limited use to the novice trying to deepen his or her own smarts if the expert is unable to communicate *why* the directives are important.

Knowledge Outside the Expert's
—or Anyone's—Domain

What happens when there are no clear patterns in the past to which the expert can compare the present situation—that is, when knowledge about the situation is primitive?

Scientists believe there are some fundamental and inherent limitations on the knowable, such as theorems in mathematics that can't be proved or disproved, or being able to simultaneously know both the position and the momentum of a subatomic particle, or predicting next month's weather. "We grow up thinking more is known than actually is," says well-known scientist Ralph Gomory, president of the Alfred P. Sloan Foundation.[25] His colleague, Professor Jesse Ausubel, applies the concept of the unknowable to finance: The future of markets "depends on what's in other people's minds, and unless I can read your mind I won't know what's going to happen on Wall Street except probabilistically." Researcher Simon Levin of Princeton University comments, "It really changes the way you deal with the world when you realize there is some ineluctable uncertainty."

At the time of our entrepreneurship study, e-commerce was new, and business models based on it untested. Who was to say that "aggregating eyeballs" was or was not a flimsy basis for making money? No one was truly expert about Internet businesses—the Internet hadn't been around long enough for anyone to have developed deep smarts. Where the guru's advice applied to generic human behavior (e.g., handling conflicts among board members) and basic business processes (e.g., setting up production, or finding and utilizing a law firm), both entrepreneur and coach were reasonably confident that this advice—even if it was based on experience with the "old economy"—still applied.

But if the issue to be addressed was tied to an understanding of how consumers would use the Internet, *neither* entrepreneur nor coach could be certain that the old rules applied. Everyone was experimenting simultaneously, and the gold rush mentality meant that there was no time to stop and learn. The suspicion by the technologically savvy young entrepreneurs that the Silicon Valley gurus "just didn't get it" was fueled in part by a belief that the old rules no longer applied and the gurus were slow to realize it. One of our senior respondents, asked to help coach an Internet start-up, at first tried to decline, saying, "I don't understand this. I can't help you. I don't understand this model, I don't know how to play this game, there is nothing I can do to help. Go find somebody else." Although he recognized that the New Economy was outside his expertise, he eventually agreed to help and make the best of it:

> "OK, I'm in. And now we've got this problem and it looks like the new model is the way to go, so I'll do my best to help get through this, but I don't know what I'm doing, and you guys need to understand that I don't know what I'm doing, but I'll try to help."

Our respondent was correct; in this case there was no experience repertoire that applied for certain. He could apply his knowledge of human behavior and certain generic business principles, but there were few patterns to be recognized. Everyone's knowledge was fragmentary. There were no experts. (We will suggest strategies for addressing such uncertainty in chapter 8.)

The coaches were in a difficult spot. They didn't know how much of their expertise applied and they were very conscious of their naiveté about the technology. Young entrepreneur Scott Rozic recalled an early strategy session that included a venture capitalist who had made many investments in Internet companies, along with a couple of other investors who were Internet innocents. Rozic and the venture capitalist were throwing out names of companies and referring to technology in a rapid-fire exchange when coach Stan Meresman intervened to plead for technical explication. "Stan said, 'Scott, you have to understand, you are cable modem and I'm 28.8' [baud rate of transmission over telephone lines]. Then [the second older investor] jumped in and said, 'Stan, if you are 28.8, then I'm tin can and string!'"

What can a coach do in such uncertainty? A number of them made conscious efforts to expand their area of expertise. When Sam Colella took on the coaching of first-time entrepreneur Kurt deGrosz, he knew little of the insurance business, as his expertise was in health care. But deGrosz's company, BenefitPoint, was in the business of building insurance industry standard platforms for the distribution and management of employee benefits. DeGrosz recalled:

> The first thing that Sam did was extensive due diligence on our firm. He took the time to educate himself as much as he could on our space. He called lots of brokers, lots of insurance companies, and did lots of interviews. I think that adds value to the entrepreneur, because you want an educated venture partner. The more educated they are in your business and your space, the better.

Colella realized that he could be most helpful to BenefitPoint if he developed the receptors that would help him understand the nature of the business. His advice could then be given in the context relevant to the decisions facing deGrosz.

False Knowing

Experts who admit that they are stretching the limits of their competence are far less dangerous than experts who believe they know what to do—and are wrong. General manager Tom Kelley of IDEO writes disparagingly of people whose expertise blinds them to innovation: "Expertise is great until it begins to shut you off from new learning. . . . Experts can inadvertently block an innovation by saying, 'It's never been done that way.'"[26] These experts may be victimizing their audiences out of ignorance, overconfidence, adhering to an old "mental set"—or all three. Each may be a cause of what we term *false knowing*.

IGNORANCE. When the situation differs from prior experience, but the experts haven't been exposed to new knowledge and new patterns, they may access incorrect patterns from their experience.

Experts are human, and often operate in a system that punishes them for fallibility or self-doubt. Those with deep smarts in one domain may find it difficult to confess "I don't know" when pressed to function in another. As a result, they may choose to protect their image or self-esteem by continuing to play the role of expert even when a wiser course would be to consult more knowledgeable colleagues. Or they may not recognize their own ignorance. The physician who confidently prescribes an acid suppressant to relieve a woman's indigestion, when in fact she is having a heart attack, is fitting the symptoms into a schema built on research about men. No chest pains—ergo, not a heart attack. Only as research reveals that women's symptoms for heart attacks differ from those of men, and as medicine builds enough knowledge to characterize this different set of symptoms, will the physician be prepared to recognize the danger of "knowing" what is happening, based on the commonly held set of false assumptions.

A recent report indicates that 60 percent of Americans suffering from depression receive inappropriate care. A major reason? Most people who are depressed are seen by their primary-care physician. Because the presenting symptoms frequently do not include "feeling depressed," the physician will often treat only the physical symptoms—for example, prescribing sleeping pills for insomnia—while the underlying disorder goes undiagnosed.[27]

And we have ample examples from business that even experts can be confused. When Enron's fraudulent accounting practices came to light, many people wondered how they could have gotten past the head of the audit committee, Robert Jaedicke, a former Stanford Business School accounting professor (and dean). No one accused Jaedicke of complicity in the accounting scandals. The accounting practices followed by the company were characterized in the press as "pushing the limits" and "convoluted"; the financial structures were called "Byzantine."[28] A man historically known for integrity, Jaedicke apparently either did not dive deeply enough into the accounting practices to discover their illegality or, along with other members of the board, was confused by them and relied on the professional auditors to watchdog any improprieties.

OVERCONFIDENCE. Of course, ignorance is compounded if the experts are so certain of their knowledge that when they encounter a new situation, they try to shoehorn the problem into what they know, making no attempt to question their assumptions and actions and therefore making it difficult for anyone to offer differing conclusions.

When coaches who are advising entrepreneurs project an air of invulnerability and infallibility, they can exert a powerful influence that may be impossible to resist. (See chapter 6.) In our study, we encountered some examples of coaches who were overly confident in their own abilities—particularly those coaches mentoring through incubators. One of the entrepreneurs we studied had deep expertise in the music industry, but was a novice when it came to using the Internet as central to a business model. One of the founders of the incubator the entrepreneur approached recalled rejecting the original presentation and steering the entrepreneur toward a more Internet-centered business:

> *He wanted to build a business where the primary use of capital was the acquisition of publishing rights for Asian music, in the belief that they were undervalued and would, at some stage, become overvalued. The platform—the digital delivery of music over the Internet—was interesting for him, but not [really central]. We listened to him for two or three hours, then I said, "Look, this is great, but frankly, (a) you're not going to get funded, and (b) this is not a scalable business. You have a chance to be worth many, many millions of dollars, and your children will never forgive you if you walk away from this opportunity [to use the Internet]."*

Who among us would wish to incur the wrath of our children! The entrepreneur took the advice, but the company was never able to reach profitability with the Internet model, and the entrepreneur returned to his original idea of developing and marketing music talent. The coaches in this case were savvy, well-connected, successful investment bankers, and were confident that they could parlay their financial expertise into creating successful Internet companies. They were wrong; the incubator itself failed after a couple years.

MENTAL SET. Decades ago, psychologists demonstrated the powerful effects of "mental set" that limit individuals' ability to break away from the familiar and comfortable.[29] For example, when chess experts are briefly presented with random or implausible chess positions and asked to reconstruct them, or when expert accountants are informed of new laws that disallow deductions and asked to complete tax returns, performance may deteriorate below that of nonexperts. In both cases, the experts were unconsciously behaving as though the novel were the familiar.

We all get in ruts (or, if things are working out well, grooves). But mindlessly continuing to follow patterns that have worked well in the past can have negative—even tragic—consequences. After the space shuttle *Columbia* disintegrated upon reentry on February 1, 2003, a panel of distinguished experts reviewed the physical evidence and concluded that a piece of insulating foam broke off from the external fuel tank and struck the wing of *Columbia* shortly after liftoff, breaching the thermal protection system. During reentry, superheated air melted the unprotected structure of the wing. But the investigation also went beyond the physical cause to identify organizational and decision-making problems at NASA that contributed to the disaster. Consider the following observations by the panel:

> *With each successful landing, it appears that NASA engineers and managers increasingly regarded the foam shedding as inevitable, and as either unlikely to jeopardize safety or simply an acceptable risk. . . . NASA and contractor personnel came to view foam strikes not as a safety of flight issue, but rather a simple maintenance . . . issue.*[30]
>
> *The history of foam-problem decisions shows how NASA first began and then continued flying with foam losses, so that flying with these deviations from design specifications was viewed as normal and acceptable.*[31]
>
> *So ingrained was [NASA's] belief that foam debris was not a threat to flight safety that in press briefings after the* Columbia *accident, the Space Shuttle Program Manager still discounted the foam as a probable cause.*[32]

As this example suggests, experts can become wedded to their pet theories and hypotheses, and it can take a great deal of physical evidence to convince them otherwise. (When experts possess personality traits such as defensiveness or dogmatism, their receptivity to new information that challenges their expertise may be further limited.)

Table 3-1 summarizes the foregoing discussion of distinctions between those with and without deep smarts, and the dangers and limitations inherent in deep smarts. While we value the benefits, it is wise to acknowledge that deep smarts do not come risk-free.

TABLE 3-1

Characteristics and Limitations of Deep Smarts

	Experts	Novices	Limitations of Expertise
Speed of Decision Making	Make decisions swiftly, efficiently, without reviewing basic facts	Need to review all facts and choose deliberately among alternatives	Overconfidence; expert may ignore relevant data
Context	Take context into account; knowledge is "contextualized"	Rely on rules of thumb that minimize context	Difficult to transfer contextualized knowledge; novices prefer general rules
Extrapolation	Able to extrapolate from novel situation to find a solution	Lack of receptors limits basis for extrapolation	Mental set; expert may base solution on inappropriate pattern
Discrimination	Able to make fine distinctions	Use of rules of thumb obscures fine distinctions	May not communicate well to a novice who lacks receptors to understand distinctions
Awareness of Knowledge Gaps	Know when rules don't apply	Don't know what they don't know	Ignorance; expert may assume expertise where none exists
Pattern-Recognition Ability	Have large inventory of patterns drawn from experience	Limited experience constrains number of patterns	When no patterns exist, expert may perform no better than novice
Tacit Knowledge	Extensive tacit knowledge drives decision making	Knowledge is largely explicit	Difficult to access tacit knowledge, so difficult to transfer

Implications for Managers

Experts really do think and behave differently from novices. Because the term *expert* is overused today, we should distinguish true expertise from competence—and not pay for the former when we are getting the latter. On the other hand, we should seek out the special brand of expertise we call deep smarts—because those who possess it are so much more effective (and, usually, efficient) in making decisions. There is a proven and remarkably large gap between the best software programmers and average ones; we suggest that there is a similar gap between even the apprentice (let alone the novice) and the true master who has deep smarts.

Many managers (including leaders in public office) appear to fall prey to a couple of misapprehensions about deep smarts. First, they may recognize that they themselves make decisions based on "intuition," but without fully understanding how they built that swift pattern-recognition ability. As a consequence, they underinvest in building similar, experience-based knowledge in their junior leaders. (They may also underinvest in traditional training—but that's a well-documented and better-understood gap.) We are concerned here with the lack of investment in the specific *kind* of experience-based education that builds deep smarts—and of course, we have much more to say about that in subsequent chapters. In chapters 7 and 8, especially, we describe what managers can do to cultivate, transfer, and recreate deep smarts.

A second and more dangerous consequence for managers who don't understand expertise is that they may make decisions without the deep smarts based on a strong experience repertoire. That is, they know themselves to be expert in some situations, but falsely extrapolate that expertise to contexts and situations with which they have little direct experience. People immersed in a given context are often rightly critical of the decisions made from afar, without experience "on the ground," that is, without basis in deep smarts. Examples include decisions made at headquarters that adversely affect operations in a far-flung regional office, but without consultation with the employees in the field; decisions made about entry into a foreign culture by people who have never lived outside their home country; decisions made by top management without consulting the people who "do the work." We hear people say, "that was really stupid" of a given decision (say, to outsource a key knowledge-building activity; insult a foreign supplier or government; acquire a company and then destroy the knowledge assets that made it valuable to begin with). What the speakers mean is that the actor had insufficient wisdom and experience to appreciate system wide implications, or to foresee the consequences of the decision.

We've always been told that nothing worthwhile ever comes easily—and deep smarts are no exception. If (1) deep smarts are based on the ability to recognize patterns accumulated over many years; (2) much of expert performance is tacit and the rules difficult to explicate; (3) unusual or rare situations can stymie experts as much as novices; (4) novices often lack the receptors to respond to expert knowledge; and (5) not all experts are good teachers, sensitive to the level of the novice's knowledge—then it will be a real challenge to cultivate deep smarts in protégés. However, the major point of this chapter is that by understanding the *nature* of expertise, and especially the kind we call deep smarts, managers will be better prepared to create the *means* for developing leaders in their organizations.

Keep in Mind

- Deep smarts in a complex area of study normally take about ten years to develop—the Ten-Year Rule.

- Deep smarts are promoted through deliberate practice, a process that can be facilitated by a skilled coach.

- Because their knowledge is deep, abstract, and contextualized, experts can make decisions swiftly, without reviewing basic facts.

- Because experts have built up a broad experience repertoire, they are able to recognize patterns in current situations and match them to events they have encountered in the past, resulting in decisions that are richly contextualized.

- Because their knowledge is relatively abstract, experts are able to see specific situations they have not previously encountered as representatives of a more general class and thus to generate and evaluate possible outcomes.

- Because of their extensive experience repertoires, experts are able to perceive in situations small variations that would escape the novice.

- Because experts are more aware of the boundaries of their knowledge than are novices, experts are more likely to know when they are encountering a rare event.

- Intuition or insight is actually the result of a rapid and efficient pattern-recognition process.

- There are limits to expertise. Because experts draw on tacit dimensions of their deep smarts, they are often not able to communicate the reasons behind their insights. Experts are subject to "false knowing," offering erroneous advice because of ignorance, overconfidence, or mental set.

FOUR

Assembling Deep Smarts

IN THE PREVIOUS CHAPTER we discussed how individuals develop and express deep smarts. And in much of the rest of this book we will be considering how they then use those deep smarts to lead, manage, or make decisions effectively and creatively. But while we often need to cultivate individual deep smarts or create organizational capabilities, it is not always possible, or even desirable, to grow all the expertise we need in-house. First of all, as we saw in the previous chapter, it takes *time* to become an expert; the Ten-Year Rule sets limits on how practical it is to adopt a "grow" strategy. And second, for any project, particularly innovative ones or otherwise unprecedented situations, we do not expect one individual or group to possess all the requisite experience, to have knowledge of all possible scenarios. We need people with different *kinds* of deep smarts to bring their distinctive talents to bear on the problem. Deciding what kinds of deep smarts to cultivate internally and which to borrow or buy is clearly a strategic decision. One can mistakenly outsource the development of critical experience-based knowledge (e.g., subcontracting new product prototyping), but one can also wastefully reinvent knowledge assets that are readily available outside the organization.

In this chapter we will consider how knowledge gaps can be filled through assembling the deep smarts of others into a larger, more expansive, perhaps more creative experience repertoire than one person or group can expect to own. We deal with assemblages of expertise within rather than across organizations. For a thorough discussion of inter-organizational alliances and partnering, see Kanter.[1] Assembly may be as simple and straightforward as reaching out to those in our personal or professional networks to import the expertise needed to solve a problem. Or our organization may need to hire the people who embody the deep smarts we lack. Or the assemblage may not be people, but the products or components that have the deep smarts of their creators embedded in them, representing years of accumulated experience. Putting a management team together in fact constitutes a kind of assembly strategy, because each individual contributes special knowledge. The coaches for the start-ups in our study differed as to whether they tried to "grow" the founders into CEOs or assembled experienced management teams, but many assumed that inexperienced entrepreneurs could not possibly learn management skills fast enough to grow with the company, and so hired more experienced people as soon as they could to take the company forward.[2]

Assembly Models

There are three related but conceptually distinct assembly models. All involve bringing together different "components," or repositories of deep smarts. Sometimes these components are literally that—hardware or software that has been developed over many years and in which much knowledge is embedded. More typically, however, the deep smarts are embodied in people. The assembly models vary in terms of whether the components can be readily merged or are modified by the assemblage, how the interfaces among the components must be managed, and where deep smarts come into play. While the following sections discuss these three models in their "pure" forms, the distinctions are somewhat artificial, as one model may shade into another.

Plug and Play

In some knowledge assemblies, the competitive value of individuals or groups lies in their ability to plug chunks of knowledge into an architecture—to manage the whole distribution and work at the intersections and boundaries—rather than to represent deep pockets of specialized knowledge themselves. This ability is itself based on deep smarts, grounded in experience and perfected over the years. In plug and play, there is minimal or no attempt to modify the components; each represents a deep slice of expertise needed for the final product. The value added by managers in this model is in managing the overall architecture and the interfaces among the components. Each component may continue to develop its specialized deep smarts, independent of the actions of the overall manager. A writer editing a book assembles the individual chapters of the various authors and may write brief introductions that smooth the transitions from chapter to chapter. Such an editor needs deep smarts about the overall framework of the book and how to manage the connections between the chapters, but he may not be an expert in any of the chapter content. Many entertainment media also exemplify this type of assembly. For example, Cirque du Soleil is a highly successful "plug and play" assembly.

Cirque du Soleil is a group of more than fifty talented performers from fourteen countries. At a time when circuses have been disappearing, this novel approach to constructing an evening's entertainment has been a tremendous success. As of 2002, over 18 million people had attended one of their productions. The Bellagio Hotel in Las Vegas hauls in $1.2 million every week from the Cirque du Soleil shows, and Disney World has built a 1,671-seat facility to host the show. Cirque du Soleil is unusual not only because it very successfully revolutionized and revived a venerable but rather shopworn circus spectacle, but because the skills and expert know-how were assembled rather than grown organically over years—although of course, the show continues to evolve and build talent. But at its inception, the show resembled a Hollywood production—an assemblage of talented individuals, each of whom embodied decades of experience and deep smarts.

A company such as Dell Computer, which buys its components, has special knowledge that has accumulated over time—the ability to assemble and distribute computers—and 60 percent of its patents focus on operational know-how, such as streamlining assembly lines and reducing working capital by turning over inventories in as few as three days.[3] Dell's deep smarts as an organization are in logistics and selection of partners rather than the technology of the computers, and it is these deep smarts that have provided the company with a competitive advantage.

When the components in this assembly mode are people, the individual experts do not have to absorb each other's expertise. The relationship is essentially transactional. Each needs to know only just enough about the other's know-how to communicate and coordinate effectively. For example, the lawyers, recruiters, and real estate agents who assisted the start-ups we studied did not need to transfer much knowledge to one another or to the entrepreneurs whom they advised. The entrepreneurs merely needed to convey their needs, and the only knowledge that the technical specialists needed to transfer was enough about their service provision processes for a smooth interaction and coordination. In our study, that coordination was normally directed by a coach, who had the necessary deep smarts to envision the overall architecture of the company and its needs.

Plug, Modify, and Play

Some of the most inventive organizations in the United States are those where knowledge is assembled from many disparate sources, but instead of simply being plugged together, the components are modified before they are assembled. As in the plug and play model, deep smarts are embedded or embodied in the components. However, the individual or team that is assembling them also possesses deep smarts in scanning the environment for candidate components and envisioning a process for combining, recombining, or modifying them. To return to our hypothetical book editor, he may not simply identify the contributing authors and merge their articles to make a book as in plug and play, but may be deeply involved in suggesting changes to each author and adding integrative introductory and concluding notes to create a cohesive, novel book that is more than the sum of its chapters.

Thomas Edison assiduously cultivated his image as an inventor, and for many decades the myth of the lone genius prevailed in U.S. business. In fact, however, Edison's genius lay as much or more in his ability to combine existing technologies, convene smart people, and network with important contacts as in his personal engineering expertise. For example, Edison didn't *invent* the incandescent light bulb. It had existed for twenty years before he improved it to the point of commercialization.[4]

A more modern example of similarly assembled deep smarts is the renowned product development company, IDEO, headquartered in Palo Alto, California. David Kelley, founder of the company (which itself originated as a merger of a design company with an engineering group), says that his talented product developers aren't expert in any particular technology. They are experts in a creative *process* of design, which involves the innovative reuse and combination of knowledge—but not invention itself. So, for example, a valve designed for the mouth of a water bottle for bicyclists turned out to be a good holder for a computer stylus attached to a medical device. The designers at IDEO have the deep smarts to recognize valuable ideas and recombine them—in part because the company is itself an example of assembling diverse experience backgrounds: engineers and designers to be sure, but M.B.A.'s and psychologists as well as history, biology, or music majors.[5] The company also has a physical library of potential component parts housed in a cabinet of drawers dubbed the "technology box," and a software program that allows designers to locate such parts in other offices. The components are fragments of knowledge encapsulated in physical form. The drawers of the "box" have labels such as Thermo Technologies and Amazing Materials, and contain items with unusual properties that might solve a particular technical problem. For example, in one drawer is a small collection of soluble hollow beads smaller than the diameter of a human hair that can be filled with liquids or gases and then dissolve to deliver their contents; in another are strips of metal that can be contorted into many different shapes—but return to their original configuration when heated. The artifacts in this cabinet help in brainstorming sessions and serve to remind the designers of past solutions to knotty problems, enabling them to assemble knowledge not only across projects but across time.

Creative Fusion

The third assembly model also involves bringing together a variety of people, each with deep smarts, and in very different domains. The goal is to co-create something new, something that is greater than the sum of the expertise embodied in the different components. Creativity comes from fusing these different components to produce an innovation. That is, the individuals involved deepen their own smarts even as they combine their experience-based knowledge with that of others, and they share the responsibility for, and ownership of, the creation. The manager of a creative fusion process must have deep smarts in envisioning the ideal team and managing the creative abrasion that is likely to result when people with different kinds of deep smarts interact.[6] The manager is ideally a person who can orchestrate the blurring of boundaries between disparate disciplines to allow for a creative solution. For example, one of us was involved in a book project that had a novel approach: have a group of international experts from disparate fields—game theory, decision theory, small group theory, among others—and have them present rival analyses of two case studies (negotiating the Single European Act and negotiating the Uruguay Round of the General Agreement on Tariffs and Trade). The authors wrote drafts of their chapters and then convened to debate the merits of each, attempting to convince the others of the superiority of their own approach. The resulting creative abrasion was expertly managed by the book's editor, a professor of conflict resolution and international organization.[7]

The history of innovation is full of examples of invention that grew out of unlikely linkages across networks of expertise. Robert Langer was a chemical engineer with a new Ph.D. from the Massachusetts Institute of Technology when he went to see noted surgeon and cancer researcher Judah Folkman. Langer solved a problem standing in the way of testing Folkman's theory that cancer tumors could be killed by inhibiting the proteins that recruited blood supplies feeding the tumors' growth. The problem was how to slow the release of the proteins long enough to study them. The solution was to trap proteins inside tiny plastic capsules from which the proteins eventually escaped—but slowly. Not only did the invention allow the study of angiogenesis (the process by which the tumors recruit their blood supply), but enabled new ways of delivering chemotherapies and other drugs.[8]

A common example of creative fusion is a task force drawn from multiple levels in the organizational hierarchy, or a cross-functional team. One of the great benefits of such teams in organizations is the opportunity to tap into different experience bases to cover different contingencies. For example, in the design of new products or services, the manufacturing expert has a very different perspective from the financial wizard or the marketing guru. And deep smarts can be found on the factory floor as well as in the boardroom.

Toy company Fisher-Price's vice president of marketing and the vice president of product development struggled with how to develop a line of action figures that would be "Mom-friendly"—that is, nonviolent. Product Development argued that a line of action figures was crucial for the company; Marketing insisted on the sanctity of company values against violence. The creative abrasion between the two different approaches resulted in an innovative solution: Fisher-Price's "Rescue Heroes" such as Jack Hammer, Billy Blazes, and Rocky Canyon each carry a special tool appropriate to the "hero's" profession that does something dramatic when activated by a trigger. The Rescue Heroes line has been highly successful, yet has not sacrificed the company's values.[9]

Sometimes the particular problem under consideration has so many atypical characteristics that those engaged in its solution have to cast a wide net to find an expert who understands the rare context.

The task force manager must create an experience distribution by aggregating deep smarts that together represent both common and rare experiences. In the United States after the 9/11 terrorist attacks, for example, the Homeland Security task forces that have been mobilized in federal, state, and local governments often pull in experts from very different disciplines, such as religion, sociology, satellite communications technology, and nonverbal communication.

Within organizations, such fusion is possible only if internal boundaries are porous and divisions will lend even their best people to help an endeavor. Through creative fusion, 3M's Optical Division developed a thin plastic membrane to cover computer screens. The membrane reduced glare and electrostatic charges but also provided privacy through embedded microlouvers (like tiny venetian blinds) that made viewing impossible except for the person positioned directly in front of the screen. The team drew on expertise from some apparently highly unrelated divisions: The Specialty Film Division contributed expertise in film lamination, and the Corporate Process Technology Lab advised on surface adhesion. More surprising was the contribution of an engineer from the Surgical Products Division who was an expert hardware designer. The resulting computer screen turned out to be a highly profitable venture for 3M.[10]

Assemble Experts—or Grow Expertise?

The decision to assemble deep smarts or to grow them has strategic implications for both individuals and organizations. The decision rests at least in part on whether control, ownership, and continued development of the knowledge assets are important.

For the individual specialist, expanding one's experience repertoire is valuable—and indeed, that is where most of this book is focused. However, over time the deep smarts of some specialists (e.g., in fast-moving technical fields) can become outdated if there are no opportunities to update their knowledge base. This erosion of expertise can occur if an expert is constantly called upon to contribute knowledge to an assemblage, as, for example, when a software developer works on one cross-functional new product development team after another. If she has no time left over from sharing her experience base to devote to renewing her knowledge, her failure to renew will eventually undermine her value. She will no longer be able to represent the latest thinking. Therefore, she has to push for time to continue deepening her technical knowledge. On the other hand, a marketing expert might find that he deepened his knowledge by working on teams serving different markets. Either way, the organization (and the employee) will need to invest in continuing opportunities for the individual to develop deep smarts—and be a valued member of a knowledge assembly.

For an organization, the choice is often between growing a capability internally and outsourcing it for expediency's sake. In our start-up study, some of the novice managers chose unwisely whether or not their small company should own and control certain knowledge assets. Managers at one of the failed companies launched with money from an incubator rued the day they outsourced development of the heart of their software technology. The entrepreneur had been persuaded by the incubator funding his start-up to invest 40 percent of his total capital in software development by a third party. When the targeted market failed to materialize as expected, the start-up quickly went broke—with no owned assets to leverage. Moreover, the entrepreneur concluded that he could have had the same technical work done in-house for less money. The most successful of the thirty-five start-ups we studied built and retained control over intellectual property, so that they had assets to fall back on when the economy soured and marketing over the Internet proved difficult.

A build strategy requires a dedicated effort to develop deep smarts by exposing the particular individuals or groups to opportunities for direct experience over time. The actors individually and collaboratively create and absorb knowledge. For specialized know-how, most managers in large organizations prefer to hire consultants to do the work and thereby avoid incurring the costs of growing such expertise internally. But what if the expertise is knowledge that one anticipates needing for the foreseeable future?

In 2002, Best Buy CEO Brad Anderson foresaw that although the company was riding high at the time, future success depended on a higher level of innovation. He decided to invest in building the capability to innovate consistently rather than simply hiring a consultant to identify new business opportunities. Strategos Consulting promised to build an internal innovation capability that would remain in place when they left—to embed the capability in the DNA of the organization. Anderson made a huge commitment to the build strategy when he agreed to release thirty-five employees from their regular jobs for six months so they could learn the techniques, tools, and practices that would sustain ongoing innovation practices.[11] As we will discuss in more detail in chapter 8, the consultants and their temporary protégés were charged with two missions: to identify new business opportunities to be exploited in the near future and simultaneously to create a cadre of people capable of seeding the whole organization with innovation know-how.

In this book, we focus on this kind of knowledge building and cultivation, and on the largely uncodified knowledge embodied in people, more than on assembly of knowledge. We do not mean to suggest that building, as opposed to assembling, automatically confers strategic advantage. But we have three reasons for focusing on building deep smarts. First, in all three assembly models we have discussed, deep smarts reside in the components, whether those components are embedded in software or hardware or are embodied in human beings. (If the components lack deep smarts, why bother to assemble them?) Those deep smarts have had to grow through experience, so ultimately we need to know the nature of that process and how to facilitate it. Second, we do believe that assembly can be a successful strategy for individuals and organizations, but only if the assembly process itself becomes a competitively important capability—that is, if people build up deep smarts in *how* to assemble. The deep smarts may comprise logistical knowledge or excellent networks of talented people. But if there is no experience involved in the assembly, if *anyone* could go out on the open market and assemble the knowledge, it is difficult to see how assembling knowledge from ready-made parts, so to speak, could be a lasting advantage for an organization. Third, assembled expertise is only as stable as the cohesiveness of the systems holding the components together. Once an assemblage disbands, the knowledge it brought dissipates unless measures have been taken to capture or transfer the knowledge created by the assembly. But if deep smarts are grown within the individual or within the organization, then there they remain (so long as employees do not leave), contributing to the overall reservoir of knowledge.

We turn now to consider another form of deep smarts that grows over time as a consequence of one's life experiences—our personal and professional networks.

Know-who as Deep Smarts

Many times in life, who we know is at least as important as what we know. As one former CEO once (overmodestly) joked: "I don't know a lot, but I know a lot of people who do." While sometimes know-who is equated with being "well connected" for nefarious or at least unfair reasons (e.g., insider stock trading, or helping a child gain entrance to an elite school), we are concerned here with how know-who is used *legitimately* to access needed knowledge. Headhunters, venture capitalists, and publicists are expected to develop personal networks as part of their jobs. But know-who is also a crucial form of deep smarts for any individual or organization needing to bridge a knowledge gap. Just as broadening one's experience repertoire (chapter 2) can add to one's deep smarts, so can expanding one's know-who.

Deep smarts will depend on the extent of one's personal and professional network and the knowledge contained within that network. The extent of the network results from both serendipity and purposeful construction, and we will discuss how people deliberately cultivate know-who later in this chapter. The ability to access knowledge depends on one's store of social capital.

Cohen and Prusak define *social capital* as "the stock of active connections among people: the trust, mutual understanding, and shared values and behaviors that bind the members of human networks and communities and make cooperative action possible."[12] One can, of course, have extensive know-who, a rich network of highly knowledgeable individuals in the network—and still not have *useful* know-who. Without a reservoir of "trust, mutual understanding, and shared values," one is limited in being able to use the knowledge of others. An individual's social capital can be bolstered by the reputation of an organization or group to which he belongs, because those institutions are known for powerful connections (for example, a well-known university or venture capital firm). However, how the individual uses that institutional social capital in knowledge exchanges ultimately determines the person's own social capital.

Know-who, and the social capital flowing within the network, can be used for various purposes, including purely as influence—to persuade an executive to switch organizations, for example, or to obtain resources. However, we are most interested in those situations in which know-who provides access to essential knowledge assets. Perhaps you have a problem to solve and no one in your immediate circle knows how to approach it—or they think they do, and you want a second opinion before you act. Perhaps you have a hypothesis and need to test it out. Or you need help in launching an innovation and know you cannot act alone, because you don't have all the deep smarts required.

Know-who as Knowledge-Once-Removed

One option for accessing needed knowledge, considered earlier in this chapter, is to hire consultants or other experts to solve the problem for you or to help you solve it. But if you have built up enough social capital, you can use your know-who to access the deep smarts you need—without having to navigate the organizational bureaucracy or pay the salaries or consultant fees. Accessing another's deep smarts is both efficient and effective.

In 1979, then-CEO of Monsanto Jack Hanley was searching for someone to head up a revolutionary initiative for the chemicals and agribusiness corporation: life sciences. He approached a candidate, Howard Schneiderman, dean of the biological sciences at the University of California, Irvine, and posed a question from a field outside Schneiderman's expertise: "We're about to make a big investment in a silicon plant in the United States. Is silicon the material of choice for the semiconductors of the future?"

Schneiderman recalled, "I asked: 'How long will you give me to answer that—one day, one week, one month?' Hanley responded, 'Play it by ear.' " And Schneiderman responded:

> *"Well, if I had one day, I would call up the top biologist at the Massachusetts Institute of Technology, whom I know, and I would ask to be introduced in a telephone conference call to the top materials scientist at MIT. Then I'd pose the question to that person and ask him to think about it. I'd tell him: 'I'd be happy to give you $2,000 for an answer, and I'll call you back tomorrow.' I figured that guy would get on the telephone, and he would ask colleagues and in twenty-four hours, I could give Hanley a reasonable answer, although it wouldn't be perfect."*
>
> *"If I had a week, I'd get people together through my contacts at the National Academy of Sciences and MIT and Caltech and Stanford. Smart people know smart people and if I spoke to the best biologist I knew, or the top physicists at Cornell where I had been a professor at one time, they would point me in the right direction."*[13]

Schneiderman got the job, not only for what he knew, but also for whom he knew—for his ability to access knowledge stored in various human nodes in his networks. We have come to think of this process as using *knowledge-once-removed* (although, of course, it may be twice or thrice removed). In our entrepreneurship study, the coach often served as a connector, knowing another "expert" whose deep smarts could aid the fledgling company.

But what if we don't have direct access to the needed experts? The studies show that, even with limited know-who, each of us is only about six intermediaries away from a random stranger we wish to contact (see "Six Degrees of Separation"). This finding seems to promise that whoever and wherever we are, we can readily close the gap between ourselves and that faraway target—if we are sufficiently motivated to do so.

Our own findings in start-up companies resonate with those of "small-world" research. Time and again we saw coaches and entrepreneurs cut through a maze of uncertainty with the words, "I

Six Degrees of Separation

IN 1967, social psychologist Stanley Milgram published his research on the "small-world phenomenon." Milgram identified a random group of about three hundred people in the United States and asked them to try to get a letter to a target person. The catch? The target was identified by name, occupation, age, and geographical location—but not by specific address. The three hundred people needed to get the letter to the target by sending it to someone they knew personally. That person in turn would try to reach the target through a personal acquaintance . . . and so on until the letter found its way to the target's mailbox. Milgram found that it took only five or six intermediaries to link two strangers in the United States.

The study has spawned a Broadway play, a movie, a popular game ("Six Degrees of Kevin Bacon," in which players attempt to link the actor Kevin Bacon to some other actor through movies in which they have jointly appeared), and some serious information science and sociological research (for example, mapping e-mail networks).

How does one account for the small-world phenomenon? As Robert Matthews has pointed out, if we assume that we each have an average of three hundred people we can call by their first name, then there are two extreme conditions. If our three-hundred-friend network is highly insulated from everyone else's network—that is, if know someone who . . ." As we have written elsewhere,[14] Silicon Valley forms a large "commons" based on contributing and withdrawing expertise of its "guild" members. Venture capitalist Heidi Roizen says:

If an entrepreneur friend of mine comes to me and says I need this [expertise], part of what I'm doing is trying to understand what the person needs. Then I look in my Rolodex and try to

each network is an exclusive clique—then it would take about a million contacts on average to reach a stranger in another clique.[a] On the other hand, if there is no exclusivity at all and our friends are spread randomly around the country—if we are as likely to know Jack Welch as the car mechanic down the street—then the degrees of separation shrink to about four.

Reality seems to lie between these two extremes. If the United States is characterized essentially by exclusive cliques, but a small number of people in each clique have random links to other networks, then these random links can short-circuit the large network, and Milgram's six degrees of separation hold true. Watts and Strogatz tested a computer model in real life with the database much loved by the Kevin Bacon game crowd: the Internet Movie Database, containing over 200,000 actors and their filmographies. On average, they found, an actor has worked with sixty other actors; and any two actors can be linked on average through just three intermediaries.[b] The "short-circuits" in this case are actors who bridge different genres: the Kenneth Branaghs who star in both Shakespeare adaptations and Harry Potter films.

a. Robert Matthews, "Six Degrees of Separation," *World Link*, January–February 2000.
b. Duncan Watts and Steven Strogatz, "Collective Dynamics of Small-World Networks," *Nature* 393 (1998): 440–442.

*figure out who has the skill set needed. Is it someone who is a team
builder or is it someone who is a great CEO coach? Is it someone
who gets engineers and turns them into terrific contributors?*

But within this ecosystem are subgroups, many of which are based
on national origin, such as the Indian and Chinese subgroups. Within
each subgroup, there are very few degrees of separation—it takes
only a couple of phone calls to connect two Indians in the Silicon
Valley business community who do not already know one another.
Know-who often has a provincial flavor; in order for members of
two different subgroups to connect, there has to be a connecting
"node," someone who operates within both subgroups. Few of our
non-Indian respondents had heard of any of the Indian coaches we
interviewed, but many knew Kanwal Rekhi, who could then serve
as the short-circuit between the Indian and non-Indian entrepreneurial networks.

The ability to draw on the deep smarts of others rests on two
major factors. First, setting aside those situations in which assistance is paid for in cash, one must have developed social capital to
"spend." In our study, this generally meant that the person asking
for help was part of the "commons," part of the community in
which knowledge was bartered. Because membership in the commons was determined by one's demonstrated ability to provide
value, one could withdraw from the bank of expertise in the expectation that in the future the favor could be reciprocated.[15] Schneiderman's commons was academia—people with whom he had taught
or served on National Science Foundation committees. (However,
either he did not feel he had enough social capital to ask for the knowledge without financial reimbursement, or simply wanted them to be
compensated for their time.) In the case of Roizen, the price she paid
for providing the knowledge was the right of that person to draw on
her knowledge at some time in the future. Second, once one is an acknowledged member of a knowledge commons, then a level of trust
is assumed among members.

As Cohen and Prusak note, "trust is a precondition of healthy
social capital."[16] Suppose that a coach arranges a meeting of her

protégé entrepreneur with a venture capitalist to review the entrepreneur's business plan. The venture capitalist may trust that the coach would not have arranged the meeting without some expectation that the entrepreneur will have something of value to provide. Alternatively, if this is not the case, then the venture capitalist may assume that the coach will provide him with some future value. As Larry Prusak is fond of saying, "trust lowers the cost of transactions." We deal more easily with people whose competence and willingness to reciprocate, should the occasion arise, we trust.

In our study, coaches varied both in the extent of their knowledge networks and in their ability to count on a response to a request. The more expert the coach, and the more social capital he or she possessed, the deeper the knowledge-once-removed was likely to be. We asked the coaches in our entrepreneurship study to examine the names of all the other coaches we had interviewed, to indicate whether they had heard of them, and if so, to estimate how easily each of those people could elicit a response from anyone they wished in Silicon Valley. By far the highest rating was given to Kleiner Perkins venture capitalist Vinod Khosla. This collective judgment was borne out by the two founders of Zaplet, Brian Axe and David Roberts, who provided several examples of Khosla using his personal and institutional social capital to persuade experienced managers and even CEOs to lend their deep smarts to the Zaplet team.

Know-who as a Second Opinion

Even people possessed of deep smarts themselves often want to check their opinions against those of other experts. In the entrepreneurship study, coaches and entrepreneurs alike also used their know-who to validate their own expertise—to obtain a second opinion from a trusted evaluator. In the best of cases, getting a second opinion either challenged the coach's assumptions or reinforced them—that is, it served as a reality check on their intuition.

Although he himself was an ex-entrepreneur and had such impressive coaching merit badges as having been an early advisor to

Yahoo!, Fred Gibbons frequently brought other experts from Silicon Valley into discussions of young companies. Gibbons especially valued the tough wisdom of a man he referred to as "Moses," Jack Melchor. "He is a Depression-era guy, with steel-cold toughness," said Gibbons. "There's no touchy-feely with guys like him. His integrity is beyond belief. . . . When he's in the boardroom, he uses the Socratic method. He keeps asking questions until he just wears you down." Gibbons specifically consulted Melchor to get a second opinion on ActivePhoto, the nascent company he was mentoring:

> *Jack was in the first five meetings with me, shaping the ideas with these kids. At the Friday meeting, they presented it, and I had the kids go get a cup of coffee while we discussed it, before we gave them a thumbs-up or a thumbs-down. And I said, "Jack, okay, what's the deal?" You might as well hear from Moses, right? So I said, "Moses, would you invest in this company?" He says "yes." I said "why?" He said, "Well, I like the people, they've come a long way, they seem to have morphed their ideas, they've picked a market they can probably go after: emergency services, real-time photo communications. It'll probably morph into some bigger opportunity. We don't know what it is, but let's get out there and play."*

Know-who as a Filter

Once a person is professionally established, she may have more demands from her extended network than she can reasonably handle. In such situations, the core network is used to filter contacts from outsiders or bare acquaintances. Nowhere is this more true than within the commons of Silicon Valley. For example, members of the commons rely on one another to screen or "prequalify" potential entrepreneurs. When a member of the "guild" passes along a business plan that he has personally vetted, this represents a deposit into the bank. Foundation Capital's Mike Schuh has learned that certain mentor capitalists can be depended on to add value: "Of the hundreds of things that I look at every week, if it's got one of those [mentor's] names on it, I don't even bother reading, I just make the appointment." The mentors in turn benefit by being brought in on future deals. (As the market for entrepreneur coaches diminished following the dot-com crash, a number of the mentor capitalists we interviewed subsequently were hired by venture capital firms —another way in which bread cast upon the waters may return in another form.)

Such filters are increasingly important as the World Wide Web enables complete strangers to contact people asking for help, including sizeable investments of knowledge. For example, as academics, we receive e-mails from around the world from students, some of whom offer little evidence of having done any work themselves before asking for customized treatises on huge topics such as "innovation" or "technology management." And were we to agree to all the e-mailed requests for informally reviewing and commenting on articles, books, brochures, white papers, and business ideas, we would have no time for anything else. So, like our venture capital coaches, we respond with more alacrity to those sent to us by someone we know. As Cohen and Prusak write, "Social capital bridges the space between people."[17]

Cultivating Know-who

Know-who begins in nursery school. Of course, most of us are unaware of the value of those relationships until we are launched professionally. Moreover, we are fairly casual about our networks. In fact, sometimes our upbringing or culture makes us feel that it is bad manners to think about a web of acquaintances as a knowledge asset, particularly when networks are "worked" strategically. Building a network comes naturally to some and only awkwardly to others. Some people are intensely uncomfortable asking for help, or feel that deliberately cultivating acquaintances is somehow manipulative. But many people *enjoy* sharing their knowledge. K. C. Branscomb, who has had a very successful career as an entrepreneur and coach, says, "I think people like to help. If I'm not overly burdensome, I have never found anybody who wouldn't give me advice."

Cultivating know-who is critical in bridging knowledge gaps and providing access to resources. But there are significant differences in the way that women and men build and use their know-who—in no small part because the organizational settings in which they work affect access. For example, men tend to have strong ties with other men, from whom they derive both friendship support and also job-related advice, political access, and resources. Women tend to obtain social support from other women, but access job-related knowledge and resources through men.[18] For both, know-who is invaluable, whether it forms serendipitously or is formally nurtured.

INFORMAL SYSTEMS. One prominent coach has described venture capitalist Heidi Roizen as "just a virtuoso at driving reactions and responses, positive and constructive responses, from her network." Here is what Roizen herself says about building and using know-who:

> I'm a very active e-mailer. I go to a lot of industry events; I host a lot of events. I make an effort to go out and do things. Whenever a member of the press is here I make an effort to meet with them. Is it part of my job to meet periodically with people who run business development in other corporations? Am I like a salesperson who has a list of my prospects to network with for this week? No. Definitely it is much more ad hoc. But my husband and I have concert tickets for next month and we said, "Who are we going to invite? Let's invite someone we haven't seen for a while." Make sure you spread around and see people, because like most people we tend to get into a rut—these are our ten best friends and we spend all our time with them and our kids are used to their kids and all that kind of stuff. So my networking is highly evolved, but not methodical.

Sometimes building know-who is just a matter of focusing energy in informal settings. Former mentor capitalist and now venture capitalist Stan Meresman recalled of a former boss: "He would go to a cocktail party after a conference. You're tired at the end of the

day, and there are a hundred people sitting around, and it's some-
place I really didn't want to be. As we walked in, he would stop and
survey the room and say, 'There are four people I want to talk to.'
We'd go in and when he had talked to those four people, he'd say,
'We're done.' "

FORMAL SYSTEMS. In some professions, such as venture capital or executive search, networking is part of the job. While Heidi
Roizen describes her networking as ad hoc, some of the venture
capitalists we interviewed were very systematic. Beckie Robertson
of Versant Ventures describes her careful building of a contacts file
to help start-ups that Versant funds:

> *[My networking] is almost embarrassingly formulaic. I have a list
> of people in various categories—business executives or stars that
> some day I want to recruit to one of the companies I've invested
> in, talented clinicians and engineers who are likely to be sources
> of new ideas that require funding, service providers who really
> will help our companies. We want to make sure we have an unfair
> mind share with these categories of people. I just rotate among
> them. Every week I try to set up x number of calls. My assistant
> gives me the list. I say, "These are the folks that I'd like to see in
> the next week." I make the call myself to people who are new or
> the first couple of times that I meet with them, but after that I
> leave it to her, or I'd spend all my time setting up appointments. I
> don't always have a particular agenda, although I almost always
> end up having one because I'm always trying to recruit someone,
> or deal with an issue. But sometimes it's just chatting: "So how
> are the kids?" and "What are you going to do for your vacation
> this summer?" It's just building a personal relationship. But it's so
> important. It's part of the profession.*

Robertson's networking contributes to keeping her deep smarts
competitive. But why shouldn't keeping track of talented people be
part of *all* managers' jobs? Being able to reach into one's Rolodex
to locate talent is becoming increasingly important as people switch
companies—and careers—more frequently.

Limits of Know-who

If you know someone who is knowledgeable, but whom people do not like to approach—someone who is unfailingly negative perhaps, or inflexibly convinced of a single best way to approach every problem—you are not alone. Rob Cross and colleagues discovered in a recent study of networking within organizations that there are "de-energizers" in the workplace whom people avoid, even if they are experts. "While energizers have a disproportionate [positive] effect on group learning," the researchers write, "the expertise of de-energizers often goes untapped no matter how relevant it is." [19] In such cases, identifying the expert may not aid the transfer of deep smarts.

Highly specialized networks also limit the usefulness of know-who, as they don't help us reach unrelated knowledge—at least not through direct contact. In our study of start-ups, the novice managers often had strong ties to technical communities, but needed help getting to financial and managerial networks. Moreover, there is a temptation to believe that an extensive network translates into access to deep smarts—but the person may lack the social capital to extract knowledge from the network, or the network may be empty of the particular knowledge needed. In our research, we have found instances of would-be entrepreneurs and incubator founders who believed that their networks in the financial world were an adequate basis for starting a new business. Sure, they knew people who understood financing and venture capital. But these individuals did not necessarily have any deep smarts about how to launch, build, and sustain a new venture. So networking helps only if there is accessible knowledge available within the network.

Implications for Managers

Every useful organization has a mission (even if it's not framed on the wall or carried around on a laminated card), and that mission is rarely accomplished by cultivating internally all the knowledge assets needed. Often knowledge is borrowed, copied, or purchased to fill gaps in the internal capabilities. However, even if an organization is designed to be a pure "plug and play" assembly of component parts, it must have some distinctive capabilities, some knowledge that distinguishes it from competitors. This knowledge can be an unusually effective ability to assemble what others have grown (the Dell Computer model).

More often, organizations have multiple internal capabilities, and the managerial task is to decide what knowledge would be more efficiently grown by someone else and imported, and what constitutes core capabilities for the firm. Such decisions are not easy. We have seen leaders struggle for months to decide what their core capabilities are, while managers throughout the organization claim that those capabilities reside within their particular internal division or function. And we have seen cases in which managers undervalued in-house deep smarts because no one really understood their contribution. For example, in a large steel company, one of us was sitting in on a top-level meeting when the CEO posed a question: What is a humane way to "let go" a small group of "advance sales" people? "What does the advance sales group *do?*" he was asked. He was flummoxed. He didn't know. Neither did any of the other top managers seated around the table. Investigation into the work of the group uncovered a pocket of deep smarts: The five people followed regulatory, social, and economic trends in the country and anticipated market demands. The work of one individual alone had repaid several times over the entire cost of the group after he found that regulations making their way through Congress would require a lower level of toxic emissions from home furnaces. Realizing that caustic fumes would therefore necessarily be trapped in furnaces, and hence the steel in furnace flues would have to be more corrosion resistant, he alerted the division selling into the residential market that they should sell to their customers the kind of steel currently being produced for the nuclear division. Because of this knowledge, the company's residential division had an almost two-year lead over its competitors. After the top managers discovered this anecdote (and a number like it), they downsized the group through attrition—but they did not eliminate it or its function.

As this example suggests, in order to know which knowledge to protect and what can be assembled or outsourced, the manager has to have a good idea of what deep smarts exist within her organization. However, she must also know what relevant ones have been grown elsewhere that could be appropriated, adapted, or merged. And when the only deep smarts available are embodied in people rather than embedded in artifacts, the manager has to know how to access those individuals and their knowledge, and ensure that their deep smarts continue to reside in the organization.

Some of the world's most important inventions have come about through the process of creative fusion—the amalgamation of deep smarts achieved by assembling wise, experienced, and diverse individuals into a team. The variety in perspectives that enhance creativity and performance can often be found by cutting a vertical swath through the organization, to access not just the knowledge and experience of upper managers but also the deep smarts possessed by people working the machines, keeping operations flowing in the offices, or spending their days face-to-face with customers.

Individual managers assemble knowledge when they access and use deep smarts that they do not personally possess—nor are likely to. Managers need to cultivate their know-who. Knowledge networks are communal banks in which social capital is often the coinage of the realm. An individual cannot forever withdraw from a knowledge bank without contributing, that is, cannot spend social capital of his own or that of his coach without returning some to the community. (We will discuss how to do this in chapter 9.) However, knowledge-once-removed is an asset underutilized in many organizations and by many individuals.

Keep in Mind

- It is sometimes preferable to assemble deep smarts rather than grow them in an individual or organization.
- A "plug and play" model brings together components (hardware, software, or individuals with different kinds

of embodied deep smarts) with little attempt to modify them. Rather, the interfaces among the components must be managed.

- With the "plug, modify, and play" assembly model, deep smarts are embedded in the components, but those components will be adapted or modified in the final product.

- Creative fusion is the third assembly model, in which very different kinds of components are assembled with the goal of fusing them into something very new.

- Growing expertise is preferable when the individual or organization must own the knowledge. If assembly models are used, it is important that deep smarts develop around the assembly process itself.

- Knowledge can be embedded in personal networks, so know-who can be an important type of deep smarts, as know-who "experts" are able to access needed knowledge readily ("knowledge-once-removed").

- Know-who can also be used to validate an opinion or to prequalify people seeking access to one's expertise.

FIVE

Beliefs Shape Deep Smarts

PHILOSOPHERS have defined knowledge as "justified true belief." Why *belief*? Because knowledge is subjective, and it is
shaped—*justified*—by many influences. Beliefs are important to
deep smarts in at least two ways. First, beliefs build up just as deep
smarts do—over time, by life experience, and through the influence
of people around us. Beliefs are often largely tacit and unquestioned.
Pushed to explain how they know something is true, people will often
trace their knowledge back to some fundamental belief system. Does
this mean that beliefs are part of our deep smarts? To the extent that
we base decisions and actions on beliefs and assumptions, yes. We
do not wish to retread well-tilled epistemological ground here to
decide "what is truth"—that is, whether deep smarts have to be
infallible. Part of our point here is that "truth" may depend on one's
viewpoint. It is sufficient for our message to acknowledge that people build, transfer, and react to beliefs as knowledge, and therefore
for them beliefs are indeed a part of their deep smarts. For our own
sakes, for the sakes of those we manage or those whose careers we
influence, we also need to be aware of how beliefs affect *our* interactions, our decisions, our acceptance of change. (See figure 5-1).

FIGURE 5-1

Deep Smarts and Knowledge Framing

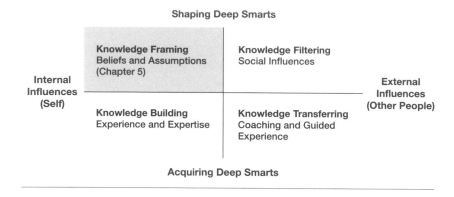

Some of our beliefs are inconsequential, such as believing that Pepsi tastes better than Coke, or that the Boston Red Sox will some day win a World Series. While such beliefs may be very strongly, even passionately, held, they are inconsequential in the sense that they do not underpin many other beliefs. Other more consequential beliefs may influence critical decisions that we make in our professions. As we shall see, our education and disciplinary bases lead us to believe in and value certain kinds of knowledge over others, to believe that our assumptions are more correct than those of other people. Still other beliefs are core to our sense of who we are—our identity. These are our highly *central* beliefs that support a large number of other beliefs and behaviors. Such beliefs are unquestioned—taken for granted as truth, even when challenged by other "truths." Therefore, they are more important to our understanding of deep smarts than are less influential beliefs. These central beliefs are largely tacit, and highly resistant to social influence.

The second way beliefs are relevant to deep smarts is that they determine what we take in from our environment as true. Strongly held beliefs are lenses that refract our view of the world and define what is real—even when "objective" evidence is to the contrary. One person's truth is another's myth. That is, the opposite of a truth is not necessarily a lie—but another truth. Our beliefs filter incoming knowledge from other people (their smarts) and test those incoming messages against what *we* believe.

On June 30, 2003, an explosion tore apart a mosque in Falluja, Iraq, killing a half dozen people. Some eyewitnesses recounted seeing an American helicopter or an F-16 overhead and insisted that Americans had fired a missile "to prevent the sounds of prayer in the mosque." Other eyewitnesses said, "All the windows were open and we heard no aircraft." The Americans vehemently denied any military strike and maintained that their analysis showed the explosion originated within the mosque—most likely from stored explosives. "The reaction to the blast," the *New York Times* reported, "showed that American troops are being held responsible for every violent act that happens here . . . no matter who actually did it." The report continued, "What caused the explosion is so deeply contested, so ideologically colored, that it seems it will be hard to ever reach a consensus. . . . But in the end, the truth seemed almost irrelevant."[1] Americans believed that the Iraqis had been sheltering illegal explosives with malicious intent and unintentionally detonated them; the Iraqis believed that the Americans deliberately destroyed a hated symbol of Islam. Each side's perception of the truth was highly colored by its belief systems. Regardless of what evidence either side would muster, each "knew" the truth of the incident.

We see such evidence of the power of belief systems to shape knowledge all the time. People feel passionately about the dangers or benefits of global warming, fluoridation, or child day care, often ignoring, dismissing, or selectively attending to scientific evidence. Consider another complex example, the O. J. Simpson murder trial, in which the famous athlete and actor was acquitted despite DNA evidence against him. The U.S. public divided along racial lines in their beliefs about the validity of DNA evidence and the fairness of the justice system. As a result, people concluded either that a rich and privileged man had succeeded in literally getting away with murder or that, for once, a black had beaten an unfair system in which planted and spurious evidence was often used to convict innocents.

In the remainder of this chapter we take a tour of beliefs, showing their power and influence on behavior and on deep smarts. We then explore how and when beliefs can change.

A Hierarchy of Beliefs

We are not born with beliefs; we absorb them from our experience in the world, including what people around us believe. We can think of beliefs as forming a kind of hierarchy that includes central or core beliefs (most basic and least open to change), less central or more peripheral ones (more malleable), and finally the inconsequential ones. (See "The Centrality of Beliefs.") We are interested here in only the

The Centrality of Beliefs

HOW DO we know which of our beliefs are central or core, and which are more peripheral? Beliefs are central to the extent that many other beliefs and behaviors depend upon them.

Psychologist Milton Rokeach has argued that central beliefs are those that are tied to our sense of identity, are supported by significant other people in our lives, and have been experienced directly. So, for example, a belief that you are a moral person will be central if friends and family share that impression of you, and if you can easily recount examples where you behaved in an ethical manner. The centrality of the belief will be weakened to the extent that it is not related to your self-concept, is not supported by others, and is not linked to direct experience. Rokeach designed a study to test some of these ideas. Subjects in his experiment first filled out a questionnaire assessing their beliefs. Some of these beliefs were highly central—containing all three of the defining characteristics—while others were increasingly peripheral, including matters of personal taste. Each person was then hypnotized and some of his or her beliefs were undermined. For example, the subjects were told that they were *not* Catholic (if they indeed were), or that soap that floats in the bathtub is superior to soap that sinks (if they in fact believed the opposite). They were then given a posthypnotic suggestion that first two. Beliefs, psychologists maintain, depend for their centrality on three factors: (1) the extent to which the belief is tied to our identity or sense of self (itself an outgrowth of our gender, family background, physical attributes, personality, and education, or, in the case of organizations, of the founders' beliefs and early decisions about brand); (2) whether we have had firsthand experience with the object of the belief; and (3) the degree to which the belief is supported by those we associate with, particularly those we admire. When a belief relates directly to one's identity, has been supported

when they awakened they would still hold the new (changed) beliefs. Rokeach found that few people changed their most central beliefs (e.g., denying their religion), but that the more peripheral the beliefs were, the more likely they were to change (floating soap is great). Of further interest, Rokeach found that when a *relatively* central belief was changed, then many other related but less central beliefs also changed, even though they had not actually been manipulated. (Finally, all the subjects had the posthypnotic suggestions removed and all of the original beliefs were restored.)[a]

More recent studies have shown that beliefs about ourselves can be a powerful influence shaping our own knowledge. In one intriguing line of research, Asian American women were given a challenging mathematics test. Prior to testing, either their gender or their ethnicity was subtly "primed" by the experimenter. When their gender identity was activated, their performance suffered, presumably because they were confirming the belief that "women do poorly at math." But when their Asian identity was activated, they did particularly well, thus confirming the belief that "Asians do well at math."[b]

a. Milton Rokeach, *Beliefs, Attitudes and Values* (San Francisco: Jossey-Bass, 1970).
b. Margaret Shih, Todd Pittinsky, and Nalini Ambady, "Shifts in Women's Quantitative Performance in Response to Implicit Sociocultural Identification," *Psychological Science* 10 (1999).

by personal experience, and is buttressed by a consensus from other people, the belief will be highly central and largely impervious to change. More peripheral beliefs lack one or more of these three and are therefore more malleable. We will postpone discussing the third, the influence of associates, until the next chapter, Social Influences. Here we focus on the belief systems grounded in personal identity and experience that are especially important to the transfer of deep smarts at four different levels: individual, discipline-based, organizational, and cultural.

Individual Beliefs

Our personal identities are made up largely of our distinctive set of beliefs, particularly those that are central to who we are. Individual belief systems thus comprise a significant part of our deep smarts, in that they are the product of many years of experience and are largely tacit in nature. Individual beliefs also serve as filters, influencing how we perceive the world and what we find acceptable, immoral, or satisfying. For example, entrepreneur Randy Paynter's personal background and beliefs deeply influenced the kinds of knowledge he accessed to design his start-up—and the belief systems he tapped into to build a customer base. Care2 began as an electronic greeting card company where 10 percent of revenues went to nonprofit environmental organizations. As the company evolved into a portal, it retained its roots, driven by the founder's central beliefs in environmental causes:

> *The environment has always meant a lot to me. My father is an ornithologist, my mother loves the environment, nature, all of that. . . . Our market is the light green consumer, people who would like to do something good for the environment but generally don't have the time or energy. Probably between 75 and 85 percent of Americans would consider themselves light green. We are trying to provide them with everyday services such as e-mail,*

Web search, and news but in a context that lets them do some-
thing good for the world at the same time. They can read the
same news that they would read elsewhere, but by seeing it on
our site they're helping generate donations to environmental non-
profits, and also we provide some environmental news so they
can learn as they go. We're working with Nature Conservancy's
Adopt-an-Acre Program, so every time you click the button
you're generating a donation to help save rainforest land.

But Care2 had to be a real business, one that would attract investors who expected to make money. Paynter described how his
coach, Fern Mandelbaum, helped him walk this tightrope:

In positioning the company, she's helped me with this thinking.
[She says:] "Don't even mention the word charity. Donations are
okay, but in terms of marketing, this is a for-profit business, a
huge business, a $900 billion market." It is a challenge to attract
people who've been investing in high-tech or have been successful
in high-tech, because they'll say, "Well, you're involved with
some of these nonprofit organizations. This isn't a real business
opportunity. I can feel good about it, but I'm not going to make
any money on this." That's definitely been a challenge for me.

The business model that Paynter had to present in order to obtain funding conflicted with his motivation for starting the company and his deep belief that he could "do well by doing good."
Was Mandelbaum right? Paynter did not have to change his business model to conform to the belief systems of his investors. But he
did have to change his communications with them, to acknowledge
their own motivations and beliefs, which included that identification with nonprofit businesses would be the kiss of death for their
investment.[2] As we shall see in chapter 6, complying with a request
to modify a behavior does not alter one's central beliefs or deep
smarts. But if Mandelbaum had asked Paynter to change the beliefs
that motivated him, he would have had to choose between serving

the business and compromising his own identity—what he "knew" as the right basis for business decisions, namely an abiding conviction that business should also serve society.

Discipline-Based Beliefs

Every discipline has a set of lenses through which its members view the world. In fact, individuals often gravitate toward a particular function or discipline because their own worldview is supported and reinforced by that discipline, and therefore their work life harmonizes with their core beliefs. These lenses quite literally affect what an individual perceives; they shape experience and hence heavily influence the nature of a person's deep smarts.

For example, in new product development, designers are generally concerned with aesthetics (form) and engineers more with function. The designers of a BMW "skin," as the outside is called, worry about the sensations that a good design elicits from consumers: reactions to the reflection of light off the car surfaces and the flow of contour lines. They develop deep smarts in the ability to differentiate shapes at the level of a millimeter—and they believe in the importance of such minute differences to the customer, even if consumers do not consciously register such variation. The engineers deal more with the "package"—motor, wheels, steering, climate control, exhaust. At BMW, as at other automotive companies, designers are emotionally attached to the process of building the exquisitely precise, full-size clay models used to assess and perfect aesthetics. Their beliefs about the importance of this process to the BMW brand were challenged when the company decided to move to a computer-aided styling (CAS) process. Chris Bangle, head of worldwide design at BMW, described the challenge:

> It helps if you understand how cars are traditionally done—by hand, using clay tools. This creative process allows for an enormous amount of human interaction with the surfaces being developed . . . you have an idea, a direction, and you're trying to caress,

*love, and stroke it, and pull it out. There is truly a sensual rela-
tionship between the creator and the object that is often written
about in art. The same is true in cars. . . . CAS basically says that
we will simulate that effect and replace it with synthetic methods.
Is it really the same? We used to joke: How many people would
choose a wife or husband from a picture on the Internet?*[3]

Reactions such as these are often dismissed cavalierly as "resistance to change." But what is the basis of the resistance? These individuals deeply believe that BMW customers *love* their cars—and in
no small part because they are produced with so much intimate, af-
fectionate attention. While the first 80 to 95 percent of design could
be accomplished through CAS, the designers (and many BMW managers) believed that the last 5 percent made a huge competitive difference—and could never be accomplished using computers. Such
beliefs are difficult to dislodge because they are tied to the designers'
identities as artists and their pride, even passion, for the product.
When they retire, they will be proud of what they have done with
their lives because they believe they made a difference. These beliefs
were important not only to the employees, but to the image BMW
promoted in the market—that of a company producing finer cars
than competitors because of handcrafting.

In the end, BMW used a hybrid approach: CAS to take the design as far as it could—but also a few clay models. The beliefs in the
competitive worth of the last few percentage points of design performance prevailed. These beliefs were not only central to the designers, but also to the firm, and shaped corporate strategy.

Organizational Beliefs

Beliefs in what constitutes success and in the strategies that lead to
success originate in the early days of an organization and become
entrenched over time. In effect, such beliefs become part of the deep
smarts of the organization—based on firsthand experience and tied
to its identity. Mary Tripsas has traced many of Polaroid's problems

in trying to move to electronic imaging back to beliefs that originated with founder Edwin Land and were deeply held by subsequent CEOs and top management.[4] Four beliefs in particular shaped the way that Polaroid approached electronic imaging: (1) Success was attributable to difficult, long-term, large-scale research projects. Land wrote in 1980: "Do not undertake the program unless the goal is manifestly important and its achievement nearly impossible. Do not do anything that anyone else can do readily."[5] (2) Customers wanted a physical print (and therefore video camcorders were not competition). (3) Prints had to be as high quality as traditional 35-mm; one senior manager said that this notion was "indelible in the DNA" of the company. (4) "Finally," Tripsas added, "there was a strong belief in the razor/blade business model,"[6] that is, that all the money was to be made from selling film (which they called "software")—not from cameras (hardware).

Not surprisingly, then, an electronic imaging group created within Polaroid set its sights on developing an instant digital camera with a detachable printer. They also invested heavily in another product consistent with the prevailing belief system: a technically complex medical imaging system called Helios, profits from which were expected through the sales of the media used. Despite the fact that the company was well positioned technically by 1989 to develop a digital camera, it did not place one in the market until 1996. A good part of the delay was occasioned by a "clash . . . driven by fundamentally different beliefs" between the old guard and new hires into the Electronics Imaging Division. A new hire described to Tripsas and Giovanni Gavetti how discussions went with senior management:

> The catch [to our product concept] was that you had to be in the hardware business to make money. "How could you say that? Where's the film? There's no film?" So what we had was a constant fight with the senior executive management in Polaroid for five years. . . . We constantly challenged the notion of the current business model, the core business as being old, antiquated, and unable to go forward. . . . What was fascinating to me was that

these guys used to turn their noses up at 38 percent margins. . . .
But that was their big argument: "Why 38 percent? I can get 70
percent on film. Why do I want to do this?"[7]

In 1996, Polaroid sold the Helios division, as digital imaging
had lost $180 million in 1994 and $190 million in 1995. CEO Gary
DiCamillo, who took over in 1996, shifted emphasis from technology to marketing; the number of internal employees devoted to digital imaging research fell from a one-time high of three hundred to
about fifty in 1998. However, the new CEO continued support for
the razor/blade philosophy of the company. On October 12, 2001,
the company filed for Chapter 11 bankruptcy. The stock price fell
from about $60 a share in 1997 to about 10 cents a share at the
time trading was halted. Many onlookers found it incomprehensible how such a formerly vibrant firm, full of intelligent people,
could have failed to move successfully into a business that seemed
so related to prior product lines and markets. The "new" and imported knowledge about opportunities in the digital markets failed
to fit with the entrenched belief systems about what was a good
business model.[8]

As this example suggests, belief systems, when they are central
to the identity of the organization and reinforced by early experience, can become as strong as ideology—almost a religion. And
they can stifle innovation and learning.

Cultural Beliefs

Finally, beliefs build as part of deep smarts at a cultural level as
well. Culture is a very broad and useful term, encompassing language, norms of behavior, artifacts—all those visual, verbal, and
behavioral cues that tell someone newly arrived that this place has
different beliefs from those left behind. A visitor from France is
startled at the common sight of guns mounted in the back of pick-
up trucks in Texas; "spirit houses" mark the sites of downed trees
in the yards of houses in Thailand; cows meander through traffic in

Calcutta. The values assimilated from one's culture are reinforced daily through family, friends, organizations, and media. The result is that culturally derived values are often so deeply ingrained that people are entirely unaware of using them as knowledge for decision making—until those values are challenged. Cultural values influence virtually all individual behaviors, and behaviors related to business are no exception.

Despite the high degree of global interdependence in business and the fact that so many managers have breakfast on one continent, then dinner on another, there is a human tendency to believe in one right road to prosperity—and of course it is *ours*. Nobel laureate economist Joseph Stiglitz castigates the International Monetary Fund (IMF) for forcing hasty privatization, fiscal austerity, and market liberalization on countries with little infrastructure to manage the sudden change from centrally controlled economies.[9] This global battle over what we "know" to be the best way for an economy to develop has affected hundreds of millions of lives. The IMF is not the only organization to believe that the Western way is the only way. Tarun Khanna and Krishna Palepu, who conducted extensive research within a number of developing nations, have written:

> As emerging markets open up to global competition, consultants and foreign investors are increasingly pressuring these groups to conform to Western practice by scaling back the scope of their business activities. The conglomerate is the dinosaur of organizational design, they argue, too unwieldy and slow to compete in today's fast-paced markets. . . . There are reasons to worry about this trend. Focus is good advice in New York or London, but something important gets lost in translation when that advice is given to groups in emerging markets. Western companies take for granted a range of institutions that support their business activities, but many of these institutions are absent in other regions of the world.[10]

One important something that "gets lost" is the realization that the apparently very rational economic policies promulgated in the

West are *beliefs*—born of experience to be sure, but experience in a very different context from that of developing nations. With the notable exception of a few companies such as GE, Western multinationals (e.g., Microsoft or Intel or Caterpillar) have tended to cluster their businesses within a single industry. However, the trading company history in Asia has led to Indian or Chinese conglomerates with businesses encompassing industries as diverse as cooking oils and steel. The Tata Industries group in India, for example, has businesses in information technology, process controls, advanced materials, and oil field services, among others. As Khanna and Palepu explain, such diversification allows the group to substitute internal labor, capital, and product markets for those that are maintained externally by established institutions in developed nations.

The belief in the extreme importance of focus early in a venture's life was promulgated by many of the coaches in our entrepreneurship study. Even the coaches who had grown up in developing nations tended to sing from the same Western hymnal when they came back to Asia. However, the entrepreneurs in Asia were more resistant to this advice than those in the United States. Looking around them at established, successful holding companies, the Indian and Chinese entrepreneurs wondered at the wisdom of the advice they were being given. Why not seize opportunities to make money, even if the markets that welcomed their products were not related?

Subinder Khurana, a venture capitalist in New Delhi, reflected on the advice offered by one of the firm's advisors, a successful Indian-born U.S. entrepreneur:

One big message he preaches is to focus narrowly on something. That is a big difference from the way traditionally businesses are run in India. Business here has always been very reactive: When some opportunity comes up, you say, "okay, why let it go?" You just pick it up. That is [behavior] we fight against day in and day out. All our entrepreneurs, in fact any business plan we get, the first thing we have to do is hack away 90 percent of what they are trying to do, saying, "This is where your strength is, this is where

you can go, just focus on this." Their mind-set is, "well, why
should I let somebody else take it over?"

The argument here boils down to different cultural beliefs about
the model of successful business: tight focus versus diversified efforts.
And in each case, the belief is based on firsthand experience. This is
what we see around us; this is what works.

Central Beliefs: The Example of Innovation

As the preceding examples suggest, anyone attempting to transfer
deep smarts needs to be aware of the beliefs the target recipient is
harboring—but also be cognizant of his *own* beliefs. The more central those beliefs, the more difficult it will be for either knowledge
source or recipient to relinquish them. Less central beliefs are more
malleable, more transferable. Let us take the coaches in our entrepreneurship study, and the set of beliefs that they tended to hold in
common, as an example. They had built their careers, reputations,
and personal wealth on technological innovation (the base of the
pyramid in figure 5-2). They thought of themselves as innovators;
innovation was part of their identity. Many had earned their entrepreneurial stripes in Silicon Valley, where innovation was "in the
water"—the natives' way of saying that the value of technological
innovation was such a deeply held belief that no one could fully explain the preoccupation with creativity.[11]

This powerful central belief in the value of innovation spawned
the belief that innovation always required risk taking and implied a
certain amount of failure (the second level in the pyramid). Both
venture capitalists (whose business models assumed false starts) and
mentor capitalists (most of whom hailed from an engineering background, where experimentation and failing forward is common-
place) believed that there was no gain without some risk of failure.

If risk is necessary, and if the possibility of failure is a likely
consequence of risk, then coaches should not discourage entrepreneurs from experimenting with new business models, including these

FIGURE 5-2

A Belief System of Some Coaches

odd new ones based on e-commerce (the topmost levels of the pyramid, representing more peripheral beliefs). After all, decades before, the transistor had opened up worlds of new business. The personal computer had changed us all into cyber denizens. Graphical user design had transformed communications between user and machine. This latest wave could be just that—the newest and best in a long history of technological advances. So the coaches were predisposed to believe that perhaps there *was* a New Economy, with some new rules—but that there were continuities with past innovation revolutions. It was, nonetheless, unsettling, as such beliefs were not grounded directly in their own deep smarts (central beliefs and experience). The comments of veteran entrepreneur and coach Robert Maxfield in 2000, at the height of the Internet excitement, reveal the conflict that coaches felt in trying to figure out what parts of their prior experience applied to this new situation.

> *You get into a mode where you can no longer really trust all of your previous expertise. But the key thing to being successful in something like that is to not quit using your past experience altogether. Look at it as: We're all experimenting in this together, let's just go and do what seems right. But I'm not going to apply all*

my old experience and try to force you down a path because I'm pretty sure that it is going to be wrong.

As this comment suggests, the coaches' beliefs in innovation, and their humility in the face of continuous technological change, led them to suspend disbelief and give the new order a chance.

In the following sections we explore some of the beliefs that spring from the central belief in the value of innovation, beliefs that go to the heart of business. For example, expand your thinking beyond niches to large business opportunities, or be willing to take risks. If the result of the risk is failure, view that failure as an opportunity to learn, not as a badge of dishonor.

Because such beliefs were internalized (not always even recognized as beliefs), the coaches unconsciously transmitted them along with advice about best business models and management practices. As we will describe, protégés had various reactions to the attempts at transferring knowledge that included this set of embedded beliefs. The decision by the inexperienced managers to either follow the advice from their coaches or resist their efforts depended on: (1) whether the coaches' beliefs differed enough to threaten the protégés' own belief systems, and (2) how central were the beliefs being threatened. If the coaches' beliefs were congruent with their own—or the beliefs that differed were not central—the protégés accepted them and factored them into their own decisions. In some cases, the protégés actually distorted the coaches' beliefs because they accepted them, but at a very superficial level. In other situations, the protégés and coaches solved conflicts by compromising (accommodating each other); and in yet others, the protégés simply rejected the coaches' belief systems. This process of sorting beliefs into acceptable, actionable knowledge versus unjustified or irrelevant assumptions goes on constantly in organizations. Anywhere in the organization that knowledge is being created, captured, or transferred, some portion of that knowledge is based on beliefs. That is why it is important for managers to recognize belief systems as part of deep smarts.

Accepting: "Think Big"

Coaches with an abiding love of innovation believe in the admonition to "think big." In the United States, as the funds managed by the venture firms grew (from $19.2 billion in 1998 to $48 billion in 1999 and $81.3 billion in 2000[12]), the investment values grew as well, and each partner had increasingly to limit his attention to just a few big bets. One of the biggest names in Silicon Valley was Kleiner Perkins venture capitalist Vinod Khosla, who was considered the man with the Midas touch. He had funded Cerent Corporation, which was acquired by Cisco Systems for $6.9 billion, and Siara Systems, which was bought by Redback Networks for over $4 billion. As a result of his very successful experience with some very big bets, he adopted the adage, "Aim for the sky and you hit the trees; aim for the trees and you hit the ground." David Roberts and Brian Axe, founders of Zaplet, recalled their first meeting with him, when they pitched the idea for the nascent company:

> *Vinod got it. And he got it really quick. Immediately, he expanded it. I remember before we went in to see him, we expanded our own number of how many pages per day we thought we might be able to handle with this technology. I think we went in with ten thousand. And I remember when we told him that, he just looked, like, "What are you guys talking about?" And then he added four zeroes to it! "That's the number you guys need to architect for." At that point I remember the room went quiet for a moment. Brian and I were not expecting that kind of explosive growth. I think it was 100 million pages a day.*

Khosla convinced his partners at Kleiner Perkins to invest in the company, and then began to translate his vision into reality:

> *I was getting the sense that this was a much bigger play than [the young founders] realized, and I started pushing them on increasing the engineering budgets. When they started, they were probably*

thinking ten or fifteen engineers. I was probably thinking fifty or seventy-five. By January it was clear to me the number needed to be north of a hundred because we needed to build a platform, platform services, user management tools, and then the applications themselves. So each area was twenty to thirty people. This doesn't always make sense, but occasionally the opportunity set justifies this approach.

Axe and Roberts had no direct experience that would counter the belief that bigger is better, and they understood from the first moment they approached the venture capitalists that they could not tie their personal identities too tightly to the original business plan. That is, the notion of "think big" challenged no central beliefs. They therefore had no reason to reject Khosla's vision—or his advice. And he was a well-respected expert. (As we will see in the next chapter, experts have a lot of power in transferring their beliefs along with their more mundane advice.)

Distorting: "Think Big"

Other entrepreneurs (including a few in our study) bought into the idea of "think big"—but distorted it into "spend to impress." Designer chairs, shiny mahogany boardroom tables, impressive waiting rooms—some start-up companies had the overdressed air of a preteen who has raided her mother's closet and makeup cabinet. One of the Indian entrepreneurs in our study admitted: "We did not spend money the way we should have. For example, we spent a lot of money building a general manager's office. We bought a car for everyone! Looking back, I think we could have done without a lot of it."

The entrepreneurs who had adapted the "think big" belief to their own uses did not really understand the concept. They had confused *appearing* big with *thinking* big. This superficial grasp of the deep smarts embedded in the coaches' beliefs characterized the reaction to a number of the mantras being chanted around the investment community at the time. The beliefs were distorted by cir-

cumstances and greed and by people who wanted to copy the results of prior innovation without understanding deeply the sources
and conditions for innovation. As we will discuss further in chapter 6, superficial imitation is often a hazard in attempts to transfer
deep smarts.

Accommodating: Take Risks and Fail Forward

Perhaps no other belief is as central to innovation as the willingness—even eagerness—to assume personal and organizational
risk. Our language is replete with overused testimonials to the value
of risk—from "Nothing ventured, nothing gained" to "You can't
make an omelet without breaking an egg." Risks are, of course,
calculated; few managers would stake their personal fortunes and
those of their investors on a 100-to-1 shot. Nonetheless, a willingness to assume long odds on the likelihood of a huge payoff, then
to work hard to reduce those odds, are characteristic of innovative
activity. But such willingness to take risks can be taken to extremes.
As beliefs in the New Economy took root at the turn of the twenty-
first century, many prior assumptions about how business worked
were considered obsolete. An angel investor who put $150,000 in
an "incubator" started up by a couple of undergraduates at Yale
early in 2000 said: "This is the wave of the future. My generation
is passé when it comes to the New Economy. It's a foolproof investment." A venture capitalist in the same article called the cam-
pus incubator "an interesting science project. But I'm not sure it
will be a good experience for the guy whose money they take."[13]
(Which gentleman, we wonder, is more likely to want his words
memorialized?)

If risk taking is such a highly valued innovation belief, then the
inevitable failures that follow from high-risk endeavors have to be
viewed as a natural outcome, even as welcome evidence of firsthand
experience—so long as one learns from the failure. And the best
coaches, those most capable of transferring useful knowledge, are
therefore those who have taken risks, have experienced both success
and failure—and learned from the experiences. Venture capitalist

Vinod Khosla characterizes Bill Campbell, entrepreneur, coach, and CEO, then chairman of Intuit Corporation, in these terms:

> *That's why I like people like Bill Campbell, who are basically qualified to coach. They've done it right, they've done it wrong, and they sort of know, right? In the end this is all about judgment. And judgment comes from having the experience, having built companies before, having done some things right and wrong. And if you ask Bill Campbell, he learned as much from [early company] Go, which was a complete screw-up, as from anything. And he's much better for it.*

So in Silicon Valley, the notion of failing forward, underpinned as it was by more central beliefs about innovation, was acceptable, even laudable. That is, Californians believed in the power of learning from iterative attempts—including failed ones. The same was not true elsewhere in the world.

In the mid-1980s, Hewlett-Packard was setting up a new research and development organization within the Computer Products Division in Singapore. The U.S.-based engineer who relocated to Asia to direct the process, Larry Brown, recalled that he had to foster an environment that encouraged experimentation: "Initially, it was difficult for people to understand why they should risk offering a design that might in fact prove not to work." Brown found that the engineers wanted to spend much more time in testing their ideas than would their American counterparts. "We had to work out an approach toward risk that would work culturally. We spent a lot of time on computer simulation, feasibility studies, and statistical design of experiments to decrease the actual risk of failure, because failure is unacceptable in Singapore. However, all this work had unexpected benefits in the end; we had the fastest, most trouble-free production ramp-up I ever experienced." [14]

The HP experience was an example of accommodating each other's belief systems; the Singaporeans learned to experiment more, and the Western manager learned to move more testing up front than he was accustomed to. Both parties were open to learning from the other, and this mutual benefit added to their deep smarts.

Rejecting: Fail Forward

As we have discussed, belief in the value of risk taking and failure based on the central value of innovation differs among cultures.
In much of Asia, businesses have traditionally been run by families,
and a failed business is a very personal matter. Local laws are also
much more severe for bankruptcy, with exclusion from ever serving
on boards or even jail terms as possible consequences in some countries. No surprise, then, that Western innovation beliefs that are tol-
erant of risk meet resistance in Asia.

In early 2000, Yusumitsu Shigeta, founder of Hikari Tsushin,
saw his cell phone and Internet company's share price collapse. As
reported in *The Wall Street Journal*:

> *There are two things Japan loathes in a businessman, and Mr.
> Shigeta . . . embodies aspects of both. In a society that likes to see
> itself as both egalitarian and tasteful, most are turned off when a
> young turk becomes a swaggering success. Much worse is a busi-
> ness failure. Start up a company here, then flop, and you're prob-
> ably finished. . . .*
>
> *"If all these venture companies are cropping up, there are
> bound to be people who fail," says Yuichiro Itakura, founder of
> a pioneering Internet advertising company called Hyper Net. In
> America, entrepreneurs frequently fail, only to bound back up
> with a new brainstorm and new backing. "But there's absolutely
> no system here to recycle these people."* [15]

One of the reasons (besides the legal ones) that failure is not as
accepted in Asia as in the United States is that a failing business may
put relatives out of work. The value placed on personal relationships
leads to the practice of hiring family members and close friends—
not only because of the complex interwoven links that will presumably ensure loyalty and honest dealings, but because in many Asian
countries employment opportunities are limited, and one naturally
cares for family and friends first. Nobody likes to fail, but in India
the entrepreneur who fails is stigmatized, and his family is shamed
as well. As one Indian entrepreneur, now working out of both India

and Silicon Valley, put it, "In India, if you are laid off it's a big thing—not so much because of what the person is losing, but there is a social element to it. People don't want to talk about it."

The beliefs that risk is bad because it inevitably means some failure, and that failure is personal, even in business, were both challenged in the Asian start-ups we saw. The entrepreneurs began to find that prudent business practices required them to violate some of their beliefs; and the coaches, many of whom were expatriates, imported from the West a set of beliefs that were incompatible with those in the country of their birth. These conflicts between highly central beliefs—innovation beliefs clashing with traditional beliefs about family and failure—made it very difficult for both entrepreneurs and coaches to know what was wise, which of their smarts applied.

The entrepreneurs in the Asian companies where we interviewed were particularly reluctant to fire employees who did not turn out to have the requisite skills when the company morphed or grew. As we saw in chapter 2, many entrepreneurs in the United States also confronted this dilemma, and a number said that they should have acted sooner to fire people whose skills no longer fit the company needs. However, in India, because there are so many people competing for jobs and because many of them may be related, firing is even more difficult. The conflict was therefore between a professional assessment of the competencies needed in the company and the sense of personal obligation to the individuals hired. Saumil Majmudar, twenty-nine-year old founder of Bangalore start-up QSupport, reflected on the difficulty of balancing personal loyalties against the need to find a team that could grow with the company: "I built the team through serendipity, hiring friends who had skills. But not all friends scale. It's hard to fire someone who joined you when no one else would even listen to you."

When B. V. Jagadeesh met with the top management team of Bangalore start-up iNabling, he explained that the reason for laying some people off in a timely manner was to protect the investors, and used Cisco as an example of a company that took strong measures, including laying off ten thousand employees. Jagadeesh had recently cut staff at his own most recent start-up, Netscaler, to extend the life of the company, a decision he described as "very difficult—I was very emotional." The response to Jagadeesh's recommendations by the iNabling team was skeptical. The CEO reminded the coach that there is no support system in India for laid-off workers, and besides, "In India, head count is not so important, because it's not the single largest expense. We always hire easier."

The beliefs promulgated in the coach's new society (in the United States), reinforced by his own entrepreneurial experience, conflicted with the beliefs in his old haunts in India. In both places, innovation was highly valued—was, in fact, a central belief. However, the more peripheral beliefs about how to *manage* innovation differed—and the protégés often rejected, or at least resisted, the coach's advice.

As these examples demonstrate, advice flavored by beliefs and unspoken assumptions may be rejected, and we don't mean to suggest that such rejection is always inappropriate. However, in many managerial situations, conflicting beliefs and rejection of coaching can hurt the organization as well as the individual. We are thus led to the next question: If necessary, can beliefs be changed?

Can (Some) Beliefs Change?

When beliefs are central, that is, based on direct personal experience and linked to the identity of the individual or organization, they are extremely resilient and unlikely to change. They are part of a person's deepest smarts. The more peripheral the beliefs, the more amenable they are to change. However, a few influences appear to affect all kinds of beliefs.

Challenge Assumptions

Consulting company Strategos guides its clients through experiences that challenge deeply held beliefs about the organization in order to help them learn how to innovate. One of the "lenses" around which the consulting coaches organize a team is the challenging of one kind of belief system, "orthodoxies," or assumptions about the company, its products, and its competitive advantages. When Whirlpool employees went through the exercise of probing the orthodoxy, "Why we consider all of our customers to be women," they discovered that this belief was standing in the way of considering men as a potential customer base. Then, upon going out to observe men around the house, the Whirlpool team recognized that men needed appliances and other equipment in the garage. This insight in turn led to the development of the rugged Gladiator line of appliances (e.g., the Beer Box and Freezerator, both designed to withstand extremes of temperature) and the Gearwall workshop modules for the garage. This product line moved from concept to prototype in an unprecedented six months and was touted by some as Whirlpool's first major new brand in fifty years. It is expected to generate sales of $300 million by 2007. CEO David Whitman was so pleased with this project's results that he increased the company's "skunk-works" budget by 60 percent to $80 million.[16] None of these new products would have been created if the innovation team had not confronted deeply held organizational beliefs.

Change Frames

A second way of affecting beliefs is to *frame* a situation differently. Amy Edmondson uses the term framing to describe a set of beliefs that influence how people view the world. Her research identified two different frames held by surgical teams implementing an innovative surgical procedure at four hospitals. "Learning" frames include three factors: an "aspirational" purpose (e.g., a belief that the team is accomplishing something important for patients); interdependent team leaders (e.g., head surgeons viewed themselves as part of a team whose members depend upon one another); and empowered teams (e.g., a sense of ownership of the new procedure and its goals by the team). "Doing" frames include a "preventional" purpose (e.g., viewing the procedure as a necessary evil); individual experts (e.g., a head surgeon who views himself involved in an essentially technical exercise); and support teams as mere enactors (e.g., following procedures). Edmundson found that although the four hospitals did not differ in terms of expertise, support by management, resources, or status, the two hospitals with a *learning* frame became successful implementers of the new procedure, while those with a *doing* frame abandoned the procedure. Edmondson draws one important implication from the study—that it is possible to *reframe* a situation to succeed in a novel situation. This can be done, for example, by convincing oneself that the situation represents a new and exciting opportunity, that other team members are vital to its success, then communicating this sense of excitement and interdependence to the team.[17]

Create Counterexperiences

Since beliefs—especially central ones—are based on experience, it is contrary experience that is most likely to alter a prior belief. In the twenty-first century, among countries in which belief systems are rigorously controlled, North Korea is surely at the top of the list. The extent to which perceptions and experience are orchestrated is almost incomprehensible to the citizens of a free society. There is only one source of mass media—the government. Refugees who have successfully fled to neighboring countries tell of their own difficulty in assimilating information that so contradicts what they have believed all their lives. One defector, for example, who had obtained a radio with illegal access to Seoul broadcasts while he was still in North Korea, disbelieved what he heard: "[W]hen I heard Seoul saying that one car company was producing a hundred new taxis I didn't believe it, because that meant there were taxis in South Korea, and for that South Korea had to be very, very rich."[18] Not until these refugees saw for themselves the incredible riches of their neighbor to the south did they change their beliefs.

People need not be brainwashed, however, to hold beliefs so strongly that only direct experience can change them. In the 1990s, Cross Corporation ran into a rare problem: Their employees were being *too* attentive to quality! That is, faithful to the company's deeply held commitment to quality, and exercising their historic right to reject any pen that didn't meet their personal standards, manufacturing personnel were filling the reject bins with pens that had no design or mechanical problems. Rather, with increasingly sophisticated tools, the workers were able to detect microscopic visual flaws. Management tried to reeducate them to consider quality from the point of view of the customer by hefting the pens, checking their function, and examining them only with the naked eye. The workers rebelled. They believed in the sanctity of visual perfection—under magnification. Then a number of workers were invited to view, through a one-way window, customers sorting writing instruments (not just Cross pens) into three piles: flawless, high quality, and substandard. Next the focus group members explained their criteria for the judgments: how the pen felt in the hand, how well the mechanism to extend or retract the writing nib worked, and how smoothly it wrote. None mentioned "flawless appearance." The workers (and their colleagues, who subsequently viewed a video of the focus group) changed their assumptions about what comprised quality.[19]

Similarly, after the 2003 *Columbia* space shuttle disaster, one member of the *Columbia* Accident Investigation Board (CAIB)—NASA research director G. Scott Hubbard—insisted on directly testing whether or not the foam hitting the orbiter during liftoff could have inflicted fatal damage. The computer modeling, the video record of the launch, and analysis that ruled out other possibilities had convinced most, but not the hard-core believers at NASA, that "the foam did it." NASA opposed a test of the launch accident, but Hubbard "argued that if NASA was to have any chance of self-reform, these people *would have to be confronted with reality*, not in abstraction but in the most tangible way possible."[20] CAIB director Hal Gehman acquiesced, explaining, "when I hear NASA telling me things like, 'Gotta be true!' or 'We know this to be true!' all my alarm bells go off. . . ."[21] The test was conducted: A piece of foam was fired at a segment of the extremely expensive ($700,000 per panel) components. When the foam hit the panel at

500 miles per hour at a 25-degree angle (a conservative reenactment of the actual event), it knocked out a large hole. "Immediately afterward an audible gasp went through the crowd" of engineers assembled to watch. Gehman said later that "their whole house of cards came falling down."[22]

So people are likely to change strongly held beliefs, that is, ones that are part of their deep smarts, only when they confront a more central counterbelief, or when they encounter the evidence of their own direct experience—and of course, not always even then. (In the next chapter we will consider the possibility of changing central beliefs when influenced by powerful role models or reference groups.) However, managers who understand how belief systems shape deep smarts are better equipped to influence behavior and to work to replace or modify beliefs that are impeding progress.

Implications for Managers

If strongly held beliefs are altered only through experience that contradicts the beliefs, what can managers do about beliefs that are dysfunctional, harmful to the organization, or barriers to progress? The most powerful counteraction, of course, is to expose employees directly to disconfirming experience: a trip to the foreign office, a face-to-face encounter with customers, a trial of a competitor's product. But if such experience is too expensive or difficult to set up, simulations are a powerful second-best option. A simulated experience that is designed to replicate reality as closely as possible is often convincing. The engineers who had worked on the space shuttle *Columbia* could not really believe that foam hitting the side of the orbiter could cause the serious damage that led to the midair disaster until they *saw* the damage in a recreation of the incident.

But what if *you* are the one who needs to change your beliefs? What if the direct or simulated experience contradicts what *you* expected? Suppose in the case of *Columbia* that the strike of the foam on the orbiter had proven the engineers to be correct, or suppose that the focus group members sorting through Cross pens had picked them up and scrutinized them closely for visual defects, thus reinforcing the workers' belief in the nature of the quality desired? Then the *leaders* would have had to change their beliefs. None of us is exempt from the possibility that what we hold to be truth is in fact a belief, an assumption—and one that can be contradicted by experience.

The difficulty of countering beliefs that are destructive to the organization or to relationships among groups is that it is possible for two belief systems to be "true" when the circumstances in which they are applied differ. That is, knowledge in one context often does not apply in another—so it is tricky to decide whether the generic knowledge is correct or whether the local knowledge is paramount. As we have seen from examples in this chapter, the obvious best way to manage in the Western world may be far from obvious or best in Asia.

When uttering a truth to another, or advising a subordinate, therefore, managers need to be aware that their beliefs may be masquerading as facts. Their knowledge may indeed be "justified true belief" in their minds, but to the recipient of the knowledge, only the last word may apply. There may be no objective knowledge; when experts attempt to convey their deep smarts, whether they intend to or not, they also convey tacit dimensions of their knowledge, including basic assumptions and beliefs. Because beliefs include so many dimensions of tacit knowledge, we are often unaware of the extent to which our "truths" are subjective. This is particularly true when communicating cross-culturally. Social psychologist Richard Nisbett has written about East-West differences in decision making. For example, Westerners are far more likely than Asians to recommend that an employee with fifteen years of good performance followed by one year of poor performance be fired.[23]

Because truth is so often subjective, managers are often well served by asking someone on their staff to serve as a devil's advocate. As we shall see in the next chapter, our belief systems are heavily influenced by those around us, and therefore we need to build in checks against the potential for "groupthink," that is, for everyone unconsciously to base their decisions on the same assumptions. A minority opinion (particularly a minority of more than one) is usually very valuable—not because that opinion is likely to prevail, but because challenging prevalent views often leads to more thoughtful review of options and a better decision in the end.[24] Research has shown that a devil's advocate who really believes in the position she holds is more effective than someone who is merely asked to take the role—but debate often stimulates a more creative response to a problem.

In fact, in the best of all worlds, managers create an environment where beliefs and assumptions are routinely challenged, because dissenting views are almost always useful. Intel touts "constructive confrontation" as an organizational value—and trains new employees in the skills of debate. Dissenting from a belief held by a superior in an organization is especially difficult. In the wake of the *Columbia* disaster, the investigative board found ample evidence that people who held important information were afraid to speak up. William Langewiesche reports a telling exchange between Linda Ham, head of the Mission Management Team that denied engineers' requests for satellite photographs of the *Columbia* to see if damage had been done by foam hitting during takeoff, and an investigator of the accident. The latter inquired:

> *"As a manager, how do you seek out dissenting opinions?" According to [the investigator], [Ham] answered, "Well, when I hear about them . . . "*
>
> *He interrupted. "Linda, by their very nature you may not hear about them."*
>
> *"Well, when somebody comes forward and tells me about them."*
>
> *"But Linda, what techniques do you use to get them?" [The investigator said] she had no answer.[25]*

As discussed earlier, Ham was not alone in her belief that the foam striking during takeoff was immaterial—but the few voices in the organization questioning that belief had no way to be heard. The result was so tragic in this case that NASA is being castigated for a culture that encourages arrogance; but is the NASA culture unusual? Unfortunately, no.

Deep smarts cannot build in a culture that allows no questioning, because in such an organization, only top managers are assumed to have relevant experience; only their beliefs are assumed to be "true." Obviously, this cannot be the case. One important managerial skill is the ability to identify assumptions (including one's own)—and question them. (More on this in chapter 8.)

Keep in Mind

- Knowledge has been defined as *justified true belief*. Belief systems are part of our deep smarts.

- Central beliefs, those that form part of our identity, are supported by significant others and by direct experience, underlie and influence many of our other beliefs and behaviors, and significantly shape knowledge.

- Because people consider their personal, professional, organizational, and cultural central beliefs to be true and because they are largely tacit and immune to change, it is very difficult to accommodate them to other belief systems.

- When belief systems conflict, the result can be acceptance (one belief system prevails), resistance (neither belief system changes), or accommodation (change in one or both—compromise). Sometimes beliefs are accepted with so little real understanding that they are distorted.

- A central belief in the value of innovation is an example of a foundational belief—one that underlies other beliefs, such as risk taking and failing forward. These beliefs, in turn, leave an innovator's mind open to new business models, such as those spawned in the New Economy.

- Conflicts between beliefs are particularly intense when they are supported by different cultural belief systems. For example, Western beliefs in focused business models conflict with Eastern beliefs in holding company models; Western beliefs in tolerance of failure conflict with Eastern beliefs that failure is personally shameful.

- While many belief systems are largely impervious to change, recognizing them as assumptions that may not be shared by others paves the way for discussion and mutual understanding.

- The most powerful way of changing a belief is to provide direct experiences that contradict the old belief.

SIX

Social Influences

WHEN WE GET UP in the morning and look in the mirror, we like to see a stalwart, independent decision maker—sure of our beliefs and uninfluenced by people around us, perhaps even by our supervisors. But if knowledge is "justified true belief," who justifies it? Often, other people. Even before our infant eyes were able to bring into focus a parental face bending down over our crib, we've been influenced by others—those who have power over us and those we like or admire. While we learn through experience, we are social beings, and we look to others to define how we should act and what is real, especially when we are unsure of ourselves and our convictions. Social influences are so pervasive that even a basic listing would be encyclopedic (e.g., media, sales tactics, political campaigns). However, here we are concerned only with the way that friends, organizations, and experts shape—*justify*—our beliefs and knowledge, specifically as we build and transfer deep smarts. (See figure 6-1.)

In broad terms, others influence us through mechanisms ranging from overt arm-twisting at one extreme to more complex "brain-washing" at the other (although we would rarely characterize it as

FIGURE 6-1

Deep Smarts and Knowledge Filtering

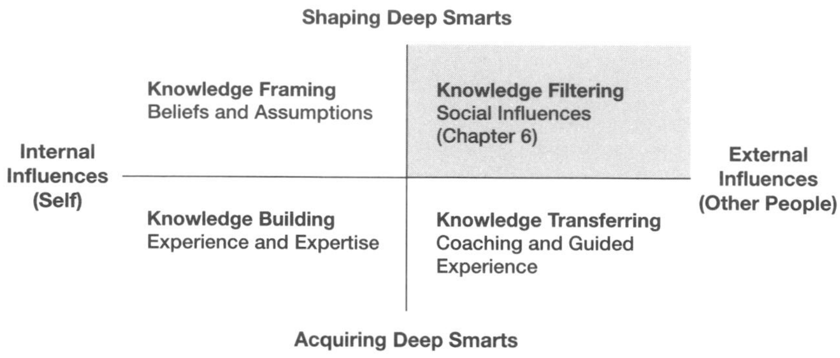

Shaping Deep Smarts

Knowledge Framing
Beliefs and Assumptions

Knowledge Filtering
Social Influences
(Chapter 6)

Internal
Influences
(Self)

External
Influences
(Other People)

Knowledge Building
Experience and Expertise

Knowledge Transferring
Coaching and Guided
Experience

Acquiring Deep Smarts

such). The difference between these two extremes is the extent to which we engage in a behavior because we are merely complying (without fully believing in what we are doing) versus acting out of conviction—and passion. That is, the more that social influences approach the right-hand side of figure 6-2, the more that deep smarts—our own as well as those we are responsible for developing in other people—are strongly affected, and the harder it is to change the resultant convictions if we need to do so.

As the examples in this chapter will reveal, social influences can range from pernicious to beneficial. We cannot wholly escape their influence, and for the most part, we don't wish to. Our deep smarts are enriched by our social contacts, our role models. The aspirations of individuals and organizations are often raised by those who model possible future realities. And as leaders, if we can shape the values and beliefs of our organization so that it constitutes a tribe attractive to the best employee applicants, we have an advantage. However, we do want to be aware of the power of social influences to shape what we *know*. Advertisements, to take one form of social influence, are usually open and obvious in their purpose to sway our judgment. The effects of herd mentality and the allure of tribal

FIGURE 6-2

Social Influences on Beliefs

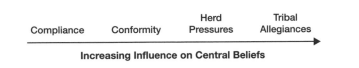

membership are more subtle. As we shall see, we can build knowledge as a result of these influences, and we can transfer deep smarts to others by exerting social influence. But the more aware we are of how that knowledge is screened and shaped, and the greater choice we exercise on how we ourselves are influenced, the better.

Compliance: Just Do It!

When do we comply with someone else's directives? We may do so because we agree with her judgment, of course. But we also comply when we think she is more expert than we are—or more powerful in some other respect (such as completing our annual review or signing our bonus checks). Compliance can create receptors (see chapter 2), and it may be appropriate for an expert to induce a protégé to take action, in order to expose him or her to some new situation and thereby *create* receptors. However, it is unlikely that deep smarts can be built through mere compliance, because there is no real transfer of knowledge or beliefs.

In chapter 3, we briefly discussed how the founder of an Asian music company was persuaded to change his original business model to one focusing on the Internet. The entrepreneur, David Loiterton, had almost twenty years of experience in the music industry, working for companies such as Bertelsmann, when he approached Hong Kong incubator Tech Pacific with a business plan for his company, Gogo. As he recounted that first meeting to us in 2000:

Ilyas [Khan] went down the list of things that I wanted to do and he circled the one that I had always put as number 12, which was build the Internet platform. He said, "That's what I'm interested in. I understand what you're doing. Content obviously is very important. But we're an Internet investment company and that's what we want to invest in. You've clearly got a piece of your business plan which is Internet related. Is there a possibility that instead of acquiring and building content, and then building a platform to exploit it, that we can do it the other way around? Can we build the platform and then go into content acquisition?" And I said to him, "I have to think about it," because that was a different approach, it was really turning the company into an Internet company that acquired content, rather than the other way around.

As the incubator coach, Ilyas Khan, recalled the meeting:

When David came to us he actually had a business plan that was very, very definitive, but it did not sound feasible. So the business that he envisaged required some very detailed retooling. . . . We then asked him to refocus his resources. That required a different business plan and that is the one that is now [in 2000] being executed.

Khan and Tech Pacific had all the ingredients of social influence to persuade Loiterton to comply with their insistence on remaking his business into an Internet platform: presumed superior expertise (at least in the Internet space), coercion (the original idea would not be funded), and rewards (the promise of wealth). But by 2001, the business had reverted to Loiterton's original plan, in which the Internet played a small supporting role. The heady prospect of wealth had dissipated, but the entrepreneur had retreated to a business—a record company—based on his own deep smarts.

Loiterton had complied in deference to superior power and changed his business plan. However, if the directives given by a superior conflict with strongly held personal beliefs, the person being coerced may find it impossible to reconcile the two—and have to remove himself from the influence. Consider the dilemma of John Brady Kiesling. A nineteen-year Foreign Service veteran, Kiesling was a supporter of the first President George Bush and the 1991 Gulf War. So why, in early 2003, was he suddenly a minor celebrity, his letter of resignation printed in the *New York Review of Books* and the *Washington Post*? Kiesling could not reconcile his role as spokesman for U.S. policy in Iraq with his views on international relations. At a party he hosted in Athens for a few pro-U.S. Greek friends who opposed war with Iraq, he spent hours trying to toe the official line, but realized how unconvincing his case had been. He later recalled being told by his superiors to telephone a Greek professor who had written a commentary, "Blood for Oil," in an Athens newspaper. Kiesling, in fact, did not believe the looming war was based on oil. "But I didn't have an answer to his next question, 'So why are you going to war?'"[1] Kiesling's international friendships (he is reported to speak eight languages, many of them learned during his various postings) and strong belief in international cooperation to solve disputes conflicted with the positions he was expected to espouse—and he chose to resign rather than continue to live with the inconsistencies.[2]

In Loiterton's case, the conflict was between what an apparent expert told him and what he believed. In Kiesling's case, the conflict was between what he personally believed, as reinforced by friends in the international community, and what his superiors wanted him to believe. Kiesling resigned rather than continue to comply; Loiterton was only too happy to return to his original business model. Although social influences affected both men's behavior for a short time, neither appeared to be confused in his own belief system by the directives. Nor was either really convinced. There was little or no transfer of "justified true belief" in either case; no beliefs were internalized to inform deep smarts.

But do people have to be our superiors or experts in our eyes to get us to conform our behavior to their beliefs? Not according to a large body of psychological research.

Conformity: If You All Say So

Imagine that you are in a room with six other people, being asked to make a very simple judgment, and to make it publicly: which of three lines displayed on a card is the same length as a fourth line. You can see very clearly that line A is the correct answer, but all of the others in the room announce in turn that line B is correct. Now it's your turn. "How can I be wrong?" you think. "I have the evidence of my own eyes. But maybe it's an illusion of some sort, a trick of the eye like those three-dimensional pictures that leap out of a background if you squint just right. How can six apparently intelligent other people be wrong and I be right?" When this experiment was conducted over fifty years ago (and confirmed many times since), the majority of people went along with the rest of the group (actually comprised of the experimenter's paid confederates) on at least one such "critical trial." Interestingly, they were far less likely to conform when they made their judgments privately—writing them on a piece of paper—than when they announced them out loud. And when they had an ally—that is, one of the six confederates gave the correct answer while the other five gave the same incorrect answer—conformity also declined dramatically.[3]

But that was a laboratory experiment, right? Probably college students in Psychology 101. Perhaps you believe that such conformity to an "obviously" wrong decision is much less likely in business or other professional organizational settings. But neither large organizations nor start-ups are immune to conformity pressures. Scandals at Enron and WorldCom, to name two notorious examples, come to mind. (See "Compliance and Conformity at WorldCom.") And if we take the start-ups in our entrepreneurship study and their investors as an example of social influence, we find a lot of people squinting hard to see if they can't see what others around them apparently view clearly as a marvelous opportunity. A first-time entrepreneur lamented, "I let other people convince me that we should spend more money than we needed to and hire faster than I thought we should. But they convinced me that it was okay." A more experienced entrepreneur rued the day when he was persuaded to abandon the service, work-for-hire side of his company in favor of a more focused online model: "In hindsight I would not have killed it. But it was drummed into me by all of the board members, that mantra about focus, focus, that this other thing is distracting, it's in the way, it doesn't let you focus on this big thing. . . . My conservative gut said to keep it going. We made that decision [to focus on the online business], but it's not the one that I felt was right."

Compliance and Conformity at WorldCom

ON OCTOBER 10, 2003, Betty Vinson pleaded guilty to two criminal counts of securities fraud and conspiracy. Her crime: As a senior manager in WorldCom's accounting division, she helped cook the books over the course of six quarters, falsely crediting the telecom giant with $3.7 billion in profits.

In October 2000, Vinson's boss, Buford Yates, told her and a colleague, Troy Normand, that his boss (WorldCom's controller, David Myers) and the company's CFO, Scott Sullivan, wanted them to use a reserve account to pay expenses—an act that would violate accounting rules while it artificially raised the revenue line. Vinson and Normand told Yates it was improper, but went ahead with the $828 million transfer. She felt guilty about it, but reasoned that Sullivan, as CFO, must know what he was doing. The following quarter found the company in an even more dire financial situation, and this time there were no reserves left to transfer. Instead, CFO Sullivan decided to move $771 million in line costs to capital expenditures. The scheme was passed down to Myers, who passed it to Yates, and it then arrived on Vinson's and Normand's desks. The plan was clearly illegal, but they were expected to allocate the money among various capital accounts, which they did, backdating the entries. The same thing happened in the following three quarters until the scheme unraveled.

continued

Multiple forces acted on Betty Vinson to compel her behavior. Certainly there were compliance pressures: She trusted in the expert judgment of her superiors (although this might have been mostly rationalization); more likely she feared for her job in a tight economy. But conformity was almost certainly operating as well. According to *The Wall Street Journal*, "Ms. Vinson wasn't alone in these predicaments. In a report issued this month, investigators hired by the company's new board found that dozens of employees knew about the fraud at WorldCom but were afraid to speak out." Her coworkers and immediate superiors expressed doubts about the accounting schemes, but nobody resigned or refused to comply. Ms. Vinson *knew* what she was doing was wrong on the basis of her own education and experience, but she complied—and conformed.[a]

a. Susan Pulliam, "Over the Line: A Staffer Ordered to Commit Fraud Balked, Then Caved," *The Wall Street Journal*, 23 June 2003, A1.

Conformity was not limited to the entrepreneurs in our study. Even those with deep smarts—the coaches—went along with new beliefs because everyone else did. As one of our experienced coaches said at the height of the bubble, "I'm from the school of slow, steady growth. It's completely different right now—you've got to paint the billion-dollar picture. Everyone looks at me and says, 'think big.'"

Acquiescence to such pressures to comply or conform does not motivate people to build a deep understanding of the issues; they are merely "going along" with those around them. Therefore, both compliance and conformity in the absence of true belief may indeed build receptors for further experience, but the motive for learning or understanding comes from outside the individual. And there is strong evidence that extrinsic forces—rewards, threats, and the like—may induce people to work hard, but do not promote learning or creativity nearly as much as intrinsic motivation—from *wanting* to learn.[4] In short, building deep smarts requires commitment from the heart as well as dedication from the brain—and doing something just because others think you should doesn't inspire that kind of effort.

The Psychology of the Herd

Few of us like to believe we run mindlessly with the herd. But many times we get swept up in a general belief that touches emotion as well as reason. While compliance is based on power, and conformity is based on a desire to avoid looking odd or out of step, herd behavior is a bit different. First, unlike people who conform even though they know better, those caught up in herd behavior are *uncertain* of what is true. When we find ourselves in such an uncertain state, where our previous experience is no guide to how we should behave (we have no deep smarts on the issue), we look to the behavior of others to help us. And if everyone else seems to know what is real, we will use their behavior to guide our own. Second, observing the herd can be an emotional experience. We may feel fearful at being left behind, or excited at the prospect of joining a mass movement. The major point here is that decisions made while galloping along with the herd may not be based on deep smarts, but those decisions still influence what we perceive as actionable knowledge, as well as what knowledge we dispense to others. Perception becomes our reality.

For example, when everyone seems to be heading in the same direction, pursuing the same goals, the "psychology of scarcity" kicks in (see "The Scarcity Principle: Going, Going . . . Gone"). If there are only so many seats on the bus, so many opportunities for "first mover advantage," then I'd better get moving—fast! And along with scarcity goes its evil twin, greed: "If this is the new reality and I move fast, I can make a quick killing."

Uncertainty rules the herd. During the Internet bubble, nobody really understood the economic basis of the New Economy, or how long it would last—what the new rules were for starting companies

The Scarcity Principle:
Going, Going . . . Gone

How much would you pay for a 792-square-foot, one-bedroom, one-bathroom house in Palo Alto on one-twentieth of an acre? $409,000? That was the asking price in the spring of 2000. It made national headlines when it sold instead for $550,000! The tendency for investors and entrepreneurs alike in Silicon Valley to see Internet territory in terms of the great Oklahoma land rush—territory to be claimed in a wild dash, by any means—was exacerbated by the other types of scarcity so evident around them. Because of the dot-coms' heavy dependence on relatively new Web-based software development skills, such talents were scarce and highly prized. As a result, software engineers and programmers flocked to the small geographic area, causing an intense real estate shortage for both offices and residences.

Scarcity makes suckers of us even when we suspect or *know* that the scarcity is being artificially manipulated. How many of us experienced the buying frenzies (and accompanying astronomical prices) surrounding "scarce" Beanie Babies, Tickle-Me-Elmos, or Pokemon

and making money. In this state of heightened uncertainty, people looked to others to discover what was true. Laurence Siegel of the Ford Foundation is quoted as saying, "You can be right and with the crowd—which is fine . . . you can be wrong and with the crowd, which isn't actually so bad. . . . Or you can be wrong and alone and then you really look like an idiot."[5] Veteran entrepreneur and coach Robert Maxfield's comments at the height of the Internet bubble in 2000 reflect the shifting beliefs in reality at the time:

> *The models that are used for criteria of success in the marketplace now have no relation to the old ones. Maybe there really is a new economy and all of this stuff is right, and all of the models that*

cards? As we observe the actions of others, we see them snapping up the scarce items, even at what would normally be considered ridiculous prices, and we panic, afraid we will be cut off from the scarce goods. In Silicon Valley in 1999 and 2000, there was a kind of contagion among different kinds of scarcity that led to a general sense of urgency to claim ownership before someone else did—ownership of scarce skills, scarce office space, scarce housing—and scarce market space on the Internet. Investment money was *not* scarce, which sometimes led to leaving money on the table—cash that could have been put to good use when Niagara Falls ran dry.

Psychologist Robert Cialdini writes of the difficulty of defending against the psychology of scarcity: "Knowing the causes and workings of scarcity pressures may not be sufficient to protect us from them because knowing is a cognitive act, and cognitive processes are suppressed by our emotional reaction to scarcity pressures. In fact, this may be the reason for the great effectiveness of scarcity tactics. When they are employed properly, our first line of defense against foolish behavior—a thoughtful analysis of the situation—becomes less likely."[a]

a. Robert Cialdini, *Influence: Science and Practice*, 4th ed. (Boston: Allyn and Bacon, 2001), 228.

guys like me have operated with all of these years just don't apply anymore. One of the big problems that I had with Fogdog [a start-up Maxfield had been involved with] was getting myself out of the mode of insisting on a plan that was going to show profitability. I was on the attack for a long time and I finally had to say to myself, "Look, these guys are committed to going into e-commerce, so if I'm going to continue to try to help them I've got to put my head in the mode of all of those other guys out there, because this is a whole new game." [Emphasis added.]

"These other guys" (other investors and venture capitalists) were promoting a different kind of business model, and helped define for

Maxfield what the rules for that new model might be. In order to function as a coach to the start-up, he adopted their perspective—despite his own long experience to the contrary. And if such a savvy veteran could be swayed, how susceptible were the first-timers who found themselves the objects of the financiers' affections?

The herd mentality of the times drove investors in 1999–2000 to formulate a standard set of characteristics for a potentially interesting start-up: huge potential payback; based on sophisticated technology; founded by (usually young) technical hot-shots who were the perceived experts on the Internet. In Boston, a group of investors (The Common Angels) reviewed dozens of business plans during the peak of investment frenzy. Interviewed right after emerging from such a meeting, one of the participants commented that it was difficult for an older entrepreneur with a less high tech concept to stir the passions (and open the pocketbooks) of the angels. His account of the reception accorded two different presentations that morning highlights the way that investors had coalesced around a common model:

> *The founder presenting the Internet software proposal was a man in his mid-forties who had been a VP at Digital Equipment. After Digital began to change, he moved and became president of a small software company. He did a reasonable, workmanlike job and sold it, making some money. This Internet deal was his chance to go for the gold. He had an interesting idea and he had assembled a team of professionals that he had worked with at Digital and/or had been customers. They made a PowerPoint presentation; they had a business plan and they had done their market analysis. It wasn't particularly high tech, but they knew the market and it was very workmanlike—a classic kind of presentation that we would have seen in a venture company years ago. [The Common Angels] is not an investment club; we all make our own decisions. When the presentation ends, the [presenters] leave and then we all discuss it a little bit. Then people express their individual interests and that becomes a subgroup that follows up or not. So we asked who was interested and maybe one or two hands went up.*

The last presentation in the morning, two kids come in. One is a twenty-something-year-old from Harvard, a skinny little guy (his neck doesn't fill out his shirt) who makes the presentation. He brings with him his partner, who is sitting there in the corner sort of looking at his shoes, a little embarrassed, not wanting to talk in front of the group. This partner is introduced as having come to this country when he was fourteen years old, not speaking any English, graduating from Harvard when he was eighteen. Now he is twenty and he is already a scientist of some stature at IBM. He has this technology that searches the Internet, a particular mechanism, and together with his buddy they had this idea. They were going to put up this Web site and search site. There was no business plan per se; they had the elements of invention and idea; they didn't quite know how to price the thing. The entrepreneurship class at MIT showed them how to wrap the idea in a strategic context. So they came to the table with an idea, phenomenal intellect, an understanding of this technology and the potential of the media, and an openness to mentoring. [They said,] "The reason we are here is because we don't want just money, we want people to come in and help us put it together." They walked out of the room. "Who is interested?" Every hand went up around the table. They hadn't gotten from that room to downstairs and they already in effect had their financing in place.

Why did the investors believe in the second opportunity more than the first? It wasn't just the people in the room who influenced them. There was a kind of global "groupthink,"[6] in which everyone was working with the same stereotype of the great opportunity. The more public the commitment, the more friends talking about the huge potential payback, the more likely that individuals were persuaded to believe. The New Economy was real: "Aggregating eyeballs" was a legitimate marketing strategy! Profitability didn't matter—maybe later! Fortunes were to be made by staking out claims to Internet territory.

Start-up coaches around the world were guilty of following popular trends and of force-fitting business plans into the desired Internet mold. But their behavior was hardly unique. Lemmings and teenagers are far from the only ones to engage in herd behavior; the "rational" analysts on Wall Street are also particularly vulnerable. And perceived scarcity is only one stimulus for a stampede. Rumors that inspire fear or anger can spark emotional, contagious reactions among organizational members. Because herd behavior is so rooted in emotion and uncertainty, people under its influence focus on what others around them are doing—and act without considering disagreement or another route. Herd behavior, in short, is based on shallow smarts.

So far in our examples of social influence, we have observed mostly negative effects on the construction of deep smarts. But what if others' beliefs link to your deep convictions—either beliefs you already have, or those you have developed as a consequence of having joined a "tribe," that is, a community of like-minded individuals? Membership in a tribe can be a very powerful emotional experience, leading to acceptance of new behaviors and beliefs— becoming a "true believer." And tribes are often excellent places to develop deep smarts.

Tribes "R" Us

We choose some of our tribes—for example, professional associations, book groups, graduate school alumni networks. Others are ours by birth or geography—being Muslim or Indian or Asian American. So long as we remain members (or aspire to membership), and particularly if a part of our personal identity is invested in membership, we are likely to be influenced in how we select and process information and, more important, how we transform that information into knowledge. And as we will see, tribes can be global, even if not all their members know each other but share certain norms and beliefs.

Drinking the Kool-Aid

Joining a tribe may be a mostly dispassionate decision, affecting one's view of the world, to be sure, but not necessarily involving strong emotional attachments to the group. Professional athletes, for example, who are frequently traded from team to team, often treat such transactions as part of the sport. They may play their hardest for each team, but reserve their emotional attachments for other groups. However, in some tribal situations emotional connections play a very important role. The expression "to drink the Kool-Aid" has come to mean buying into a fervent, mass (and perhaps mistaken) belief system—to succumb to a promise of a bright future, to become a true believer. Drinking the Kool-Aid can powerfully influence people's beliefs, and can cause them to behave against their own interests. (See "The Tragedy of Jonestown.")

When group beliefs lead to such a grisly outcome as Jonestown, outsiders are aghast. How could people end their lives in obedience to such a leader? How could parents give their children the fatal drink? Two decades later, in March 1997, a similar scenario played out in a suburb of San Diego when thirty-eight young men and women, plus their leader, Marshall Herff Applewhite, each ingested up to fifty phenobarbital pills. The "Heaven's Gate" cult (which doubled as a successful business designing Web sites!) apparently had been convinced by the charismatic Applewhite that it was time to "shed their containers" and be transported to a spaceship hiding behind comet Hale-Bopp.

The Tragedy of Jonestown

ON NOVEMBER 18, 1978, 913 members of the People's Temple, including at least 270 children, drank Kool-Aid laced with cyanide. With the urging of the Reverend Jim Jones, founder of the People's Temple, and under the watchful eye of armed guards, the adults first administered the toxic brew to their children before joining them in what Jones described as a "revolutionary suicide." Earlier that day, Congressman Leo Ryan and four of his traveling

continued

party had been shot as they boarded planes to return home from Jonestown, deep in the jungles of Guyana. Seeing the end of the People's Temple as imminent, Jones ordered the suicides, and then fired a bullet into his brain.

Many attempts have been made to explain what to most people is an incomprehensible act. Audiotapes of the final moments do indicate indecision on the part of some of the parents, and the presence of armed guards enforcing compliance no doubt left dissenters with little choice. However, in general the people appeared to accept what was asked of them. When the horrific scene was surveyed some days later, adults and children were found lying arm in arm. A more powerful explanation than mere physical coercion was the influence of Jones himself. Jones was a father figure—in fact, he liked to be called "Dad" or "Father"—but he was a demanding parent. Even the mildest disobedience or violations of rules were met with harsh punishments or public humiliation. Absolute allegiance to Jones was a given. Despite the rigors of life in Jonestown, however, members wanted to believe in the utopia that Jones held out for them. His "healings" of cancers (the usual charlatan's trick of miraculously extracting chicken-gizzard "tumors"), the glowing testimonials of the multiracial membership, and the charisma of Jones as he promised a more just society all combined to create a powerful reference group for members. While resistance was, indeed, futile, few had the desire to resist the call to murder and suicide. On the arm of one woman found among the 913 was scribbled, "Jim Jones is the only one." [a]

a. Neal Osherow, "Making Sense of the Nonsensical: An Analysis of Jonestown," in Elliot Aronson (ed.), *Readings About the Social Animal*, 8th ed. (New York: Worth, 1999).

Jonestown, Heaven's Gate, the Charles Manson gang—all are easy to dismiss as bizarre, if tragic, aberrations. But in fact they are merely extreme examples of the tribal influences to which we are all subject, every day. As social creatures, we are born with a strong need to belong to some collective, to learn through socialization within such groups, and to pattern our beliefs and behaviors after those whom we admire and love. A cult demonstrates how potent a tribe's influence can be, as it combines pressures to believe, conform, and please with an aspiration to imitate the leaders of the group. As the preceding examples show, groups and their leaders can exert their influence even when members' most deeply held values are challenged. So if a charismatic leader of an attractive group can induce parents to murder their children, how likely is it that the groups we choose can influence far more mundane behaviors?

At the height of the Internet frenzy, some aspiring entrepreneurs were walking away from lucrative unvested stock options in established companies to start businesses with even greater upside potential for personal wealth. Dot-com Epinions was launched in 1999, twelve weeks after its founders left their former companies, such as @Home and Yahoo!, and started writing code. They left behind up to $10 million each in stock options that would have vested in a matter of months. Why? A *New York Times* reporter quoted one entrepreneur who "talked blatantly about wanting 'plane money,' and how you weren't even a player in the Valley with less than $100 million."[7]

"Plane money," as you might guess, does not mean first-class tickets; it means owning one's own jet. The "players" in Silicon Valley were a powerful reference group for this young man, a tribe to which he wanted to belong.

Some start-up companies went a bit overboard in ensuring that employees were willing to drink their Kool-Aid. TheMan.com was formed to provide men with online ideas for dates, along with an opportunity to purchase all the trappings of the date on TheMan. com's Web site. In a *Time* magazine article, the CEO explains how members were inducted into the tribe:

> *The newest hire . . . is forced to carry a Rugrats doll and order take-out Chinese food, the nightly company meal. "How do you indoctrinate people into your culture? You baptize them," [CEO Calvin] Lui says. "We want everybody to drink out of the same vat of Kool-*

Aid."... Lui says the foldout desks and below-average salaries keep his employees "hungry" for the eventual IPO. "We say, 'If you're willing to take a pay cut now so that your equity is worth more later, that's great.' If people don't jump at that, they don't fit." [8] *[The company ceased operations 11/1/2000.]*

One wonders if this CEO understands the difference between building a tribe around a mission and building one around a specific (reasonably superficial) goal—in this case, an initial public offering. Once the IPO is over, what incentive remains to build lasting smarts into the company?

But when drinking the Kool-Aid is tied to deep smarts, it can be helpful. Indeed, many successful organizations are founded and sustained because their members believe deeply in the mission. Working for a cause can move people to heights of performance and satisfaction that receiving a paycheck never will. Apple's young founders were excited by the opportunity to change the world. One original team member recalled the early days: "Everyone who worked there identified totally with their work—we all believed we were on a mission from God." [9] Harley-Davidson is another company whose employees feel passionate about their work. Former CEO Richard Teerlink explains:

We wanted people to be excited about what they do, to have an emotional attachment to our company.... It was the excitement they got when they were standing in line in the supermarket wearing a Harley T-shirt and someone said, "Do you work at Harley? Wow!" We got people who wanted to work for this kind of company, who wanted to make a difference." [10]

Warring Tribes

The sense of the whole organization as a tribe usually promotes knowledge sharing and the development of common smarts. But what happens when separate tribes evolve, and we-they feelings develop? The consequences for the overall functioning of the organization can be disastrous. A degree of "tribalism" has been implicated in the 2003 space shuttle tragedy (discussed earlier in chapter 3 as resulting in part from "mental set"):

> [Columbia *Accident Investigation*] *Board member John Logsdon blames the problem, at least in part, on so-called tribalism: NASA has "a particular culture, has its own rules and its own behavior." As an example, Logsdon cites the competitive and sometimes strained relationship between Johnson Space Center in Houston— the nucleus of NASA's human space flight—and Marshall Space Flight Center in Huntsville, Alabama—the propulsion hub. "Foam is Marshall's problem. Orbiter is Johnson's problem. Who looks at foam hitting the orbiter? There's kind of a hole in the middle," said Logsdon.*[11]

In the past couple of decades, businesses have created cross-functional design teams to speed up new product and service development and avoid the kind of "hole" mentioned above. Yet silos of knowledge remain in many organizations, in no small part because humans *like* tribes, and the tribes often encourage knowledge hoarding.

Communities of Practice as Tribes

But tribes *can* form across internal or external organizational boundaries. It is much easier and more comfortable to share knowledge with people who speak the same disciplinary and organizational language. Communities of practice—groups of individuals who coalesce around a particular kind of job—also constitute tribes.[12] They are important knowledge communities—especially for geographically dispersed members of groups with a common work interest. For example, the World Bank has encouraged the growth of what they term Thematic Groups, which are intended to share smarts—and build them. The need for such knowledge-based communities was clear. As one World Bank employee complained in 1999:

> *When my clients [in Africa] asked me what do we know about the technical, financial and economic feasibility of using solar*

energy in low-income countries, my staff told me that there was nothing available. It took them a week to figure out that there was in fact high-quality know-how on this very issue in the Environment Network.[13]

Some informal knowledge exchange groups already existed at the World Bank. A group of people working on highways had regularly held discussions for more than fifteen years. But the bank managers decided to support and fund more formal communities of practice, such as one addressing urban poverty—a growing problem, especially in Asia, Latin America, and Africa, that affected approximately one billion people, 200 million of them under the age of five. People living in high-density slums typically lacked basic services, such as water, sanitation, waste collection, security, street lighting, paved footpaths, roads for emergency access, and schools and clinics. Although the bank had set up an Urban Department in the mid 1970s, the department gradually shifted focus to citywide initiatives, and in a reorganization in 1987, the staff were dispersed into more than two dozen small units. Knowledge became extremely fragmented; teams were "fractured," "atomized," and "blown to the wind." Such knowledge as was produced on the topic was seen as overly theoretical by those who had experienced the problem firsthand.

In 1997, a Thematic Group on Services to the Urban Poor was set up. Their mission, as they saw it, was to help "the Bank, its clients, and practitioners, promote and deliver basic services to the urban poor. The group gathers, generates and shares knowledge on slum upgrading from practices inside and outside the Bank." The group began developing simple tools for colleagues working with urban clients. For example, they created an "electronic toolkit" containing reference materials, video and text information to guide the design and implementation of large-scale upgrading programs, and an electronic newsletter. They began to hold in-person and video-conferenced brainstorming sessions to aggregate experience and stimulate innovation among the "urbanists." The network of people in the thematic group also helped with an ambitious plan called

"Cities Without Slums" that set targets to improve the lives of 5 to 10 million slum dwellers by 2005 and 100 million by 2020.

Such communities of practice help in the building and transfer of smarts in multiple ways: They help members locate relevant processes rather than reinvent them; they foster the kind of creative fusion among experts mentioned in chapter 4; and they socialize new members into the belief systems of the group. Perhaps most important, they serve as the focal group for tribal passions—the love of the mission that draws these people together. Who but colleagues in the same line of work can appreciate the nuances in a task exquisitely well done and share excitement over details in the job that might be meaningless to someone outside the tribe? As Brown and Duguid point out, participants in such tribal communities gain more than knowledge *about* a given field of practice; they learn *to be*, that is, they learn know-how.[14] In short, communities of practice provide the focus necessary for providing the practical, experiential basis for deep smarts.

Disciplines as Tribes

For similar reasons, disciplines can also serve as tribes. As discussed in the previous chapter, for example, engineers have strong beliefs about function, whereas designers focus on form. Common beliefs can shape identification with profession, role, or job. One may identify more strongly with a disciplinary culture, such as engineering, than with the organization for which one currently works. People change jobs with some regularity but disciplines more rarely. As a result, one's deep smarts are shaped through an immersion in one's discipline. Entrepreneur Ash Munshi, originally trained in mathematics and computer science, remarked, "When you're a technologist, every problem looks like a technology problem." He went on to say that a couple years of leading start-ups had given him an appreciation for sales, marketing, and customer interactions. He had joined a new tribe.

Table 6-1 summarizes these various social influences on beliefs and suggests the increasing difficulty of changing behavior once individuals identify themselves with tribes.

TABLE 6-1

Varieties of Social Influence on Beliefs and Knowledge

	Compliance	Conformity	Herd	Tribe
Nature of Influence	Explicit: "Do this because I know more than you do" or "Do this or else."	Explicit: "I know this is wrong, but everyone else is doing it."	Largely explicit: "I don't know what to believe, but everyone else seems to know what to do."	Largely tacit: "This is how my tribe does things, what they believe in. So do I."
Basis of Influence	Direct exercise of power: reward, punishment, expertise.	Indirect influence: whatever "everyone" is doing. Fear of looking bad, odd, "out of it."	Emotional arousal caused by, e.g., scarcity or greed.	Desire for belonging; emulation.
Uncertainty Level About What Is Real or Correct	Generally low.	Generally low.	High.	Generally low unless conflicting views of other tribes are made apparent.
Type of Change	Shallow: behavior change; peripheral beliefs may change; may build receptors.	Shallow: behavior change; peripheral beliefs may change.	Moderate: behavior change; peripheral and moderately central beliefs may change.	Deep: behavior and central beliefs may change.
Direct Contact Necessary?	Normally yes. Monitoring of behavior enhances compliance.	Yes. Influence diminishes when not face-to-face.	No. *Perception* of consensual beliefs is important.	No. Person need not be a member of the tribe to be influenced. Role modeling is possible with no personal contact or interaction.
Countermeasures	If possible, leave the relationship.	Seek allies to reduce conformity pressures.	Counter with other, more central beliefs.	Reframe beliefs to align with goals; seek guided experience for reality check; draw on other tribes for support.

Imitating Role Models

We are influenced not only by the tribes to which we belong, but by those we *want* to join. Individuals and groups alike select models of behavior they wish to emulate. These reference groups or role models define what is possible for us. For example, the entrepreneurs in our study compared themselves to their peers in order to define appropriate aspirations. Randy Paynter, founder of Care2, was only half joking when he reflected on his success as an entrepreneur compared to that of his Stanford Business School classmates:

> *The Stanford network is unbelievable. We get a lot of help from them, but also you get a lot of inspiration. Our class—I was Class of '95—has Jeff Skoll, one of the founders of eBay. And Tom Adams, who joined eBay later. Steve Jurvetson from Draper, Fischer, Jurvetson. They have all done phenomenally well. They're very motivational and inspirational. They also, of course, raise our expectations unbelievably. I mean, if we've only made $100 million, what are we in this for?*

We don't even have to know people personally to be influenced by their achievements, to have them shape our perceptions of what deep smarts are needed to reach a goal. In fact, in these days of near-instant communications, role models are increasingly global. In 1996, Rajesh Reddy was a young, ambitious computer engineer in Bangalore, India. He had an idea for a company, little cash—and a role model. On his wall, Reddy had posted a *Newsweek* cover photograph of Marc Andreessen, a similarly young (twenty-four), ambitious, and now suddenly wealthy entrepreneur, whose company, Netscape, had recently gone public. "Netscape had just happened in the U.S., and it was a big story. I remember putting that [photograph] up on the notice board in my room. I thought, 'Here's how it's done. I have no idea how we would take it from here to there, but we can do something like that.'" This aspiring entrepreneur went on to found Unimobile, a company with offices in India and the United States. Because Netscape's Andreessen was also young and did not come from a privileged background, young people all over the world viewed him as a role model—someone they admired and who was not that dissimilar from themselves. They could imagine themselves in his position.

Aspiring to be like the very wealthy and successful spread rapidly in the late 1990s—a combination of emulating role models and following the herd of fellow business school students and computer programmers. In 1999, *Time* magazine reported:

> *Stanford's Graduate School of Business . . . has become a hothouse for aspiring Internet entrepreneurs. Forty-five students out of this June's graduating class of 360 have already started their own Internet business, more than double the number in 1998. The reason is simple. Stanford M.B.A.s spend two years schmoozing A-list Valley executives and VCs—and other people don't. Garth Saloner, a professor at Stanford, says it works like this: "You're 27 years old, you are sitting in an auditorium, there's a billionaire in front of you, and you are thinking 'Gee, why not me?'"* [15]

But can one acquire deep smarts through imitation? Groups, even whole organizations, can be persuaded to emulate a model. The concepts of benchmarking and "best practices" are based on the idea that imitation is more than just the most sincere form of flattery—it is also a path to distinctive capabilities, if the role model is not a direct competitor. If you can find some organization that excels in a particular process or system—one outside your own industry or market—and figure out how they do it, you will have an edge over your competitors. Sometimes the attempt to transfer knowledge from one organization to the other ends up benefiting both, as in the partnership between Timberland and City Year. (See "The Timberland Company's Role Model.")

Both kinds of reference groups, the ones to which we belong and the ones to which we wish we belonged, shape knowledge. However, selecting role models does not necessarily mean that we are *able* to imitate them. Much depends on how well we understand

The Timberland Company's Role Model

THE TIMBERLAND Company manufactures high-end boots and other outdoor apparel. Timberland's founding family had a long history of philanthropy, but had never integrated these beliefs into the company. Jeffrey Swarz, the current chief operating officer and grandson of the company's founder, put it this way: "I just knew Timberland needs to be part of its community. It's in my heart, it's in my being." When Alan Khazei, cofounder of City Year, a Boston-based community-service and leadership-development organization, cold-called Timberland's headquarters for a donation of seventy pairs of work boots, not only did Timberland make the donation, but this initial act of charity also set in motion what would become an intimate partnership between the two disparate organizations. When Khazei drove up to New Hampshire to express his thanks for the donation, Swarz recalls saying to him, "You are out there actually saving lives. I am making boots, but I have always wanted to save lives." Khazei then proceeded to tell Swarz how he and his company could do just that. Over the next few years, Timberland increased its commitment to City Year, including large monetary contributions, boots, and uniforms, and encouraged hundreds of employees to work on City Year projects. Swarz took a position on City Year's board. City Year, in turn, helped Timberland with its diversity and team-building programs.

Clearly, City Year was functioning as a role model for Swarz and his company's employees, providing a means for putting personal values into action. Eventually, Timberland created its own Community Enterprise division, providing employees with thirty-two hours a year to work in community service programs, including City Year. A senior manager of the division described Community Enterprise as "the keeper of the company's beliefs." Those beliefs were described in a public statement by Swarz as "the belief that each individual can and must make a difference in the way we experience life on this planet. . . . As a company we have both a responsibility and an interest in engaging in the world around us."

Source: Details and quotes in this box are from James Austin, "Timberland and Community Involvement," Case 796-156 (Boston: Harvard Business School, 2001).

their deep smarts, that is, what knowledge we need to transfer and absorb in order to replicate their success.

Beware Morphing Role Models

Distance is no barrier to at least superficial imitation if the template is available through the Internet. The founders of the Hong Kong incubator Tech Pacific subscribed to the start-up stereotypes favored by the tribe of investors in 1999–2000 and pushed applicants to shape their business plans accordingly. However, Tech Pacific designed its own internal business model in imitation of an incubator in Silicon Valley, Garage.com. Under the leadership of founder and CEO Guy Kawasaki, Garage.com was a combination of venture capital firm, investment bank, and management consulting firm. As Garage.com attracted thousands of business plans, selected the most promising ones, worked with the founders to refine their plans, and arranged early-stage funding for them, they enacted their informal motto: "We find 'em, fix 'em, and fund 'em." Garage.com's Web site included a "Heaven" section, where interested investors could contact registered entrepreneurs directly.[16] Tech Pacific's imitation of the Garage.com template ranged from superficial similarity in marketing communications ("We find, finance and build Asia's technology companies") to more substantial process emulation: matching investors and entrepreneurs (with "Nirvana" substituted for Garage's "Heaven").

Tech Pacific illustrates a problem with emulating another organization that is in the process of morphing rapidly: It becomes impossible to learn from the model what worked and what didn't. Neither the model nor the imitator survived the economic downturn unscathed. Garage.com is barely recognizable from the high flyer of 2000 when it attracted thousands of prospective entrepreneurs to its "boot camps." The renamed Garage Technology Ventures is essentially a venture capital firm, while Tech Pacific has been absorbed into Crosby, an Asian investment banking firm.

Smarts can't be deep if there has been no time to learn from experience. Caught up in all the influences highlighted in chapter 5 (e.g., the apparent need for speed), and earlier in this chapter (e.g., the pressures of perceived scarcity) the founders of Tech Pacific did not receive the potential benefits of imitation. In fact, although imitating a high-performance model is a tempting way to shortcut the deliberate building of deep smarts, successful duplication is often elusive, as the following examples will show.

Some Models Don't Transfer

Even imitating a well-established company may not work if the model conflicts with local practice. As suggested in the previous chapter, Western models often do not transfer well to non-Western markets. When Arun Jain founded New Delhi start-up Clips in 1996, he modeled it (including the play on the company name) after Staples, a company he greatly admired. After drastically morphing the original business model to a wholesale operation marketing Clips-branded products to small retailers, Jain reflected on why the Staples model did not transfer to India:

> *The reason Staples is successful is because the people running the small office actually go to a stationery shop and buy their requirements. And they're willing to drive in the car, fifteen to twenty minutes, pick up all the supplies, and come back to the office. Here, stationery is viewed as a necessary nuisance to run an office, and more often than not, a [low-paid worker] will just be sent to buy the product from the closest retailer. When such a worker came to Clips he would often say, "Okay, how much does it cost?" And we'd say, "three hundred rupees." He'd say, "I'll take it, but give me an invoice for five hundred rupees." And we'd say, "Sorry, we cannot do that." One of the lessons I learned is that you have to be very, very careful when you apply concepts and ideas that might have been successful in one environment into another environment.*

Even a native-born Indian (albeit with an American M.B.A.) was not aware of basic obstacles to running an Indian business using an American model. Jain didn't want to follow the traditional Indian business practice of paying middlemen, but found that this was not possible in the office supplies business. This example suggests the hazards of incomplete experience and experimentation to test assumptions. Jain unquestionably had deep smarts about business and about his own country—but not about the intermediaries between supplier and customer in this business. Clips had to morph dramatically in order to survive.

Photocopying the Features

If you want to mimic the success of Apple Computer, you need a great idea, smart employees, some money—and a garage. Why a garage? That's where Hewlett and Packard built HP's first product and where Steve Jobs started Apple. Garages are hard to come by in Bangalore, India, but the four founders of IQura, a software start-up, actually looked for one because they wanted to follow "that Silicon Valley model to the dot," according to one of them.[17] They never found a garage and had to be content with a dark basement.

The actions of the young men in this story may sound perilously close to superstitious behavior, but fads in business are often more symbolic than substantive. The producers of foosball machines hit the jackpot when entrepreneurship flowered so extravagantly in 1999–2000 and such games were the accepted badge of hip corporate creativity. All the start-ups had them. Even staid corporations began to imitate some of the outward trappings of small creative groups—partly because their employees were drawn to such groups and many were leaving the corporate world to join the hopefuls. One such corporation, in an effort to create an internal reference group for some of their e-business software hotshots, cordoned off the entire tenth floor in their fourteen-story office building. The idea was to recreate the atmosphere of a start-up. Only the inhabitants of the tenth floor were permitted entry, but they could come and go at whatever hours they chose and dress as they pleased. They enjoyed many amenities lacking on the other floors: free drinks in the kitchen, a lounge area, and—yes—a foosball machine.

Predictably, the effort caused much resentment among the rest of the employees—and had little obvious effect on the outflow of tenth-floor workers. One of the major shortcomings of the tenth floor was that while it *looked* like an entrepreneurial venture, it did not have many of the basic differentiators from the rest of the corporation, including different incentive systems. Hope flared on the tenth floor when a former entrepreneur was brought in from outside to manage the group. He was, after all, a member of the entrepreneurial community to which many of the employees aspired. However, he lasted fewer than six months before he deserted in favor of a *real* start-up.

Upper management in this corporation understood that they were losing valued employees to the strong attraction of an outside reference group—but they didn't really know how to combat that pull. While they put in place the superficial elements gleaned from the popular press of the time, they did not understand how those elements connected to the deeper sources of attraction. It was as if they were employing rules of thumb (see chapter 7)—"Install foosball and creativity will rise"—as a substitute for deep smarts about innovation. To be fair, many of the employees relocated to the tenth floor did not at first understand what constituted a start-up environment. They shared with management the desire to create a compelling reference group inside the organization—but they found that they were working with the same people they always had. They just did so now with free drinks, at odd hours, and perhaps with their pet parakeet perched on their shoulder. The knowledge gap faced by the managers in the corporation was large not only because no one in upper management had ever run a start-up, but also because there were no reliable models for creating a start-up environment within a corporation—or at least none that they knew of. The gap existed in terms both of model and implementation.

However, sometimes the gap is largest *between* the two. That is, as suggested by the preceding examples, the referent organization or group may provide a kind of template to be followed—but the imitator has no direct access to deeper knowledge that underlies the template.

Tacit Knowledge Doesn't Come with an Instruction Book

Highly regarded performers—including organizations that are admired and imitated—may trace their success to their tacit knowledge. At the height of its referent power in the steel industry, Chaparral Steel CEO Gordon Forward said that he could escort competitors through the minimill, show them almost "everything and we will be giving away nothing because they can't take it home with them."[18] If the knowledge that makes the system to which you aspire work is largely tacit, even imitating the observable operational steps will not lead to the same desired outcome.

One of the most admired role models for manufacturing and assembly in the world remains the Toyota Production System (TPS). During the 1980s in particular, when U.S. automobile manufacturers were losing market share worldwide, the flights from the Midwest to Japan were full of knowledge seekers. They came back to institute such processes as just-in-time inventory control and the "pull" system within assembly lines that enforced the principle of little or no inventory buildup between stations. Assembly plants in the United States were suddenly populated with *kanban* cards to control materials flow with visible signals and *andon* cords to stop the line in case of a quality problem. Foreign terms invaded the manufacturing lexicon: *jidoka* (to make problems visible and aid diagnostics); *kaizen* (continuous improvement). Thousands of articles about the TPS appeared in the popular press and in academic journals.[19]

Quality in U.S. automobile plants improved. However, according to researcher Steven Spear, who spent several years researching the system (including working on a Toyota line), "What's curious is that few manufacturers have managed to imitate Toyota successfully—even though the company has been extraordinarily open about its practices."[20] One reason that all the dutiful pilgrims to Japan were unable to bring back the essence of the system was that "observers confuse the tools and practices they see on their plant visits with the system itself."[21] This confusion is not surprising because the TPS was never written down and even the best practitioners of the system "often are not able to articulate it."[22] TPS is actually a kind of scientific method that stimulates both workers and managers to treat every step in the process as an opportunity for experimentation. Each assembly step is so well articulated and specified that any slight deviation from expected output is treated as evidence of a problem to be identified and treated—immediately. With every worker constantly on the outlook for any small variation from the ideal, the company is a hotbed of learning. The workers absorb the basics of this system through the kind of experiential learning discussed in chapter 8. There is a "cascading pathway for teaching, which starts with the plant manager, that delivers training to each employee."[23] Knowledge about the TPS is therefore mostly tacit, learned over time, through direct experience. Small wonder that visitors cannot bring it home with them.

Institutionalizing Role Models, Coaching, and Know-who: The Case of TiE

In chapter 7, we will discuss the chain of knowledge transfer originating in California with Kanwal Rekhi, and extending to novice entrepreneurs in India. Rekhi was a cofounder of The Indus Entrepreneurs (TiE), a remarkable institution that serves an important role-modeling, coaching, and networking function for Indians, Sri Lankans, Bangladeshis, and Pakistanis who may have thought of themselves primarily as "back room" technicians but not as creative, product-oriented managers and entrepreneurs. Part of TiE's "philosophical framework" is to "always provide an uplifting positive leadership role model."[24] Prior to the mid-1980s, it would not have been easy for an aspiring entrepreneur to find a leadership role model within the Indian community. Indians were renowned for their engineering talent (3 percent of applicants are accepted at the six ultra-prestigious Indian Institutes of Technology), but prior to Kanwal Rekhi, none had been CEO of a major U.S. company. Rekhi overcame huge odds to head Excelan, a company he cofounded in 1982 to produce add-in circuit boards to connect desktop computers into a local area network. He started the company as the only path available to upper management. Passed over repeatedly for promotion to managerial positions, Rekhi had been told by his bosses that they "couldn't afford to lose me as an engineer." When a technician working under Rekhi quit to start a company, he thought, "If [he] can do it, then shame on me for not trying." His company was sold to Novell in 1989 for $210 million, and Rekhi became a wealthy man. He became CTO at Novell; however, shortly after he was passed over for the CEO slot, he quit. Restless at being a man of leisure after more than twenty years of hard work, Rekhi began spending time at the TiE offices in Santa Clara, meeting informally with young men and women who sought out "one of theirs" who had successfully broken through the silk ceiling. He and the other twenty original founders of TiE, all successful managers and/or entrepreneurs, became a magnet for young people who wanted to believe they could also be successful—and now had the people who could provide the kind of experience-based help they needed. Rekhi recalled: "We discovered everybody had the same experience [of Indians having difficulty attaining top executive positions]. At some point, somebody said, 'You know, we ought to help our people overcome this issue. We need to help them by showing them we can become role models and provide any assistance they need.'" In the following vignette we see how conscious attention to providing aspirational role models and access to know-who can promote the smarts of aspiring entrepreneurs.

A Look at TiE in Action

*T*HE BALLROOM *at the Santa Clara Hilton is packed. The Indus Entrepreneur conference is being covered by a For-tune magazine reporter; venture capitalists, investment bankers, and angel investors mingle with TiE members; cofounder and spiritual head Kanwal Rekhi is surrounded by acolytes. But mostly the room is filled with young prospective entrepreneurs, almost all from Indian backgrounds and now residing in Silicon Valley. Two young Indian executives from a successful dot-com have just addressed the audience with a can-do message. Now comes the main event. On cue, thirty or so young men and women form a line and,* *one by one, take the microphone. They have two minutes each to make a pitch about their idea for a company. After a couple of PowerPoint slides and a parting "See me at table 17," they make way for the next hopeful. The queue of young people, armed only with an elevator speech and a couple of transparencies, have plenty of aspirations. Now they have the role models, the contacts, and—if their idea is good enough—the coaching to show that being Indian is no bar to success.*

Rekhi continues to dole out advice from the original Silicon Valley TiE offices, but there were at last count an additional thirty-eight TiE chapters around the world, eighteen in the United States. All the chapters continue to provide TiE members with coaching for their business plans and access to established entrepreneurs, bankers, and venture capitalists that would not otherwise be possible. Without this help, many new business leaders would never have started cultivating deep managerial smarts.

Implications for Managers

Social influences powerfully shape what we believe to be deep smarts as well as how we build them. The people who work for us generally want to be part of a tribe—be it the whole organization or a group within it. The social impulse is wired in. That fact has both a bad and a good side. The bad side of social influence is that when they are uncertain or confused about the right course of action, people often follow the herd—and herds don't have deep smarts. We certainly saw many cases of that shortcoming in the numerous scandals that topped the financial pages at the beginning of the twenty-first century. It takes strong leadership to withstand the power of a stampede, much less stop one. We need to develop leaders who recognize the strong emotional pull of a herd, and pause at least long enough to test the herd's attraction against their own deep smarts, including those shaped by their beliefs and values.

Another downside to social influence is that managers with considerable influence over peoples' decisions and actions can get people to do things that they don't really believe are effective. People who "just go through the motions" in complying with directives may glean some knowledge from the exercise, and may even eventually come to believe in the reasoning behind the instructions—but they lack the necessary motivation to absorb or build deep smarts. So when we ask people to take a required training course, carry out some organizational initiative, write a report, or make decisions based on criteria that we provide, we should not delude ourselves that we are transferring knowledge. We may even be killing the motivation to develop deep smarts if we cannot inspire people to accept the bases for our directives, but can only get them to comply.

The good side to social influence is that as a manager you can create a powerful motivating force in a group or organization that is a tribe people want to join—and stay with. They will enjoy working there enough that they will turn down more lucrative offers from other organizations; they will work in teams for a common goal; they will internalize and act on beliefs that others around them strongly support. The tribe will influence the kinds of knowledge these individuals value and attempt to attain. Moreover, if you and your colleagues are strong leaders, people will see you as positive role models and try to imitate you.

Positive role models inspire people by demonstrating that lofty achievements are in fact possible, and create receptors in the sense that they embody at least one visible path to some desirable goal. We see someone we admire and we think, "I'd like to be like her," and the very thought opens the mind to observe and mimic her deep smarts. Of course, there are negative role models as well, and the hazard in organizations is that managers will discourage employees from gaining deep smarts if it appears the tribe rewards only technical achievements or "making the numbers"—regardless of *how*.

When the objects of our admiration *do* have deep smarts, those smarts contain large quantities of tacit knowledge, and tacit knowledge (as we will discuss more in chapter 8) cannot be readily transferred from one set of brains to another. One of the biggest paradoxes in importing "best practices" is that those most easily imitated are least likely to provide a competitive advantage, and vice versa. Therefore, when we wish to emulate a role model—either individual or organization—we will need a great deal of firsthand observation or, better still, time working together. When Korean company Samsung decided to invest in learning how to do better product design, they transported some of their own designers to work alongside designers at IDEO, the award-winning product development company headquartered in California, on joint projects. It is probably no accident that in recent years, Samsung designers have started winning awards for their own work.

Keep in Mind

- Compliance with an expert or a powerful person's demands results in behavior change but little change in underlying beliefs. Compliance may help develop receptors but is unlikely to lead to deep smarts.

- Group pressures towards conformity can persuade people to alter their behavior, even when they know such change is wrong or immoral. Conformity generally does not affect central beliefs.

- Under conditions of uncertainty, people tend to respond emotionally, particularly to perceived scarcity. Herd behavior can influence fairly central beliefs as well as behavior. Even intelligent, strong-minded people can succumb to herd behavior.

- When we particularly admire or like a group and its members, that group becomes our tribe, and can exert a powerful influence, shaping our central beliefs, behavior, and knowledge.

- True believers, those who have "drunk the Kool-Aid," feel passionate about their groups and are intrinsically motivated to advance the interests of the group.

- One need not be an actual member to be influenced by a tribe. Adopting a tribe as a role model can provide benchmarks for one's beliefs and behaviors and can shape how one develops knowledge.

- Role modeling across cultures can have negative results when deep smarts about the role model are not effectively transferred.

- Imitation of surface features of a model tends to have symbolic value only. When deep smarts are not transferred, it is highly unlikely that a would-be emulator will succeed.

- One reason why modeling behavior after an admired reference group does not always succeed is that the model's smarts have extensive tacit dimensions—and those are very difficult to transfer.

SEVEN

Transferring Deep Smarts

U P TO THIS POINT, we have examined what constitutes deep smarts, including the social influences that shape and filter knowledge. Now we turn to a major focus of the book: how to transfer deep smarts from those who have them to those who need them. (See figure 7-1.) Knowledge transfer is obviously a process of teaching and learning, but organizations expend tremendous resources ineffectually because managers fail to match expectations and resources to transfer methods. Not all transfer techniques can deliver *knowledge* (as opposed to information).

The next two chapters explore the role of knowledge coaches—experts called upon to teach relative novices. We call them coaches because we argue that such transfer requires techniques associated more with coaching than with other forms of teaching. We call them *knowledge* coaches to distinguish the role from that of a process facilitator or executive coach. Knowledge coaches have domain expertise to pass along or recreate in others. As we will explain, not all coaches come from the top of the ladder of expertise, and every one of us may play the role of knowledge coach or protégé at different times.

FIGURE 7-1

Deep Smarts and Knowledge Transfer

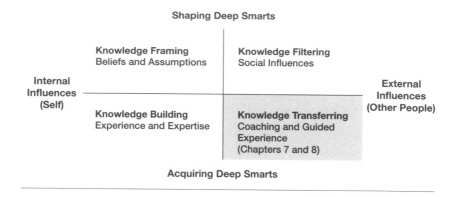

When Is Transferring Deep Smarts Important?

Many times in our lives—both professional and personal—we need either to transfer knowledge we have built up over years of experience from our heads to someone else's (our children, a junior colleague, a peer) or we have the reverse need: to somehow access those bits of wisdom accumulated in someone else's cranium. Every time we take over a new job or leave an old one, there is an immense waste of knowledge. Not that a newcomer wants to use *everything* that was in her predecessor's head—some of it was mere flotsam and jetsam, and some was obsolete. But the good stuff? Her mental Rolodex would be handy—whom to call when something breaks down or needs expediting. And how about her uncanny ability to decode behavioral cues—subtle signs of disagreement or even hostility among subordinates in meetings? How does she *do* that? That storehouse of unwritten process details—the way that certain software or hardware does or doesn't work—maybe that know-how could save some time. The *real* story not contained in the files on those customers? Definitely neither flotsam nor jetsam. These are her deep smarts—the knowledge that is vital to preserve.

Who Can Be a Knowledge Coach?
Who Can Be Coached?

Of course, much of the success of knowledge transfer depends on identifying not only what is to be transferred—but how. And the transfer will never take place without a willing, skillful coach and a receptive, able learner.

Leonardo da Vinci notwithstanding, no one is expert on everything; the Ten-Year Rule discussed in chapter 3 sees to that. An expert in one domain is a novice in another. When e-business burst on the scene, GE's CEO Jack Welch was impressed by the strategy adopted by the CEO of GE's Global Consumer Finance (GCF) division, who realized he was not up to speed in e-business. The CEO identified the brightest person under thirty in GCF and asked him to be his mentor. When Welch returned to the United States, within forty-eight hours he spread the word: All managers were to identify someone who could serve as an e-business mentor. According to Welch, the youngest and brightest would now teach the oldest.[1]

There's no rule that says the need for being coached stops when one has reached a certain age or level of expertise. Concert pianists and Wimbledon champions draw on the expertise of master teachers to guide their practice sessions. One forty-six-year-old senior vice president at Adobe Systems calls upon mentors within the company (including CEO Bruce Chizen) and out (a former supervisor from her days at Hewlett-Packard). And Chizen himself taps Intuit chairman Bill Campbell for advice and support.[2]

So who can coach? Certainly some level of expertise is required, some knowledge that is worth transferring; beyond that, a desire to coach and some skill at dealing with people who may have little or no prior knowledge. We do not always have the luxury of an expert to coach us—or of reaching mastery before we are called upon to share our knowledge. Recall that there are several rungs on the ladder of expertise: novice, apprentice, journeyman, and then master. Each individual reaching a rung above novice has knowledge to impart to those on the lower rungs of the ladder, although it is likely incomplete. A nudge in the right direction by an apprentice may be helpful to the total novice.

In our entrepreneurship study, we observed extensive chains of knowledge transfer in which a coach's protégé quickly became a coach to someone less knowledgeable than himself, who then coached a budding entrepreneur even *more* callow. In the next section we trace one of these chains from the heart of Silicon Valley to Bangalore, India. The time between start-ups grew shorter and the smarts more shallow as they were passed down the line and across the world—but some value was always transmitted.

You Don't Always Need to Be an Expert to Be a Knowledge Coach

In 1967, a young graduate of Bombay's Indian Institute of Technology, Kanwal Rekhi, came to the United States to obtain a master's degree from the Michigan Technological University. Thirty-two years later, a young Indian in Bangalore, Saumil Majmudar, started a small company. Those two events are connected by a trail of knowledge accumulation and hand-offs, of experience hard-won and generously shared.

After selling his company, Excelan, to Novell in 1989, Rekhi put his newfound wealth and entrepreneurial skills to work helping other ambitious South Asians. (Rekhi's story was told in more detail in chapter 6.) Two of his beneficiaries were K. B. "Chandra" Chandrasekhar and B. V. Jagadeesh, founders of a small company, Exodus Communications, who met him when they were days away from going broke. Rekhi bailed them out with $200,000—but he contributed more than cash. He helped them decide how to focus the company, and Exodus reached a peak market capitalization of just under $30 billion in March 2000.[3] "Kanwal's my guru and my mentor," Chandra said.[4] (Both Jagadeesh and Chandra subsequently left Exodus to found separate companies; some time later Exodus filed for bankruptcy.)

Chandra, in turn, mentored fledgling entrepreneur Rajesh Reddy, who was in India in 1998–1999 building a company called Unimobile, a provider of universal wireless solutions. As Reddy recalled his second meeting, Chandra "tore the Unimobile business plan apart," noting that the revenue projections were unrealistic and the business focus was too diffuse—but still he invested in the company.

The chain of knowledge flows didn't stop with the Rekhi-to-Chandra-to-Reddy exchange. Even after he moved Unimobile to the United States, Reddy kept in touch with people back in India, with the result that he was able to help his friend, twenty-eight-year-old Saumil Majmudar, with his start-up, QSupport, a technical support company for people with home personal computers. Reddy passed along knowledge he had newly acquired about selecting and dealing with the board of investors, honing a business strategy, building a strong core team, and managing cash carefully. The two of them also discussed mutual problems they faced, such as balancing loyalty to employees against incompetence and inability to scale up with the company.

In interviewing Majmudar, we thought we had reached the end of the knowledge transfer chain. But no. He was coaching three of *his* friends who were starting up businesses in India!

Several observations emerge from this story of knowledge transfer.

- Experts can mentor novices, despite a very large gap in knowledge, if the experts are willing to coach and the novices can bear having their knowledge gap exposed. Some experts find the knowledge gap so great that they don't know where to start—and/or don't have the patience to begin with the basics. Rekhi's approach is to give novices advice, often as rules of thumb, such as "focus"—and then send them out to put the rules into practice. If they are smart enough to act on his advice and come back to report on their progress, he will give them more assistance. If they didn't get it or didn't try his suggestion, he will not see them a third time. Thus he is building their knowledge base by forcing them to practice what he preaches!

- All along the ladder of expertise, people can coach those who are less experienced. They transfer what they have learned *so far*. No sooner do they learn something from their mentor that is reinforced in their own experience, then they can pass it along. In fact, the relatively less experienced apprentice may be better positioned to coach the novice because the apprentice understands the receptors, having recently been a novice himself. An expert coach understands this. Kleiner Perkins venture capitalist Vinod Khosla was mentoring the young start-up team at Zaplet. But Khosla also sent another of his protégés, Joe Kraus (founder of Web portal Excite), to talk with the founders. Although Kraus was only in his mid-twenties, he was able to draw on his recent experiences as an entrepreneur to assist the Zaplet team. In many of our organizations, such apprentice-level individuals with experience are underutilized as coaches.

- Coaching can help shorten the time to fill some parts of the knowledge gap. That is, when Rekhi passed along the knowledge it took him years to discover, Chandra's learning curve was shortened; Chandra in turn shortened the period for Reddy to learn certain aspects of entrepreneuring, and Reddy quickened Majmudar's learning process. Contrary to the old adage about a little knowledge being dangerous, a little knowledge here was helpful. Each coach was able to help those below him on the ladder, to frame their experience as it unfolded. That is, the coaches helped their junior colleagues grow more receptors.

- By the time the knowledge reached Majmudar, it was fragmentary and incomplete, to be sure. But because those pieces of knowledge passed along were rooted in the recent experience of the coach, this was not like a game of "telephone," where the knowledge gets distorted by being passed along. Rather, the knowledge was truncated, limited by the experience of the mentor. So toward the end of the chain, the "coach" (Reddy) was still struggling with the same issues as the "protégé" (Majmudar). For example, Reddy had not yet solved the problem of how to hire people who would be able to scale up as the start-up company grew—and how to fire them if they didn't. He had been given the rule of thumb—hire people who can scale, and fire them if they don't—but he didn't know how to do that in real time. (In fact, he gave Majmudar the opposite advice at one point—hire people who will be loyal to the idea and don't worry about hiring for skills!)

Therefore, if we decide in our organizations to employ apprentices as knowledge coaches, we need to be aware of the pieces of the puzzle that the apprentices have experienced and those that are outside their repertoire. The stream of knowledge with the Indians was individual coach to learner. We also see deliberate programs in which the more expert are enlisted to help the less experienced to become coaches themselves. (See "Coaching Coaches—Online!")

Coaching Coaches—Online!

THE HARVARD Graduate School of Education offers an online (Web-based) professional development program for kindergarten to grade 12 teachers and administrators from—at last count—sixty-four countries. The objective of WIDE World (Wide-scale Interactive Development for Educators) is to help educators design curricula that integrate new technologies and improve their skills in assessment, attention to multiple intelligences, and teaching for understanding. "I've come to believe that Web courses can be even more effective than face-to-face instruction," WIDE co–principal investigator Stone Wiske says. "In a real classroom, so much gets lost—words float in and out of the air. But online, they are captured and held so that learners can reflect on their work."

However, online doesn't mean impersonal teaching. In addition to the instructors, coaches have been designed as an essential part of the course. They have learned to coach by taking the course themselves at least once, and sometimes a second time as an "apprentice coach." This second time through, they focus more on observing the

continued

coaching process than on course content. Would-be coaches also take an online course especially designed for them. The sessions include know-how about coaching—particularly online—as well as about technology and the course content. After this training, the coaches are ready to take responsibility for ten to twelve teachers in a study group. One of the coach's tasks is to moderate online discussions, a responsibility that includes everything from modeling how to treat participants with respect to keeping the discussion substantive. They also give individual feedback to learners and summarize the progress, concerns, and themes expressed by learners for the instructors. And they serve as peer consultants for fellow coaches. All of this in a few hours a week on top of their day job!

Pairing Coaches and Protégés

Suppose you want to match a knowledge coach and a protégé—how should you go about it? The evidence from the literature on mentoring suggests that forcing a pairing might not work well. Self-selected mentor-protégé teams tend to be more effective than appointed teams.[5] One can readily imagine why. Arranged marriages appear to work reasonably well for some cultures, but now even among middle class Indians, for example, the proposed match is extensively explored for compatibility (including detailed horoscopes), and both parties have the right to veto a choice. The relationship between a knowledge coach and a protégé requires some of the same commitment and mutual respect as a marriage—if not a similar lifelong aspiration.[6]

In chapter 1, we drew a distinction between a mentor and a coach, pointing out that the roles *may* be interchangeable, but that the term *mentor* implies more personal counseling and socialization in a profession or organization, and the term *coach* implies more knowledge and skills training. In the start-ups we studied, the roles were often intermingled. One of the venture capitalists confided that he had nicknamed a young founder of a company he was helping "PITA-2," for pain-in-the-ass (fondly, it should be noted). "My son is PITA-1," he explained with a grin. "Both of them tend to call me at eleven o'clock on a Sunday evening for help." From our interview with the entrepreneur who had the same filial privileges as the VC's son, it was clear that the affection was reciprocal.

Wide differences in age, experience, and level within a hierarchy make this kind of paternal regard understandable, even desirable. Certainly not all coaches would give out their home phone numbers, nor could take this fatherly approach. Coach-protégé relationships can work well without this intense personal closeness, and in fact when professional shades too far over into personal, it becomes more difficult for the coach to deliver deserved criticism. However, some degree of mutual liking and respect is essential.

The Matchmaking Game: Selection Criteria

Our entrepreneurship study provides a close look at the matchmaking process between knowledge coach and protégé, and at the differences in the criteria they emphasized. We asked each coach and each entrepreneur what they were looking for in a coaching relationship—how they selected one another. As might be expected from a heterogeneous set of knowledge coaches (venture capitalists, independent mentor capitalists, incubator founders) and mostly novice entrepreneurs as protégés, the criteria varied from person to person. Overall, however, coaches were generally more attuned to whether or not people *could* be taught. As one coach noted of a chosen protégé: "He's someone who says, 'I don't know it all; I will get help wherever I can. I will learn along the way.'" But they were also looking for a pattern they could recognize as having high potential, one that combined a promising idea with the interpersonal skills to enable the team to attract and manage outstanding employees, execute on strategy, and lead. In short, the coaches wanted to be sure that they were investing their efforts in a value proposition with potential, and in an entrepreneurial team that could build a lasting company (preferably a billion-dollar company).

For their part, most entrepreneurs lacked the experience to recognize patterns. They simply focused on the near-term value the coach could bring to the relationship—his or her experience, availability, network, and access to money. However, some entrepreneurs were looking beyond the bottom line to access deep smarts: "I was looking for somebody who has been a CFO in a multi-billion-dollar company," said one, "but was there when it was small, who had been through the various stages of growth within a company, a very strong strategic thinker, a real partner to develop a business with."

The perspectives of knowledge coach and protégé naturally differ in any situation, not just an entrepreneurial one. People with deep smarts usually need a reason to share them—be it the prospect of financial gain or the pleasure of seeing a group of talented people succeed. Protégés necessarily have different concerns, generally a desire to develop the skills that will enable them to be successful—if not in the current endeavor, then in the next. The criteria for selection frequently reflect these different motivations for entering into a relationship. In the most successful relationships, these differences are complementary, not antagonistic. A knowledge coach who wants to invest time and money in a protégé to develop her skills, and a protégé who wants only to get promoted quickly, is a relationship unlikely to succeed. (We will say more about alignment later in this chapter.)

How are a coach and a potential protégé to determine whether the relationship will be a mutually beneficial one? In the entrepreneurship study, we found one very common concern that we see also in coaching relationships within many organizations: a desire for that elusive interpersonal quality of compatibility or "chemistry." The term is a catch-all for personality traits, goal alignment, and thinking styles. When coaches in the study spoke of chemistry, they emphasized looking for people and situations that they could become engaged with. Said one, "I need to be excited about the person and the mission. Then I can give value. I can go deep with that company." Coaches also mentioned the importance of integrity and passion. More than a few times, both coach and protégé talked simply about *liking* the other person. Mutual attraction is certainly desirable, and one can draw on one's past experience to determine that a particular interpersonal style may ultimately benefit or doom the relationship. However, just as one should never select a car salesman because he's a nice guy (will this nice guy be servicing your car and dealing with warranty problems?), one should also look beyond chemistry in selecting a coaching partner.

You Can't Always Get There from Here

No matter how good the coach and how willing the protégé, when a protégé does not appear able to "scale," that is, move to the next level of responsibility, coaches may find themselves in the unenviable position of the "hatchet man" or "making the employee available to the industry."[7] There are times when the novice cannot learn fast enough to fill a particular role. Entrepreneurs appear especially vulnerable to believing they can acquire smarts at a pace that matches the demands of the venture. They are, as a class, optimists—or they would never try the daunting task of building a company. Surely, they think, I am the next Bill Gates or David Packard, not one of the nameless thousands who have gone back to a desk in someone else's company. I will, as CEO, personally take my company from three people to thirty thousand. One young Indian entrepreneur, Saumil Majmudar, noted in 2001 after he had been replaced as CEO of the company he founded, "Intellectually, I knew that someday I would be replaced, but emotionally I didn't realize it. It's hard to actually experience the exit, to know I won't be there when the company goes IPO or sells. I should have set expectations right. I thought I would take the company all the way. I won't say that next time."

When the coach sets realistic expectations from the outset, the protégé is in a better psychological position to move on. Kleiner Perkins's Russ Siegelman reflected on how he discussed up front with Vividence founder Artie Wu the likelihood of his continuing in the role of CEO:

> *I told Artie we typically would tell a first-time entrepreneur that we want to give you a shot at CEO, but probably we will want to hire professional management that has done it before. In some cases, if we're particularly impressed by the entrepreneur, we don't necessarily make it a* fait accompli. *We would give him a shot and we would make the call later on. . . . We touched base on this topic from time to time, and two years into it, when he realized that he didn't have really the skill or the experience to run an enterprise-class company, he was ready to move on anyway. It wasn't contentious at all with Artie.*

As we showed in chapters 2 and 3, complex knowledge with many tacit dimensions cannot be learned quickly. And surely taking a company from early stage to a mature, large organization involves complex, tacit knowledge. Not everyone is well suited to learn some of the needed skills, and nobody can learn them overnight. Similar limitations hold for intrapreneurs within organizations.

When a large communications equipment company was setting up new ventures within an in-house incubator, the COO was unconcerned about selecting leaders—despite a warning that intrapreneurs are a special breed, like entrepreneurs. "I have any number of excellent middle managers who could take on the role," he declared confidently. Eighteen months later, when none of the proposed ventures had shown enough promise to be supported further by the organization, he admitted that none of the managers he had selected, skilled though they were in the large corporation environment, had demonstrated the necessary skills and experience to guide a start-up. They had deep smarts, perhaps—but the wrong ones. "It's a whole different ball game," he said ruefully. Not only had this COO expended resources fruitlessly, but at the end of the experiment he was no closer to understanding the skills that were needed in ventures; he knew only that they weren't the same ones his managers had. The knowledge gap was much larger than he had assumed, and he had made no provision for calibrating just how large it was. In the following chapter we will discuss a technique that he might have used to advantage: experiments to explore multiple options.

The larger point, however, is that smart people often underestimate the depth of smarts required for a particular role and the size of the knowledge gap to be bridged. The less well structured the problem space is, the more tacit knowledge is involved. And, as will be discussed at greater length, the more tacit knowledge involved, the harder it is for a novice to come quickly up to speed. Knowledge coaches who assess the gap at the outset of a relationship with a protégé (and weigh the odds that the protégé can completely close it) can position the joint project—whatever they are doing with the protégé—as a step in a learning journey rather than as an all-or-nothing effort. Of course, the coach doesn't want to discourage the novice from striving hard by suggesting the goal is impossible, but a realistic discussion of the knowledge gap avoids delusions about the ease of obtaining the requisite deep smarts and, more critically, leaves room for the protégé to ask for help.

Barriers and Facilitators of Knowledge Transfer

In any coaching relationship—in sports or the arts as well as in business—the promise of knowledge transfer is not always realized. A number of specific factors may impede—or enhance—such relationships, starting with the extent to which the parties involved agree on end goals.[8]

Alignment Between Source and Receiver

A coach-protégé relationship is a partnership. If the two individuals involved don't agree on the direction to take, their creative endeavor—whether it is how to improve one's job performance, or market a new adhesive, or mount an art exhibit—is unlikely to succeed.

In fact, in the thirty-five companies in our entrepreneurship study, alignment between coach and founder on company strategy was one of the variables most strongly correlated with judgments of the company's success. In our second interviews, we asked each coach and entrepreneur several standard questions, designed to provide subjective measures of success[9] and alignment. Both coaches and entrepreneurs rated the success of the company compared to their initial expectations and compared to other area start-ups. In addition, coaches rated success of the company compared to all the other companies they had ever coached. Coaches and entrepreneurs also rated the degree of alignment between their view and that of the other in terms of business strategy and company management. (See appendix for exact wording of items.)

In general, the greater the perceived alignment, the more successful the company was rated. This was particularly true for the first "success" item: The greater the perceived alignment on both strategy and management, as rated by coach and by entrepreneur, the greater the perceived success compared to expectations.[10] (The converse, of course, is that the greater the perceived *mis*alignment, the less successful the company was judged.)

Misalignment can occur because of a lack of candor. It is not always wise to take at face value what the other party *says* he wants, or has to offer at the outset, as the following story from a highly experienced entrepreneur and coach reveals:

> *Before I ever got involved in the company, I asked, "What do you guys want—what's your objective?" The CEO said, of course, "We want to build a company." I said, "Okay, great." I took that at face value. But then when I got involved with the company I heard him say, "I sure will be glad when we get the IPO done so I can go on and do something else." In the old days you could say, "I'd like to build a company; and if I stay with it long enough and work hard enough and if I'm successful in building a company, I might get rich." But you had better value what's in the middle because you're going to spend a lot of years not being rich. And if building a company is not enjoyable, then whether or not you get rich at the end doesn't much matter.*

Although this coach chose to stay with the start-up, it is clear that a fundamental difference in values and goals existed. The entrepreneur was following the inescapable tendency of us all to say what we know the interlocutor wants to hear. However, lack of agreement about goals undermines the ability of the coach to transfer the desired knowledge.

It is possible to argue that successful companies breed happy coaches and entrepreneurs, which causes a warm glow of perceived alignment; that is, that they report being in alignment *because* of perceived success. On the other hand, perhaps when they are in agreement about where the company is headed and how it is being managed, the company has a better chance of being successful. We believe the latter is more likely because when coaches and entrepreneurs confessed to interviewers that they were having difficulty in agreeing on strategy or personnel management, the accompanying confusion was often symptomatic of deeper problems uncovered during the research, such as conflicting interpretation of market feedback, differing perspectives on the importance of an IPO, or the criticality of speed to market versus reliability of products. And these companies tended to be assessed as less successful.

A number of the pairs of coaches and entrepreneurs said that they were not *perfectly* aligned—but that this was an advantage, reflecting a healthy discussion about alternatives. As our earlier writings attest, we are firm believers in the power of creative abrasion to avoid premature consensus and to foster innovation. However, it is obviously a problem if a knowledge coach and protégé are headed in totally different directions. For example, in a large service organization we know of, a new venture group was set up to nurture new businesses just long enough to prove their value, and then turn them over to the business units. The business development group was supposed to transfer to the business unit recipients the requisite knowledge of the new service process and the market. However, the business units were so successful selling current products that they had no incentive to invest in these fledgling—and by definition still small—new initiatives. The business units dismissed the new venture ideas as strategically unimportant to the overall organization. Not surprisingly, with this degree of misalignment, the coaches met with a cold reception when they attempted to transfer their experience with the embryonic businesses to those in the business units.[11]

Buried Knowledge

Another barrier to transferring knowledge is not being able to locate it. One of the missions to Mars failed for lack of a tiny piece of knowledge resident in the head of one engineer. Years after the failure of a Mars Observer just a few days before it was scheduled to go into orbit around Mars, a group of engineers at the Jet Propulsion Laboratory were sitting around a table speculating about what had gone wrong. A retired engineer present asked what regulator was used, and when he was told, he said, "Well, that regulator has an inlet filter, and has some flux that is residual from the manufacturing process that's incompatible over the long haul with nitrogen tectoxide. The regulator would fail in a long-duration mission."[12] How could anyone have known this fact? The same regulator in the same propulsion system had been flown at least six times in shorter missions. The troublesome chemical reaction took place only after six or seven months—exactly the length of time for the Observer to travel to Mars.

This kind of precise, context-dependent knowledge may be critical—but almost impossible to uncover in any general knowledge sweep. The knowledge is not tacit, but such specific gems as the regulator problem are likely to surface only in the process of problem solving—unfortunately in this case, after the doomed flight, rather than before. The more that people are exposed to stories about problems and solutions from the past, the more receptors they develop (as we noted in chapter 2) and the more likely they are to ask the right questions, to consider various contingencies, and to troubleshoot extensively. At JPL, Jeanne Holm, chief knowledge architect for NASA, has instituted storytelling sessions by senior scientists about prior missions. The added value of such sessions over more structured knowledge-transfer workshops is the greater interactivity and deep context. As discussed in more detail later in this chapter, stories evoke images and details that are lost in bullet points and spare text.[13]

Tacit Knowledge

The extent to which the knowledge to be transferred is tacit limits the ability of the coach to teach and the protégé to learn. One might expect that manufacturing processes would be so standardized, documented, and well characterized (in the scientific sense of that word) that they would transfer easily. One would be wrong. For example, E-L Products, manufacturers of electroluminescent lamps (used in dashboards and wherever paper-thin displays are desirable) acquired another lamp company, Grimes, for its apparently superior production processes, very impressive documentation, computer-aided design systems, and research. E-L hired several supervisors and technicians from Grimes on three- to six-month contracts to transfer knowledge and train E-L operators on Grimes machines, which had been moved to the E-L site. During the training period, the laminating department had no problems with machinery acquired from Grimes. However, when the Grimes personnel left, the same machinery began producing defective lamps. Despite all the documentation, critical operating knowledge had not been captured or transferred because it was rich in tacit elements.[14]

It may be difficult to transfer knowledge with tacit dimensions for many different reasons:

- The experience cannot be readily articulated (e.g., how to ride a bicycle, tie a shoe, define what "good design" is).

- The expert has never tried to make it explicit (e.g., the case of the fire lieutenant recounted in chapter 3, an expert who knew to pull his men out just before a burning house collapsed).

- There are incentives to keep the knowledge tacit (e.g., in a consulting firm where one's standing depends upon being the best expert in a given industry).

- The knowledge is still too primitive to be well structured (e.g., in the early days of biotechnology, when determining how long cells should remain in a growth medium was a matter of judgment and experience).

Regardless of the reason, however, knowledge with many tacit dimensions has to be *relearned* or even *recreated* by the protégé, absorbed into that person's experience base, rather than merely received in a package. We will discuss this topic fully in chapter 8.

Cognitive Boundaries to Be Crossed

As suggested in chapter 2, people have receptors developed from their personal experience that enable them to transform information into knowledge—or not. Any coach, manager, or teacher has to keep the recipient's receptors in mind in order to shape a message and customize the learning process. Research on learning in educational settings supports this conclusion. In reviewing the relevant literature, Bransford et al. have concluded, "There is a good deal of evidence that learning is enhanced when teachers pay attention to the knowledge and beliefs that learners bring to a learning task, use this knowledge as a starting point for new instruction, and monitor students' changing conceptions as instruction proceeds."[15] In Gabriel Szulanski's study of the transfer of best practices within eight corporations, the single best predictor of successful transfer was the *absorptive capacity* of the recipient of the knowledge transfer attempt. That is, groups that had adequate "preexisting stocks of knowledge" were better able to absorb new knowledge about best practices than were groups lacking absorptive capacity.[16]

While the presence of appropriate receptors may be difficult to detect, an astute knowledge coach can guess at them by considering some generic boundaries to be crossed. Obviously someone of a different ethnic or national culture will have different receptors. Often organizational cultures can build distinctive, powerful receptors; for example, the historic emphasis at Hewlett-Packard on process has apparently left alumni of that organization with an abiding respect and need for proper systems. HP alumni whom we met in East Asia and South Asia as well as in the United States tended to emphasize setting up processes as an early requirement of start-ups. Even different disciplinary backgrounds, as discussed in chapter 5 in the context of belief systems, can build barriers or promote easy transfer of knowledge.

As the following anecdote shows, the ease of transfer is not just a matter of vocabulary, but of perception. When one of us (Dorothy) was walking with a fellow graduate student in Beijing in 1978 as a member of one of the first U.S. groups to visit after Mao Tse-tung's death, she noticed that there were fire hydrants along the streets—evidence of a standardized infrastructure and government services (neither of which existed in the countryside and in the communes we had been visiting). The engineering student striding along beside her glanced at the nearest fire hydrant and commented (without pausing) that the threads were stripped where the hose would be screwed in. Fascinated by his observation (and somewhat skeptical of the high-speed, walk-by diagnosis rendered from ten feet away), she stopped to examine the hydrant and found he was right—not only about that one, but about virtually all of the hydrants on that main thoroughfare. Where she had filtered her observation through her sociology/social psychology receptors, he had used his engineering acumen to see something different. The two observations (that there was standardized infrastructure, but not in working condition) were combined in a report fed back to students and faculty at Stanford University in both engineering and social science departments, as knowledge about conditions in China at the time.

Differences in thinking styles represent another barrier to successful knowledge transfer. Understanding others' strongly held thinking-style preferences—respecting their cognitive receptors—is essential to communicating effectively. Diagnostics are widely used today in organizations to help employees and managers identify their own inherent biases in processing information.[17] Although such paper and pencil exercises provide insight into only one small aspect of personality, they have proved quite robust over time in differentiating strongly held preferences for how individuals use their brains. The four dimensions of the Myers-Briggs Type Indicator (MBTI—to select the diagnostic most widely used) are very relevant to knowledge transfer: Extraversion versus Introversion (a preference for making decisions and processing information in a group setting versus alone); Sensing versus Intuition (a preference for hard data and lots of facts versus the "big picture" or theory); Thinking versus Feeling (a preference for analysis and choice based on what is "true" versus value-based decision making, based on what is right in the circumstances); and Judging versus Perceiving (a preference for closure and certainty versus a tolerance for ambiguity and leaving options open). These preferences, *if strongly held* (as most individuals have only weak preferences between one or more of the pairs), lead to different ways of building receptors. For example, a person with a strong preference for Intuition will want to understand the theory underlying the knowledge presented, whereas a person with the opposing strong preference for Sensing will need evidence based on observable facts and on data.

Different thinking style preferences thus have important implications for knowledge transfer. Someone who scores high on Extraversion, for example, will likely welcome a highly interactive relationship with a coach. High scorers on Introversion, who prefer to carefully consider before responding, may be uncomfortable and resistant to a Socratic dialogue in which immediate answers are required. A protégé who prefers closure may grow impatient with a coach who prefers to keep options open—and vice versa. Being aware of these preferences can help coach and protégé reach a greater degree of alignment, which, we have seen, may be critical for success.

Proximity on the Ladder of Expertise

Any coach, teacher, consultant, or public speaker knows the trauma of facing a group of people, uncertain about how much the audience already knows. Where to start? What receptors exist? While some advance exploration can give him an idea, he has to launch the topic and count on feedback from the group—verbal or physical, via body language—to calibrate the depth of knowledge and degree of receptivity that people have. In knowledge coaching, there is almost always a large gap between the level of expertise of coach and protégé. Therefore, it is difficult to gear the teaching to the level of sophistication of the novice's receptors and build on the novice's prior knowledge. When this advice is not followed and the coach presents information at his or her own level rather than that of the novice, the novice will either not receive the information at all or may categorize it in a way not intended by the coach. The greater the gap in expertise, the more feedback the expert may need in order to calibrate the level of the presentation.

One reason that so many of us who work in offices turn to a colleague for help when our computer mysteriously refuses to follow our utterly clear instructions is that the help desk is not only more distant physically, but is also more remote psychologically. The official experts try not to smirk at our ineptitude, but the gap between their grasp of the arcana of Microsoft Word and our own feeble word processing skills is likely to be large. Their vocabulary is intimidating. We and our tech-smart colleagues share many of the same receptors—we speak a common professional language, and the conversation can take place with a shared vocabulary. And the difference in our levels of expertise is likely to be smaller—our colleagues seem closer to our novice status, and may empathize more with our plight.

Motivation and Ability to Coach and Learn

Coaches need a motive to enter into a relationship with a protégé. People who are charged with transferring something they have worked long and hard to attain—their deep smarts—will be reluctant to share their knowledge if they are arbitrarily paired with a novice who lacks adequate receptors or who may not be motivated to learn, or where "chemistry" is lacking. Moreover, while some coaches find adequate incentive in the satisfaction from realizing how useful their deeps smarts are, others will need some explicit rewards for the coaching activity—recognition, if nothing else. It will take managerial wisdom to develop effective coach-protégé relationships wherein both coach and protégé are motivated to engage with one another to transfer deep smarts.

Within organizations, we see enormous variation in knowledge sharing—and the degree to which it is encouraged by structure or culture. A consulting company we know encourages coaching by promoting only those employees who have trained someone to take their place. This organization has an advantage over competitors who allow knowledge stars to hoard their smarts.

In our entrepreneurship study, motivation was almost never an issue with either coaches or entrepreneurs; they selected each other, and both wished the enterprise success. In only one instance did a coach describe his selected charge as "uncoachable." (The relationship was later terminated.) During the time of our study, coaches who were willing to take on green entrepreneurs and help them mature to the point where their company had a reasonable chance of success were scarce commodities, and the start-up entrepreneurs knew it. Similarly, the experts did not want to waste their time on founders who were unwilling to learn. When they found the right match, many coaches reported that they really enjoyed coaching. One coach we interviewed reflected that out of all the jobs he had undertaken in a very successful career, he was beginning to realize that he was better suited to coaching than any other. The mutual due diligence resulted in expert-novice pairs that were genuinely interested in advancing the latter's knowledge, and in the process enhancing the value of the company. And, of course, if the company succeeded, the coach—who typically owned part of the company—succeeded as well. The result, at least in our study, was a relationship in which the coach provided a great deal of "mind-share"—extensive periods of time working closely with the novice.

If motivation was never an issue with coaching start-ups in our study, *ability* was. During the two years of research, we saw a sobering example of the failure of what sounded like a terrific knowledge transfer mechanism: the venture incubator. (See "The Grand Incubator Experiment.") The incubators failed, of course, largely because of the critical miscalculation that equity from the start-ups being incubated would be returned quickly from IPOs or other "liquidity events." The incubators were themselves mostly start-ups, dependent on cash from investors. When the IPO market came to a sudden stop, the incubators' cash was flowing in only one direction—out.

The Grand Incubator Experiment

W HEN DOT-COM fever went beyond epidemic proportions in the late 1990s and it seemed that every bright engineer and first-year M.B.A. student had an idea for a can't-miss Internet company, a vast knowledge gap became evident.

Enter the incubator phenomenon. While there were only 14 incubators worldwide in 1995 and 63 by 1999, by May of 2000 a remarkable 348 incubators had sprung up.[a] Some simply provided space and some shared office and technology support. Others were "full-service" incubators that promised to provide the coaching, and thereby the knowledge, the hopeful entrepreneur lacked: knowledge about management, financing, recruiting, shaping the business proposition, and marketing it—just about everything needed to grow a company. And, since the ground was shifting under everyone's feet and "first-mover advantage" was crucial for success, the incubators would have to fill the knowledge gaps *quickly*. Because entrepreneuring requires deep smarts, the incubators could not fill the gaps in time.

Few incubators remain, gone the way of most of the companies they incubated; and most that are still here have morphed into more traditional venture capital firms. Of the nine incubators in our entrepreneurship study, six have shut down, one has become a venture firm, one has merged with a venture firm, and one has become an investment banking firm.

Source: The authors are indebted to Brian DeLacey, who contributed to this box.
a. Mark Veverka, "Pied Piper of the 'Net: How John Doerr Sparked the Internet Boom and Brought Home Big Profits," *Barron's*, 10 June 2002, 19–22.

However, more germane to this book was the failure of incubators to appreciate the limits of transferring quickly enough the kind of deep smarts needed to make a successful company. As we have noted elsewhere, any coach can help someone lower on the ladder of expertise, but many of the incubator coaches were themselves relative novices, with too little operational experience to be adequate guides, especially given the uncertain economy. As we saw in chapter 3, the Ten-Year Rule sets some cognitive limits on how quickly complex skills can be learned, even under the tutelage of an expert coach. It was simply not realistic to expect raw young wannabe entrepreneurs to learn all that they needed to know in the short time they had before the money ran out—especially if they were being tutored by other novices, as some were.

Modes of Transfer: Coaching Techniques

Whether your task is to take everything you have learned in the past twenty-five years and transfer the useful bits to a colleague, or the reverse—to figure out what is useful in another person's head and try to absorb it—the challenge is the same: effective and efficient coaching and learning. The great advantage of having a coach is that he or she can help reduce the noise-to-signal ratio in building up an experience repertoire. That is, if experiences are accumulated purely reactively, then one will build up the more common experiences, but very little learning will occur at the tails of the distribution. Coaches (and, as we saw in chapter 2, simulations) can be proactive in providing experiences in a more planned, organized way, and in filling out the experience distribution.

Not everyone learns exactly the same way, of course, but there seem to be some universal truths. Some modes of coaching are useful mostly for creating receptors—frameworks and mental architecture—for subsequent experiential learning. On the other hand, the more experience-based the mode, the more likely that the protégé is *recreating* at least some of the tacit dimensions of knowledge that make the coach an expert. From our study of coaches and entrepreneurs, as well as a number of coaching cases within large organizations, we suggest a menu of modes of transfer that are increasingly self-directed by the protégé and increasingly experience-based.[18] (See figure 7-2.) Most of the attempts at transferring

FIGURE 7-2

Modes of Knowledge Transfer

Active Learning	• Learning by doing (guided experience)
Increasing Cultivation of Deep Smarts	• Socratic questioning
	• Stories with a moral
	• Rules of thumb
Passive Reception	• Directives/presentations/lectures

knowledge inside organizations today fall at the lower end of the interactive spectrum. While all modes of transfer can be useful, we will argue that the less interactive modes transfer much less real knowledge than do those involving interaction and guided experience. Why is this so?

Part of the reason that coaches can't just *tell* a novice how to do something is because of the way our brains work. We remember something longer if we struggle to understand it before the issue is resolved. Puzzling over a problem and generating some hypothesized answers help embed the problem and the answer in our brains. To see how this works, try to figure out what is being described in the following sentence:

The notes were sour because the seams split.

What on earth does this mean? What kind of notes? (Did you mentally picture a notepad or musical notes?) What kind of seams? Think about it for a moment. Got the answer? No? Now look up the answer at the end of this chapter. Cognitive scientist Salvatore Soraci calls your reaction the "aha! effect," and you can see why.[19] When after a few minutes of puzzlement and confusion you are provided the solution, the proverbial light bulb flashes on, and you will remember the riddle longer than if you were told the answer right away. So there is some rationale to making learners struggle by themselves for a while.

Specific Directives

At the lowest level of self-directedness, the coach simply tells the protégé what to do, and little is required of the learner except to pay attention and follow orders. Such directives can be very helpful and efficient in two situations: when the protégés are experienced and already have the necessary receptors but the coach knows they need practice; and when the protégés are so entirely inexperienced that telling them what to do is the most efficient way of creating some receptors. An example of the latter was the case in a board meeting that we observed in which coach B. V. Jagadeesh was lecturing the inexperienced founders on setting sales targets:

> *You need to build the sales funnel. If the target is $500,000 this year, and you already have $200,000, you need $1 million in opportunity in the pipeline. When you reach 90 percent of that, go to a new projection of $1 to $3 million. You need three to six times the deals in the funnel. If next year you have $1 million in revenues for products and $4 million in services, how is it split each quarter? How are you going to achieve it? This is what the strategy is. It's easier for the board and future investors if you can show what was promised, what is delivered, what is in the funnel, what is committed for a particular date. . . . You want to be sure that the process is very clear, that everyone gives the same message to the outside world. Things should not be done on an ad hoc basis.*

This was basically a lecture, and you recall the witticism about lectures: that the information passes from the notes of the teacher to the notes of the student without passing through the minds of either. That is a harsh judgment and underestimates the value of lectures in creating frameworks in the minds of students. However, too much time is spent in organizations on this kind of knowledge transfer attempt—and too much is expected in the way of learning. The entrepreneurs in this example will use the coach's guidance to think about their sales funnel—to develop receptors. But they will learn how to create a sales funnel by *doing it*.

Rules of Thumb

The coach with deep smarts has a vast storehouse of patterns upon which to draw. Those patterns that guide the expert's decision making are hard earned over a long period of time, and there is no apparent way to "download" those hundreds or thousands of patterns to a novice.[20] There is no lexicon, encyclopedia, or wall chart of patterns that the novice can study, like a quarterback poring over his football team's playbook. Even if there were, the patterns in such a playbook would reflect the expert's experiences, with questionable relevance to the current situation. This is why experts often rely on transferring rules of thumb: shorthand, decontextualized statements that summarize a great many patterns into one simple, memorable—and *usually* reliable—rule.

Novices frequently find rules of thumb useful shortcuts to more contextualized knowledge, and coaches rely on them to transfer knowledge quickly and efficiently. Psychologists describe people as "cognitive misers"—we are forced to simplify the complex world we inhabit by taking mental shortcuts.[21] Such shortcuts as "Don't lead away from kings" in bridge, "control the center of the board" in chess, or "It's the economy, stupid!" in politics are easy to remember and, like most generalized rules, are frequently effective, at least in "typical" situations. One experienced knowledge coach, Craig Johnson, believes that many problems encountered by start-up entrepreneurs result from a failure to do things in the proper sequence. He illustrates this "sequence" rule of thumb in the following example:

A company is so worried about competition that it raises a lot of money and starts building a sales force before it has finished developing its product. And what often happens is you incur the cost of building a complete sales force, offices, and salespeople and everything assuming the product will be ready to ship on March 2, and the product isn't ready until September 30, and even then it's not really ready. I have a client that got exactly into this mode where the founders had raised $100 million but thought that was plenty of money to get the job done. They built a very expensive sales force

*and then discovered some very fundamental technical problems with
the product that required them to go back to the lab and review.
In the meantime, this sales force was idle, with nothing to sell and
burning millions of dollars per month. Ultimately the company
had to lay off the same people they had just hired, and it was very
disruptive. That's basically getting things out of sequence.*

The most common rule of thumb our expert entrepreneurs im-
parted to their novices was "focus, focus, focus." In some cases, this
translated as "focus on software, not hardware," or "focus on market A, not market B." B. V. Jagadeesh used a metaphor in urging a
start-up team in Bangalore, India, to focus: "You're throwing darts
in many places, going after too many opportunities, rather than
finding the key markets."

However, rules of thumb can conflict, as when "focus" seems to
contradict "think big." And novice entrepreneurs are not usually
able to make concrete decisions—or at least good ones—on the
basis of such abstract concepts. Coaches don't always present their
rules of thumb in explicit form. When the founders of ActivePhoto
were discussing in a board meeting the problem they were having
finding customers for their camera/software product, and the CEO
suggested "adding resources," coach Bill Krause remarked: "I'm always nervous when the solution to a problem starts with the word
hire." He wanted the current management to own the problem and
find the customers themselves.

Some coaches embed the rules of thumb in cryptic analogies.
When the same ActivePhoto founders were debating long and hard
over exactly how to work with a potential partner who had not yet
committed to the alliance, coach Fred Gibbons delivered one of his
famous aphorisms: "Before you skin it, you have to catch it." His
rule of thumb was delivered in a more humorous form than Craig
Johnson's, but the message was the same—sequence matters.

Stories with a Moral

Relating stories based on past experience can be an effective
way of transferring lessons learned from that experience, because

such lessons are very likely to be remembered. Cognitive scientists have identified several reasons why stories are memorable. For example, the "availability heuristic" demonstrates that the more vivid the images evoked by a story, the more memorable and the more likely the story will be judged true or likely to occur. Also, we are more likely to remember narratives or *episodes* than lists of facts. (Compare the number of images you can recall seeing during the past hour with the number of new vocabulary words you can learn in the same period of time.)[22] Stories are particularly likely to be recalled when the recipient of the story is led to apply the moral of the story to his or her own experience,[23] as the following example illustrates. During an ActivePhoto board meeting, one of the young founders was reporting on the company's free cash and how to invest it. Board member and experienced coach Bill Krause responded with a cautionary tale: Many years before, a CFO of his acquaintance wanted to invest his company's cash in a high-yield, high-risk instrument. A senior board member told him, "No one will remember the extra 1½ percent you made. But they will remember your losing $10 million."[24] The moral of this story was not lost on the ActivePhoto entrepreneur; the cash was invested conservatively.

The fact that stories can transmit knowledge—and make it stick—can have negative consequences as well. Consider, for example, the dilemma of the CEO of a large paper company, who was hired two years ago. A consultant has been invited to give a one-day workshop on innovation for a group of senior managers. She asks a pointed question: "What is the climate for innovation here? What happens when an innovation fails?" After a pause filled with heads shaking and a few rueful chuckles, one man volunteers, "It's awful. The CEO tells us that he wants innovation, wants to take risks, but he actually doesn't." "Really," replies the consultant. "What happens to someone who fails?" The man relates the plight of a woman in marketing who had an idea that didn't work. She got transferred to the American equivalent of Siberia. "When did that happen?" After turning to his colleagues for confirmation, he says, "about seven or eight years ago." Pressed for another example, the consultant hears of another failed innovation, this one costing the innovator his job. This one happened five years ago.

The new CEO's problem is clear. He is pushing for innovation, but the dramatic horror stories embedded deeply in the organization undercut his efforts, even though the stories predate his tenure. Until the CEO is able to replace the old stories about the dire consequences of risk taking with examples of positive responses to intelligent failures, the stories will have more power than any rhetoric to the contrary.

Socratic Questioning

Socratic questioning is as old as, well, Socrates, who realized a couple of millennia ago that his students would learn far more if they were nudged to come up with answers themselves, rather than having the master simply tell them what they needed to know. Initially U.S. law schools and then some business schools began using this form of education in order to sharpen their students' thinking. The questioning forces the recipient beyond active listening in one of two ways: first, to get the person to clarify and refine vague wording and thinking; and second, to get him to challenge his own assumptions, to think more deeply about underlying phenomena. If done properly, Socratic dialogue is an intense, very active process. Even in text assignments, questions that require the reader to actively engage the mind in summarizing, drawing inferences, or thinking about applications of the information read, as opposed to questions that simply require the reader to recognize the material, have been shown to facilitate the transfer of knowledge.[25] What makes the Socratic method particularly effective is the active engagement of the learner as he or she clarifies thinking and challenges assumptions.

Entrepreneurs are accustomed to being asked to clarify their business concept. Entrepreneur Scott Rozic recalled coach Stan Meresman asking:

> *"So, Scott, what's the one-liner? What does the company do in one or two sentences?" Then you give the pitch and he plays back, "That's not compelling" or "What is your competitive*

advantage?" And then he would identify two companies that sound as if they would do the same thing, when they're really quite different. "There are so many companies out there and everybody has funding. There is something magical about your company, but how do you distill that? Why is a customer going to deeply understand the solution that you are providing to their problem and write a check to you rather than another company?"

The final mode of knowledge transfer in figure 7-2, namely guided experience, warrants a chapter unto itself, as it is by far the most powerful—and most underutilized—way of transferring deep smarts. In the next chapter, we argue that learning by doing, *especially under the direction of a knowledge coach*, is both efficient and effective.

Implications for Managers

People with deep smarts can help others develop them, but knowledge coaches will be more effective if they understand how people learn. The modes of coaching are arranged in a rough hierarchy in figure 7-2 for a reason. The more responsibility learners take upon themselves to learn and the more coaches aim for true assimilation of knowledge rather than compliance or even just comprehension, the more smarts the protégés develop.

Most knowledge coaches will themselves need help in coaching. Their know-how and deep smarts lie in the *content* of the knowledge to be transferred—not necessarily in the *process* of transferring their wisdom. And as we have noted before, coaching is not synonymous with mentoring. Great mentors may not be great coaches. They will have the motivation and the relationship-building skills—but will they have the deep smarts to convey? As managers look around their organizations to identify whose deep smarts are essential, they often see people with deep technical abilities, who have not a clue about how to help others develop similar know-how. And such experts may have to be convinced that transferring their own deep smarts is worth time and effort. After all, unlike coaches of start-up companies, these experts will not emerge from the coaching relationship with a piece of a potentially successful company. If you ask them to become a knowledge coach, they may have a number of different reactions, depending on how the issue is presented to them. If their status in your organization results from their being the "go-to" person with questions, and they see only a diminution of their power from coaching, obviously they will be disinclined to oblige. If they see increased stature from being identified as a master, they may be more receptive.

Not all knowledge coaches will be equally adept at the different modes of transfer suggested in figure 7-2. Some people are not good at thinking about and telling meaningful stories, for example. That's just not the way their minds work. However, all coaches would do well to be at least conscious of the different modes and their relative effectiveness. Coaches can all try to develop a repertoire of transfer modes. It does not take ten years to learn to be effective at the Socratic method of questioning, for example, although of course some people excel in probing questions; others may rely on simply asking "why?" and then listening hard to the response, to compare it to their own experience and judgment.

If all the attempts to make mentoring work in organizations are any guide, we can't necessarily match coaches and protégés and expect that the relationship will work. There are multiple considerations to take into account in the matchmaking process. What people commonly think of as "chemistry" between a coach and protégé is actually a grab-bag of similarities and differences in thinking styles and personalities; the degree to which the protégé has ready receptors; and the degree to which the coach is willing to "give away" the *real* nuggets of wisdom she has acquired with so much effort.

Not all knowledge coaches have to be masters; apprentices or journeymen can help those below them on the ladder of expertise develop deep smarts in our organizations. Apprentices and journeymen even have some advantages over the masters in transferring such knowledge as they have, since they are closer to those below them on the ladder of expertise and often have a better sense of what receptors exist in the minds of the novices. Moreover, since teaching requires that the coach consolidate what he knows, the apprentices enhance their own deep smarts by coaching. There are some risks in this approach, of course. As we saw in the case of incubators, apprentices can have an overweening opinion of their own smarts and *think* that they are masters, or pass along practices that are not tested through extensive experience. However, managers can guard against that outcome—for example, by setting up a process for demonstrating and assessing progress up the ladder, so that the apprentice is not the sole judge of her own smarts; or by arranging for continuous feedback for coaches at all levels of expertise.

Keep in Mind

- Knowledge coaches need not have deep smarts in order to coach. Some level of expertise is required—more than that of the protégé. However, although knowledge transferred from a coach one rung up the expertise ladder from the novice may be helpful, that knowledge will be fragmentary.

- The most effective coaching arrangements are those in which knowledge coach and protégé select one another.

- Coaches and protégés both look for compatibility or "chemistry," but they may also have different priorities in selecting one another. For example, when choosing entrepreneurs to work with, coaches focused on coachability and the potential of the business idea. Entrepreneurs focused on the value the coach could bring to the company, such as experience, networks, and access to financing.

- Coach-protégé relationships work best when the two have aligned goals and objectives. Those companies in our entrepreneurship study where the two were misaligned were less successful.

- It is very difficult to transfer knowledge that is largely tacit, as much experience-based knowledge is. Such knowledge is best recreated through experience, rather than transferred from someone else. (See next chapter.)

- Different professional backgrounds and thinking styles may create obstacles to effective communication between a knowledge coach and protégé. If managed properly, however, such differences may enrich a relationship.

- Specific knowledge coaching techniques vary along a self-direction continuum, and range from specific directives to guided experience.

- The most directive techniques, including rules of thumb, may be useful in creating or adding to mental receptors, but are unlikely to transfer deep smarts. Those techniques that involve the protégé more actively in his or her own learning, such as Socratic questioning, transfer more smarts.

Answer to riddle: bagpipes.

EIGHT

Recreating Deep Smarts Through Guided Experience

DEEP SMARTS, we have argued, are not just nice to have. They are essential to your organization, and managers who consciously cultivate them in current and future employees are investing in a competitive advantage. In the previous chapter, we suggested four ways that those with deep smarts inside (or, sometimes, outside) your organization can coach more novice learners. Those techniques range along a continuum from highly directive (specific instructions and rules of thumb) through somewhat less directive methods (stories with a moral) and on to strategies that require more independent effort on the part of the learner (Socratic questioning). (See figure 8-1, an expanded version of figure 7-2.)

None of these techniques, however, useful as they may be in either creating receptors or building on existing ones, can provide the deep, memorable knowledge that direct experience and discovery can, especially when guided by an expert knowledge coach. If we review the definition of deep smarts, we see why. Recall that deep

FIGURE 8-1

Modes of Knowledge Transfer: Guided Experience

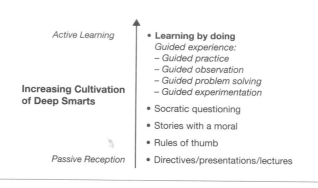

smarts are based on firsthand life experiences, providing insights drawn from the tacit knowledge that has built up over time. Deep smarts are as close as we get to wisdom about managing. There is no way to *transfer* this wisdom, all the packets of knowledge, all the lightning-fast associations, all the rich details that a single word or phrase calls up from long-term memory in the brain of a person with deep smarts. Rather, wisdom must be *recreated*.

It is a daunting task, so why even try? Because we really do have a responsibility to ensure that those deep smarts that are essential to our organization are not lost. And we owe it to the next generation of leaders to prepare them for the undoubtedly rocky road ahead—better and faster than they could prepare alone. Even if knowledge coaches cannot effect a brain transplant, they can surely help protégés develop a very similar set of deep smarts through *guided experience*.[1]

Guided Experience

The simple observation that deep smarts are neither gained nor transferred easily (see chapters 2 and 3) creates a dilemma for managers who need to preserve or grow strategic knowledge assets. One solution is to import the expertise we need (see chapter 4). But even in these days of relatively high workforce mobility, we cannot assume that we can hire in and assemble all the needed experience-based knowledge. Even if we could, it is likely that key knowledge making up our core capabilities has grown over time, is largely tacit in nature, and therefore is difficult to integrate with the deep smarts of newcomers to the organization. That brings us back to the option of developing—and preserving—deep smarts within the organization.

But organizations and the people running them are beset with constantly increasing time pressures. It is not surprising that we *want* to believe that we can capture knowledge assets from experts in our organization and transfer them quickly to novices so they can become more productive faster. Yes, information technology and particularly the World Wide Web have enhanced our ability to access and transfer *explicit* knowledge faster, better, and more widely than ever before. And PowerPoint presentations; the publishing of best practices, checklists, and guidelines; and the coaching techniques discussed in the previous chapter can create receptors where none existed previously. But none of these methods, useful as they are, will suffice to create deep smarts—managerial smarts included. Only experience will. So the dilemma intensifies: A knowledge-based reaction to complex events requires appropriate receptors, gained through an accumulation of firsthand experiences, and the process requires time that managers feel they don't have.

One partial answer to the dilemma is to encourage and structure processes that enable *guided* experience. A knowledge coach who designs a learning path and then wrings every possible lesson out of the novice's action will still demand a commitment of time. But the resulting learning will be more efficient and the resulting smarts deeper. The key is to concentrate less on the *transfer* of knowledge and more on guiding the novices through a process of *creating* their own deep smarts.

For a number of reasons, guided experience can be much more powerful than other modes of knowledge creation and transfer. First, directed action, combined with feedback from the coach, captures the essence of *deliberate practice*: The novice monitors and reflects on his or her experiences, a process that is crucial in promoting learning. Second, coaches can train their protégés to distill knowledge out of observations and planned encounters with naturally occurring situations that are potentially enlightening—if the observer has the right receptors in place. A third way that coaches can provide value beyond unguided experience is through guided problem solving, whether or not the expert knows the solution in advance. Finally, knowledge coaches can help novices reduce uncertainty through experimentation and exploration. We deal with each of these forms of guided experience—guided practice, guided observation, guided problem solving, and guided experimentation—in the next sections.

Guided Practice

Deep smarts grow out of practice, but not simple repetition. *Deliberate* practice adds reflection and mindfulness to the act of repeating a skill. But *guided* practice adds the experience and skill of a coach to help the learner reflect on his or her performance, and to provide feedback on that performance. Practice anchors know-how in the brain, but practice without reflection can lead to anchoring the wrong skills. And even deliberate practice can produce the wrong results if you don't know what part of the practice you should be reflecting on. Deliberate practice under the guidance of a coach makes the process more accurate and efficient. The knowledge coach can identify skills that the learner may not have thought of, can direct the practice that will begin to fill out the experience distribution, and then can provide constructive feedback to guide future practice. Here's a simple example from our entrepreneurship study: Few new entrepreneurs have given any thought to exactly how they are going to persuade angel investors or venture capitalists to invest in their company. Oh, they realize they will have to put together a PowerPoint slide presentation, but actually deliver a persuasive speech? Respond to pointed questions? And do all of this in a half-hour or less? Many of the coaches in our study drew on their own experience as entrepreneurs, investors, and venture capitalists to critique the novices' presentations. They ran them through practice sessions, helped them find the "sweet spot" in the business model, and pared the core message down to elevator-ride duration. With valuable feedback following each iteration, the presentation was "ready for prime time."

Other examples of guided practice come from the consulting world, where both the consultants themselves and often their clients learn processes through guided practice. At SAIC, a consulting firm that works primarily with the U.S. government, "knowledge consultants" learn their trade from more experienced consultants through first observing the expert help a client learn a particular knowledge management process, next practicing the skills by leading a client session and receiving feedback from the coach, and then teaching the skill to another consultant. This process is one of SAIC's most useful knowledge transfer tools not only in-house, but also for coaching clients. The knowledge consultants take their clients through the same "see one, lead one, and teach one" process of learning.

CECOM's (Communications and Electronics Command in the U.S. Army) Acquisition Center contracted with SAIC to coach personnel in identifying Subject Matter Experts, eliciting their knowledge (including tacit dimensions), capturing it, and then codifying that knowledge. For example, the SAIC team coached a group of twenty "knowledge harvesters" in how to elicit know-how about sourcing—how to procure materials. The task sounds pretty mundane—how could there be much tacit knowledge involved in locating vendors? But one can't just buy tactical radio systems or thermal imaging systems for tanks on eBay or at the mall! The few people who had mastered the multistage, labyrinthine process of selecting a source for a military purchase were about to retire. Finding out what they knew before they headed out the door was a high priority.

The first step in the process was a four-day general orientation to the concepts and lexicon involved (creating receptors). The next step was "see one"—observing a knowledge-transfer session in which an experienced procurer works with a relative novice. For example, one recipient of such a "peer assist" was a contracting officer just assigned to source materials—when the selection process was already halfway completed. What did she need to know? Whom should she contact? Where were the possible pitfalls? In this case, she quite reasonably wanted to have the technologies she was going to purchase vetted by outside experts. But the experienced procurer cautioned: "Don't—unless you get all the legal clearances first." This warning saved her a lot of effort, expense, and embarrassment. She would have arrived at the date set for the vetting—and found out that none of her hired experts were cleared to work for the army.

Such meetings seem such a straightforward, uncomplicated process that one might wonder why the knowledge harvesters need to subsequently practice what they have observed. Can't they just be told how to do this? Why do they need to "see one" and then "do one" (practice) in front of an experienced coach? The answer is that they will be much better interviewers, much better at selecting people for peer assists, much better at facilitating such assists if they practice—with feedback from people who are more expert at the process. The guided practice constitutes some insurance against employing the powerful forces of practice to embed the wrong processes in the brain. As any golf or tennis coach will tell you, it is very difficult to dislodge incorrect swings from the mind-body connections established by practice. After every practice session, SAIC's expert consultants also hold an "action review" to provide feedback to everyone involved. Then the final step for the SAIC clients is to "teach one," that is, to coach someone else in the knowledge elicitation process and consolidate the lessons learned from guided practice.

Guided Observation

Observation is one of the earliest modes of learning. Children observe their elders and their peers and, for better or worse, mimic what they see. (See chapter 6 for a fuller discussion of the power of role models to transfer deep smarts.) Knowledge coaches can guide observation for either of two purposes: First, observation is a powerful way of initiating novices into the practices of someone with deep smarts. Second, as suggested in the chapter 5 discussion of challenging beliefs, guiding someone to observe behaviors to which they would not normally be exposed creates an opportunity for confronting assumptions and previously unquestioned beliefs. Let us first consider how observing expertise in practice helps transfer deep smarts.

GUIDED OBSERVATION AS SHADOWING. An example of the first kind of guided observation is the relationship between Sanjeev Malaney, founder of MediaTel, and an experienced coach, Rich Zalisk. Zalisk temporarily assumed the position of president. Reflecting on his own development as a CEO, Malaney commented:

> *A lot of my education came from observation. We had an issue here, how did Rich solve it? How did Rich do this? How did Rich do that? How did changes occur? Whether it be something as simple as how you go about doing effective business planning, or how you facilitate bringing your VPs together and getting them to agree on what you are going to do next . . . I learned mostly by osmosis.*

Such osmosis is most effective when it is carefully guided by an expert who encourages pausing to reflect on the behavior observed, in order to create, capture, and reinforce knowledge. The coach draws on a wide experience repertoire to guide the novice in *what* to see—what deserves attention. A top consultant was once asked where and how he learned his skills in closing deals with clients. "I had an excellent teacher," he replied. He explained that when he joined the company, an elder statesman in the firm had asked him to sit in on client meetings. "You don't have to say a word," the older consultant told him. "Just listen and learn." The junior consultant rightly took that directive as more than a suggestion and sat at the back of the room. After the client meeting, he and the older consultant discussed what had occurred. "I learned more from those debriefs," he said, "than in four years at my prior company and two years of business school."

Observation with reflection and guidance is an underutilized mode of transferring knowledge. Some universities, for example, have adopted the practice of requiring junior faculty to sit in on the classes of master teachers, followed by a discussion of what worked and why. (And, in the best models, there are reciprocal visits by the experienced teacher to observe the junior colleague in action.) But far more common is the "sink or swim" attitude that one should learn purely from practice, with the only feedback the end-of-semester student evaluations. It is no better in companies. Perhaps it was easier in the more authoritarian culture of management that was common when the consultant just mentioned learned his trade, and an experienced manager could command the time and energy of the firm entrant. Or perhaps the perception that such guided observation is a waste of precious time is a reason that it is not used more. We suspect, however, that many managers never even consider setting up such occasions to guide learning—either because they have never been taught that way themselves, or because they don't stop to think about the value to their junior colleagues, and to the firm. A recent college graduate was frustrated because her supervisor in her new job never allowed her into any meetings in which the strategy of the department was discussed. "I know enough not to say anything," she lamented. "But how am I ever going to learn about management if I am kept in the dark about how decisions are made here?" Finally emboldened to ask permission to attend some meetings, she found her supervisor initially surprised but willing to allow it. Later, noting her increased understanding of the department needs, he began convening postmeeting discussions with her as an occasion for further learning. As these examples suggest, guided observation can be a more effective way of developing deep smarts than observation alone if the knowledge coach selects the subjects for observation and focuses the protégé's attention on salient behaviors, including subtle ones that reflect tacit knowledge.

GUIDED OBSERVATION AS CHALLENGING ASSUMPTIONS. So shadowing an expert can help recreate some of that individual's deep smarts. But guided observation can also be utilized to help people *un*learn as well as learn. True learning, and certainly innovation, depends on our ability to see the world differently. We have a natural tendency to see what we expect or wish to see, and guided observation is a powerful way of challenging those expectations. As we discussed in chapter 5, ingrained notions about how the world works are difficult to dislodge with any means short of personal experience. We need to see with our own eyes evidence that contradicts our individual or organizational assumptions. The knowledge coaches in Best Buy's innovation journey, discussed briefly in chapters 2 and 4, utilized guided observation both to help the novices learn—and to unlearn.

Recall that when CEO Brad Anderson decided that Best Buy needed a deeper innovation capability, he asked thirty-five of his upper midlevel managers to spend six months learning how to innovate from consulting company Strategos. Strategos coaches divided the group into teams, each of which approached the task of identifying new business opportunities for the company through a different technique. A team working on "customer insights" went into the field to look at other businesses and cultures in order to stimulate new ways of viewing the world. In the terms of this book, the team members first created new receptors and then built up related experience.

For example, team member Toby Nord was influenced by trips to Mexico City, to the American Girl store in Chicago, and to the Amish countryside in Indiana. American Girl specializes in a line of dolls representing historical figures. More of a "destination" than a retail outlet, the store features doll-centric activities such as getting a new hairdo for the doll, or having lunch in a special restaurant where dolls sit at the table and the menu features "American Girl Tea." Nord, along with his Best Buy male colleagues, was definitely pushed out of his "comfort zone." But he came away with specific observations that fed into subsequent brainstorming sessions and eventually, in concert with other observations from his travels, a new business idea. He realized that the dolls at American Girl were a kind of "platform" for intergenerational socializing: grandmother, mother, daughter. The store was entertaining. The business focused tightly on a community built for a given demographic—in this case, gender.

All of these insights proved useful when he went on to work with a team on a youth-centered entertainment concept: a "PCBang" where teenagers and people in their early twenties (much younger than Best Buy's typical consumer) could play computer games together, socialize, and meet new friends. Anyone could have told Nord about American Girl, but actually observing the store with a particular assignment in mind left a very different impression than a mere discussion—or just visiting with no guidance—could have made. One of the interesting outcomes of this exercise for Nord and for Best Buy was that he began to adopt some of the techniques of anthropology, including new observational skills. Even on vacation, he began to look at the world differently—to see how people around him were socializing and entertaining themselves in communities. *Guidance* inspired him to do this.

The World Bank conducted internal exercises aimed at both providing role models for imitation and also challenging ingrained thinking. Peers from headquarters, instead of consultants, guided the observations. In the spring of 2002, thirty senior leaders from the Africa region went on a two-week tour of five countries: Japan, Singapore, Malaysia, Thailand, and Vietnam. The objective was to see some "best practices" in transportation and export. Although the bank had conducted such learning tours before, either for individuals or small teams, there were two innovations: (1) the team was multidisciplinary (e.g., engineers, financial analysts, agronomists), and (2) built into the tour were specific reflection and debriefing sessions, captured on videotape for later use. The participants reflected on their observations with open-ended questions, such as "What did you learn?" "How relevant is it to the African situation?" and "What adaptations would you have to make to help the new practice work in your context?" (So, for example, if you were building a container port, how would you adjust for the lack in your region of the skilled manpower that Singapore and Japan have?) This deliberate reflection, paired with brainstorming, and the obligation to capture the learning as it occurred, stimulated improved observation and questioning as the tour proceeded. That is, the participants steadily increased their ability to observe and learn. They also gained some role models and changed some assumptions about what technology could accomplish. While they might have made some of the same observations had they just traveled, the guided observation resulted in more targeted, relevant learning—and an increased observational capability.

Guided Problem Solving

Guided problem solving may involve some observation, but serves different purposes and requires much more active engagement from the protégé than does observation. The knowledge coach may already know the answer to the problem, or may face the same uncertainty about the solution as the protégé. The major advantage of working on the problem jointly, however, is that the protégé can learn *how to approach* the problem. That is, the knowledge coach transfers know-how more than know-what. Moreover, because both coach and protégé are actively engaged in solving the problem, the coach often learns as well from the questions (and sometimes the solutions) posed by the protégé.

In an engineering company, a highly experienced design engineer was asked to "train" a younger colleague in the same kind of systems thinking for which the older man was renowned. One of the senior engineer's most valued skills was the ability to bring multiple perspectives to any design, including not only engineering knowledge about each and every component (software and hardware) in the complex systems the company manufactured, but also an understanding of how the system was to be produced. He was famous for detecting and avoiding potential assembly problems as well as possible performance shortfalls. Having developed his skills over twenty-five years of engineering design, complemented by a three-year stint as a process system engineer in manufacturing, he knew that he would never be able to transfer his ability to comprehend the overall product architecture nor his respect for manufacturing constraints through any of the knowledge transfer techniques we have discussed so far. Rather, he took his protégé down to the assembly line and had him work on problems with a test engineer for several months. The senior engineer joined many of these problem-solving sessions as well, adding perspectives that the test technician lacked, such as historic customer biases and preferences. While the protégé gained specific knowledge about component parts, the more important know-how transferred was the ability to look at the whole system, see how the interfaces worked, and understand how different functional priorities led to certain design flaws. The protégé also got to know and respect the knowledge of people working on the assembly line. This experience enhanced his organizational know-who and altered his belief systems as well as contributed more obviously to his technical expertise.

Such guided problem solving combines many of the best features of the transfer techniques mentioned previously: focusing attention, practicing process skills with feedback, providing an opportunity to mimic an expert, engaging the learner actively in developing her own deep smarts, and contributing to an experience repertoire.

Guided Experimentation

What can you do when you have to make a decision, but you lack the information or deep smarts needed to distinguish among alternatives—or even to identify potential options for action? Under such conditions of uncertainty, there is a need to experiment. David Garvin distinguishes between two types of experiments: hypothesis testing and exploration.[2] When some boundaries can be set—that is, there is a limited set of known alternatives—*hypothesis testing* can determine which of those alternatives is superior. *Exploration* is much more open-ended: the goal is to map out territory and generate options. In both cases, coaches can add value by helping to identify the types of experiments and their extent.

In familiar markets, for example, experiments yield information about whether a new product will actually inspire customers to open their wallets. Whirlpool managers hypothesized that customers might be interested in customizing appliances, and that such customizing could increase market share and profitability. With the help of coaches from consulting company Strategos, they decided to run a simple experiment, selecting two retail outlets in both Philadelphia and Dallas, and then setting up customized appliance kiosks in the stores. An advertising campaign brought in curious shoppers ("Come build your own Whirlpool refrigerator down at XYZ Appliances"). Potential customers could incorporate the design features they wanted on a computer, and then workers in a back room would quickly assemble the appliance to the customer's specifications. At the conclusion of the experiment, Whirlpool found that customization did improve market share in these four outlets. But there was an unexpected finding: Customers built in about $70 more in added features per refrigerator when offered the option of configuring their own. Using the knowledge gained from this experiment, in early 2003, Whirlpool's KitchenAid division began to offer to all customers an option to "build your own" dishwasher. Pick your model and tailor the features and external appearance attributes (door, color, etc.) that you want—and that is what shows up in your kitchen.

Start-up companies have an even greater need to experiment than established organizations, as their proposed product or service may be new to the world—but their processes fall somewhere between hypothesis testing and exploration. The number of alternative markets to be tested depends on two factors: the range of possible markets that would value their product or service and the resources available to test those markets. The ActivePhoto founders were relatively certain of the primary characteristic an interested client would have (need for instant access to photos over the Internet)[3] and their resources were limited. The team had developed ways of labeling photos and tracking them right from the camera, a capability that opened up several possible markets.

At the urging of their coaches, the team quickly abandoned their initial idea of serving individual consumers, who could use the wireless image transfer to exchange family photos. They focused their attention instead on commercial markets: public safety personnel such as firefighters, who would be able to access the expertise of a fire chief while still at a blaze by transmitting photos to headquarters; property insurance damage assessors, who already used photographic prints in their jobs; and auctioneers, who would like to display their wares online.

During the first two board meetings that the three founders of ActivePhoto had with their primary coaches, Fred Gibbons and Bill Krause, one of the critical issues addressed was *experimentation* in the market—how to discover what potential customers had greatest need for their service. The coaches were clear that the company should aim for vertical markets rather than attempt to become the image transfer platform for every type of application. But there were many subsequent decisions to be made: How many customer bases should be explored at once? What were the primary criteria for targeting a particular market? How much customization of the product should the team undertake in order to gain a customer? Should the team subsidize customer usage in order to gain feedback, or set prices at an immediately profitable level? This is how the two coaches helped guide the process of experimentation.

Gibbons advised: "If you can't get the equipment right for a customer, move on." He then told a story about another company that customized their product for an initial customer and subsequently could not sell it anywhere else. "Sometimes," Gibbons concluded, "the customers want what you don't sell. There can be bad customers." "Look for image-driven businesses," counseled Krause. Gibbons warned them not to try too many experiments at once: "Prove them one at a time. Do one wireless and one wired."

By the second meeting, the ActivePhoto team had focused on the Palo Alto Fire Department as an interested customer. Krause cautioned: "But don't focus on just Palo Alto. Try one to three other fire departments to find out if they will use it. You are dealing with a government agency, so it has to be written into their procedures. Is this service important enough to them to fight to get it into their process?" When the team worried that despite interest, the fire departments would never have the budget to afford the expensive camera necessary, the advisors focused them on usage. "If we make it free," said Krause, "and it still doesn't work, we can say we've given it our best shot."

Cofounder Valerie McGinty argued against continuing to serve the public safety market: "I am extremely uneasy about it. My personal take is that we should get out of this market now."

"What's the constraint?" Krause wanted to know. "Time or money? You don't want to give up just because you can't get Palo Alto to work. How about just one more experiment?" He worried lest the team give up too easily on their first target customer base. "The grass is always greener," he cautioned. "New customers always appear easier than the ones we have."

McGinty continued to argue against fire departments as a market: "There are so many obstacles—psychological, technical—and price is a major barrier." "You're probably right," Krause conceded, "but hang in a little longer. You have only a sample of one."

The team also wanted to try out their service in the insurance industry. Cofounder Shane Dyer argued, "I love the insurance market, because we can show quantifiable evidence of value. They have all these forms—and no pictures associated with them. It's a glaring flaw in their products." The coaches were less enthusiastic—but willing to have the team experiment. Krause advised: "Find a few showcase customers; stay focused. You may be able to handle three to five experiments, but be sure that they are with people who want to use the product and that the product works. We don't want to customize the product 100 percent for each customer. But if you have the fundamental engine, you can tune it up for a particular customer."

Gibbons laid out a few criteria for selecting the trial markets: "What will it take to get the customer to use the product? Are there enough customers? Will they pay?"

Finally, Gibbons left them with some excellent advice: "We need to learn from each experiment. The proof that it is a good experiment is when we learn and the next experiment is easier."

The ActivePhoto team was simultaneously refining their technologies while selecting their market. How else could one learn the best application for a totally new capability? One of the greatest services provided by coaches in our study was the stimulus—and often the venue—for entrepreneurs to test their evolving business ideas directly with other companies, prospective clients, and real customers. People accustomed to dealing with known markets and innovation within well-established product categories are often critical of this kind of experimentation. Why can't start-ups save money and time by doing market research? What such a question ignores is that this kind of experimentation *is* market research. In such uncertain environments, traditional market research cannot reveal the value proposition with the greatest appeal.[4] When the product category is totally new, customers' reactions to queries about their intention to buy are almost always misleading. Gerald Zaltman recounts a typical example: More than 60 percent of individuals who were trying out a new kitchen appliance in their homes said they were likely to purchase it within the next three months—but eight months later, only 12 percent actually had done so.[5] As this example indicates, experiments have to include actual market *behavior* in order to yield more useful information than the behavioral *intentions* that surveys or focus groups reveal.

In developing an innovation—a new product, service, or internal organizational process—the earlier one can experiment to learn, the better.[6] Knowledge coaches who have experience in experimenting help protégés think about how many resources should be devoted to the experimentation, how bounded it should be (e.g., three possible markets—or ten), and especially how to think about experimentation in general. The dangers of experimentation are many: overcustomization for the first viable customers identified; setting up experiments with inadequate feedback loops; designing a demonstration instead of an experiment (i.e., predetermining, or at least assuming, the outcome—but still *calling* it an experiment). However, the benefits are great—most important, contributing to experience-based knowledge. Experimentation builds experience, and it does so rapidly and systematically. In a study of twenty-nine software development projects, researchers found that teams whose members had experience developing more generations of software used significantly fewer resources. Their experience was useful in "framing and directing the experimentation strategy" so that the design process was much more efficient.[7]

HYPOTHESES IN DIRECTED EXPERIMENTATION. In directed experimentation, not only are the protégés absorbing the information gained in the experiment, but they are also developing an enhanced capacity to think in terms of hypotheses and tests, that is, a new way of learning. Participants in the innovation journey at Best Buy described earlier believed in the end that the most valuable capability left behind at the company was their own changed ability to think differently. Toby Nord, a member of the first team to go through the journey, was subsequently selected as a coach to take others through a similar experience. Speaking in his role as coach, Nord remarked:

> *You can almost see the epiphany happen; the participants understand that their role is less about passively taking filtered information from someone else and more about aggressively going out to create their own experiences, so they can learn and take that learning to help shape what they are going to do next.*

In his ethnographic work on the Toyota production system, justly famed for its high quality and unusual learning environment, Steven Spear found that an essential element underlying the outward trappings of the system was a mind-set engendered throughout the organization. As discussed in chapter 6, from operators on the line to team leaders to managers, employees were trained to pose improvements as hypotheses—and test them through quick prototyping. Furthermore, once individuals grasped the power of self-motivated experimentation, they were expected to expand their grasp in two ways: enlarge the scope of the experiments to encompass a larger segment of the overall system, and coach others in the methodology.[8] Spear attributes much of Toyota's success—and the difficulty of imitating it—to this embedded mind-set.

The mind-set of thinking in hypotheses ("Would changing this element improve the process?") was also characteristic of minimill Chaparral Steel when it was at its height in the intensively competitive steel industry. The strategy of the company was emblazoned on the brains of everyone working there: become the lowest-cost producer of high-quality structural steel. Having this clear objective enabled everyone from the president to the operators on the mill floor to think up possible improvements and try them out, so long as they lowered costs, did not degrade quality, and did not unduly interrupt production. Hypothesis testing ranged from elaborate experimental design presentations for the board of directors to "quick and dirty" (and cheap) experiments on the rolling mill floor. Production workers set up water-soaked plywood splashboards along the path of the near-molten steel to test various possible board angles and heights before investing in metal ones. Rolling mill operators, stopwatch in hand, tested innovative ideas for sequencing the ingots going through the mills in order to eke out more productivity and lower energy costs.

In all these examples, deep smarts are built in two ways: The experiments themselves yield knowledge and the individuals who conduct them learn to think in terms of options for change.

PROTOTYPES IN DIRECTED EXPERIMENTATION. Designing hypotheses in the form of physical or process prototypes is a complementary knowledge-eliciting technique. When product development company IDEO needed to determine if their new goggles for snowboarders would stay fog-free on cold ski slopes, they had a problem: It was July in the United States and the client couldn't afford to fly them to the southern hemisphere. Their solution? Get a few company volunteers to ride an exercise bike in winds produced by a fan—in a nearby family-run ice cream factory's large freezers![9] Prototypes are essential not only for such testing but for communicating new ideas. IDEO employees believe that if a picture is worth a thousand words, a good prototype is worth a thousand pictures. Many times potential customers or fellow workers cannot really understand the innovation being proposed if the new idea is presented in words—or even pictures. Whole books have been written about the value of prototyping as a means of communicating across barriers and of creating knowledge.[10] All we wish to point out here is that the most valuable experiments include some form of proto-typing, be it a physical artifact or a process.

Managers in service industries often fail to think of prototyping because they associate the term exclusively with physical objects. But services can create small trials of customer interactions that yield knowledge. Bank of America's Innovation and Development teams are conducting more than two dozen experiments in operating branches at any given time, including "virtual tellers," video monitors displaying financial and investment news, computer stations uploading images of personal checks, and "hosting stations."[11] Similarly, universities can try out services on a small scale before rolling them out to the entire community. One of us (Walter) helped develop a small pilot program to involve first-year college students in the research of faculty members. Several active researchers were recruited to develop semester-long seminars, each with ten freshmen, who in the course of the semester would work with the faculty member to design and carry out a small research project. The faculty member would also serve as the students' advisor. At the end of the semester the students and faculty evaluated the program. Slight modifications were made, outside grant support was obtained, and the program, called Windows on Research, was rolled out campuswide the following year.

Of course, with the advent of increasingly sophisticated computerized simulations, a lot of prototyping can be done less expensively by creating virtual artifacts and processes. Such simulations can yield unexpected, counterintuitive results. For example, Stefan Thomke tells of BMW's search for safety in automobile side crashes. When company analysis revealed that a section of one of the pillars connecting the roof to the chassis below the windows was dangerously prone to fold, BMW engineers first assumed that increasing the density of metal at the base of the pillar would solve the problem. When a development team member insisted on testing the assumption through an easy and inexpensive computer simulation, the group was disconcerted to discover that their intuitive re-design actually decreased crashworthiness: Reinforcing the lower segment of the pillar caused it to buckle at the height of passengers' vulnerable midsections and heads. The unexpected solution turned out to be to weaken rather than reinforce the lower part of the pillar.[12] This revelation is an example of something we have shown several times throughout this book—a change in beliefs and assumptions on the basis of *direct experience*, and a subsequent addition to a group's deep smarts.

So How Did I Do? Positive and Negative Feedback

Throughout our discussion of guided experience, we have emphasized the importance of feedback from the coach who is guiding the protégé's learning. When the coaches draw on their deep smarts to reinforce new behaviors, or correct inappropriate responses, protégés will learn more efficiently and effectively. One of the most critical aspects of guiding experience is the realization that in giving feedback to protégés, the two extremes of providing uniform praise or unremitting criticism are both ineffective. Neither directly tells the protégé how to improve. But while unqualified praise is certainly a barrier to progress, we have seen many more instances of unqualified negative feedback. Corrections and criticism are undeniably an important part of feedback, but when a coach relies exclusively on such negative reinforcers, and seldom responds to what the learner is doing successfully, that person learns only what is not working. The protégé does not learn how to move forward. And when a developing leader receives a steady diet of such feedback from a supervisor, he or she learns the same managerial approach—and may imitate it.

But in addition to hampering learning, unrelenting negative feedback can demoralize and produce a high level of anxiety, extinguishing any joy in performing the job. This is a difficult lesson for managers. Our profession has socialized us to "correct" problems, not to reinforce what is already working. But people not only need to know what they are doing well (so they can continue doing it well), but also to hear that their performance is appreciated by those who are teaching or leading them.[13]

We know of someone whose boss was extremely stingy with praise of any kind. When our acquaintance had his major evaluation, a process done every three years that involved collecting judgments of job performance from more than fifty colleagues, the responses were highly favorable. At the meeting with his boss, however, one or two minor criticisms were picked out of the report, along with an acknowledgment that there weren't any "major problems." But this rather grudging concession was tempered by an astonishing parting shot: "Of course, the fact that you lost your son this year probably made it difficult for anyone to say anything critical." A year later, our acquaintance found a different position, one where his strengths—not his deficiencies alone—were clearly acknowledged. And the boss? His career stalled, in no small part because he wasn't considered "good at managing people."

Unremittingly negative feedback is not only unhelpful to the protégé's morale and motivation, but may also damage or destroy the relationship between coach and protégé. In some situations, stinginess and lack of emotional intelligence kills the tribal instinct as well: The hapless employee gives up on the organization as a whole and leaves. The organization loses deep smarts in the making. Upper managers should never assume that because someone "makes the numbers" and performs well, she will make a good coach. Knowing how to perform well in a given environment is only the necessary first qualification for a coach—it is by no means sufficient. Poorly chosen knowledge coaches can damage more than benefit, as potential protégés will quickly see an unfruitful relationship as a time sink at best—and negative word-of-mouth about an organizational coaching initiative can doom it.

Implications for Managers

As should now be obvious, we don't believe that deep smarts can be packed up and shipped overnight to a protégé. And most managers know that. But the vast majority of organizational resources are devoted to processes for learning that ignore that fact. It is far easier to send our up-and-coming leaders to training classes on leadership—or place them in positions of leadership to sink or swim—than to arrange for guided experience. But setting up processes for guided experience can benefit our organizations in multiple ways.

First, of course, identifying people with the deep smarts important to our organization is, in and of itself, a valuable exercise. We have mentioned instances where that failed to happen—with serious consequences for the organization. Second, in so many industries and organizations, we face the same necessity that venture and mentor capitalists faced when the Internet boom was upon us: to grow leaders *fast*. As the baby boomers retire, we are going to need more deep smarts, and the sooner we start coaching coaches to help transfer those smarts, the better off we will be when the diaspora begins.

Third, coaching through guided experience focuses the teachers on what they know—and what they need to question or renew. That is, as they guide the experience of the protégés, they will themselves learn anew, because the experience that they are putting the protégé through will never duplicate exactly their own learning path. And finally, the protégés will not have to learn through the inefficient process of ad hoc trial and error. They can benefit from their elders' wisdom about *how* to learn as well as *what* to learn. As will be discussed more in chapter 9, the practice of guided experience need not be a separate, huge undertaking for the corporate university—although it could certainly be incorporated more than it is into regular curriculum. Rather, organizations that build an expectation of guided experience into their culture make the most of what managers are already doing in their daily routines. Managers in such organizations recognize that they are as responsible for deliberately cultivating deep smarts at work as they are for guiding their children's acquisition of practical knowledge. Thus, guided experience results from a cultural mind-set and a choice in managerial attention. When managers focus on learning opportunities and think of themselves as coaches, they will cultivate and transfer deep smarts.

There are situations of inescapable uncertainty, when no one has the deep smarts, the essential business wisdom, about what to do. In such cases, the only course of action is to act and then act again in response to knowledge fed back from the environment. This reactive and inefficient process of morphing, of seeking direction through a process of trial and error, may be the only possible way to move forward. The most widely recognized situations involving morphing are innovative projects, including start-up businesses, and many of today's established corporations went through a period of searching for their identity.[14] However, morphing is an ongoing process common to all organizations, and more common to many everyday initiatives than we might like. Managers, who are trained to be decisive, analytical, and careful of resources, would prefer to believe that *all* projects, all undertakings, can be mapped out well in advance. The consequence of this belief is a lot of wasted effort put into detailed plans that the planners themselves know to be fraudulent, but which "the system" requires (including the often constraining timing of budgeting cycles). This is not to say that bounding a problem, broad-based analysis, or plans involving stages and milestones are not useful; to the extent that they help managers think through different contingencies, they are invaluable. But forcing people to pretend that they have the deep smarts to set out a definite, detailed course of action when *no one* has that kind of wisdom in the circumstances can waste time and effort and—perhaps most important—undermine the integrity of the organization. What is the role of a knowledge coach in such situations? A coach can protect the fledgling undertaking as it morphs by legitimizing the process of search and experimentation, and by making certain that the managers involved actively learn from each foray into uncharted territory. As we will see in chapter 9, individuals often follow a similar morphing path as they cultivate their personal deep smarts.

Keep in Mind

- Guided experience, that is, practice, observation, problem solving, and experimentation under the guidance of a coach, will facilitate the development and transfer of deep smarts from expert to novice.

- Deliberate practice that is guided by a coach includes identifying particular skills that need to be practiced, encouraging reflection, and providing feedback that helps the learner chart progress.

- Feedback is a particularly important part of guided practice. While criticism is important for correcting errors, exclusively negative feedback does not identify steps for improvement and can be highly demoralizing. Positive feedback for good performance is an underused but essential tool for shaping knowledge and promoting morale.

- Observing deep smarts in action is an effective way for an expert to transfer knowledge. But modeling becomes even more effective when the coach guides the protégé to reflect on what has been observed.

- Guided observation is also a tool for forcing unlearning, that is, the relinquishing of assumptions and cognitive habits.

- Guided problem solving recreates deep smarts because the protégé can develop know-how and know-who as well as know-what (facts about the knowledge domain).

- Under conditions of high uncertainty, such as when a new technology is being developed or a new market is being explored, guided experiments can provide critical information. This extreme form of planned "learning by doing" creates receptors and promotes the development of deep smarts.

- When learners conduct experiments they learn to think analytically, in terms of hypotheses or "what-ifs."

- Hypotheses expressed as prototypes are particularly effective in communicating and eliciting knowledge.

NINE

Cultivating Deep Smarts

For Organizations and Ourselves

WHEN WE STARTED YOU on this journey in chapter 1, we sought to convince you that deep smarts are critical to your organization and to you as a manager—and that you cannot manage them without understanding their origins and character. We hope by now that it is clear that deep smarts constitute a tapestry of interdependent elements, woven out of direct and vicarious experience. We have seen how what we already know (the receptors in our brain) affects our perception and ability to learn more, and how expertise can be narrow or broad, depending upon the experience repertoire. We know that the design of the deep smarts tapestry is highly, if sometimes subtly, shaped by our beliefs and by other people whose influence we accept, often unconsciously. Such influences determine from whom we learn as well as what we choose to experience and what we accept as true. Managers need to understand the role of beliefs and social influences in developing deep smarts because even technical and professional knowledge often includes strongly held assumptions that block the importation of new knowledge into groups and organizations. On the other hand, our professional tribes can motivate and facilitate learning, if they are managed toward that end.

We have seen that much practical, experience-based wisdom is composed of tacit knowledge. Those tacit dimensions enable people with deep smarts to recognize patterns, but render that ability difficult to transfer. This transfer barrier is precisely what makes deep smarts competitively valuable—but a challenge to manage inside the organization. Knowledge coaches can help, especially if they recognize that not all modes of knowledge transfer contribute to the growth of wisdom. Some aspects of deep smarts must be *recreated* through guided experience: guided practice, guided observation, guided problem solving, and guided experimentation.

In many organizations, deep smarts are an endangered species of knowledge. In this chapter, we address a few of the forces that make the cultivation and transfer of essential business wisdom so challenging to managers. We introduce one of the most important tools in the manager's arsenal for developing deep smarts in the organization: dual-purpose projects. And we return to the theme of coaching to discuss the implications of this book for selecting knowledge coaches and helping them learn to coach. The last part of the book we devote to you as an individual—to your professional life, to developing your personal deep smarts. We think the understanding of deep smarts is as important to the individual as to the organization, especially as people face increasing job mobility and a greater need to take direct responsibility for their own career planning.

Deep Smarts: The Manager's Imperative

As noted several times throughout the book, many organizations face the imminent retirement of hosts of experienced managers and technical employees who will walk out the door with their deep smarts. Even if retirement is not an issue, if employees are relatively young their leadership skills need to be developed and the organization needs "bench depth" for potential successors to current leaders. For the manager, therefore, one of the first essential chores in managing deep smarts is to assess who has them in the organization and then to consider how they may be transferred.

Calibrating the Gap

There are many situations in which the distance between competence and expertise is unclear, and therefore it is difficult to decide whether or not to incur the costs of exploiting the deep smarts of the master. Perhaps competence is enough. Perhaps the expertise is outdated. Consider the problem faced by a large research laboratory when a number of senior scientists are slated to retire within a few years, passing the mantle of leadership on to their more junior colleagues. The junior scientists have excellent technical skills, superior cutting-edge knowledge about certain tools and equipment, and are unquestionably smart. What is the nature of their knowledge gap? What don't they know that their seniors do? What do they *need* to know? A different organization faced a somewhat similar need: huge data files, stored on large outdated tape reels, held valuable information. Ironically, the knowledge was inaccessible because so much had been stored that no one could separate the diamonds from the rhinestones. The antiquated technology was rendering the information—much less the knowledge—less accessible every day that they waited. And once again, people with some idea of what the files contained were retiring.

The usual approach to addressing such gaps is to arrange a series of workshops that cover technical topics assumed to be important, with the senior scientists lecturing and fielding questions. This kind of exercise is valuable, of course, but it is unlikely to cover more than the most common events, situations, and technical problems. Moreover, the tacit dimensions of knowledge are not elicited. Even asking experts to recount "critical incidents" from their lives and careers relies upon those individuals' ability to recall details without providing much context.[1] A likely more fruitful diagnostic is to pose problems in the form of scenarios or cases for the experts and the relatively less experienced individuals to independently tackle, then compare the two responses and see where the differences—the gaps—lie. The expert's analytical approach, use of resources, and exploitation of professional networks all will differ from the behavior of the relative novice, or even journeyman. That is, in order to uncover the deep smarts of the expert and determine the important differences from those of the less experienced, one has to provide *context* for the calibration of the gap. Moreover, such exercises demonstrate the expert's deep smarts in action—which can be important in several ways. First, the organization can see what does and does not comprise deep smarts and what kinds of knowledge are critical. Second, such exhibitions of deep smarts may serve to counteract the impulse of some experts to hoard their knowledge. Challenged to demonstrate their abilities, they will have to share some of their deep smarts. Finally, not all individuals with deep smarts are recognized for their knowledge by the organization—especially if they work at relatively low levels in the hierarchy. The recognition provided by such scenario or case discussion is a powerful motivator. We know of a situation in which a coach took a vertical slice through personnel levels in a manufacturing organization to address some hypothetical futures. The managers were surprised to find that some very deep smarts about the operations of their plants resided in the heads of supervisory-level workers; the supervisors were thrilled to have their knowledge revealed and used.

Why is this kind of exercise so seldom undertaken? Part of the answer, we suggest, is in our emphasis on efficiency over effectiveness.

Speed Kills Learning

Apparent "laws" of nature and assumptions about the limitations of science and technology are being overturned every year (estimates of the storage capacity of computer chips seem to be revised at least annually). Information and communication technology continues to connect us to each other ever more rapidly, extensively, and with richer media. So why do we authors remain wedded to the primitive notion that much of knowledge transfer depends on human-to-human contact, over a period of time? We cannot blame our intransigence on a lack of exposure to the most sophisticated technologies, organizations, and individuals. We are rich in those connections. Nor do we have belief systems that would preclude our delighting in imagined futures where Star Trek–like "mind-melds" could occur between consenting adults, or brain implants could instantly instill, say, fluency in another language. No, we have come to our conclusions by watching novice managers struggle to learn when speed was paramount.

In Western society, efficiency is king. Anything that can be done faster is automatically something done better. But speed is anathema to the transfer of deep smarts, for all the reasons explained in the chapters on experience and expertise. Our ability to communicate information fast has outpaced the natural rhythms of learning. Receptors—both primitive and more profound ones—can be built through lectures, through simulations, through coaching. But deep smarts are grown organically, through experience, and like any organic process, this growth takes time.

Knowledge varies in terms of its "stickiness," that is, how difficult it is to transfer from one situation to another.[2] It is not easy to transfer complex content knowledge, or "know-what," but process knowledge ("know-how") is particularly difficult to transfer because it relies even more upon pattern recognition, which in turn depends on experience and deliberate practice. Coaches and novice managers must realize that the transfer process must move at a reasonable pace and cannot be significantly compressed. Trying to proceed at Internet speed may cause an Internet-speed flameout.[3]

This simple fact challenges many managerial practices. We *want* to believe that we can make leaders out of managers if we send them to a course on leadership. We *want* to believe that smart people taking over new positions can learn what they need to know, with little or no overlapping service (or even contact) with their predecessors. We spend millions of dollars on reports, analyses, and databases, so that people who need to learn can plow through them and become knowledgeable. And we no longer have time for apprenticeships.

The practice of having a novice shadow an expert for an extended period is prevalent only in some isolated parts of our society, such as in medical training. Managers usually don't think about inviting their subordinates to observe important meetings, either because that is a "waste of time" or because—a more subtle reason—attendance at such meetings is evidence of the manager's power and can't be shared. And the subordinates generally buy in to this conceit. The result is that we do not design *guided experience* into our organizational practices. In the name of efficiency, we forsake effectiveness.

Technology Can Help—to a Point

A second reason that our basic observations in this book about how people learn run counter to current practices is that our societal fascination with the magic of bits and bytes (magic we authors enjoy employing in our own professions, of course) tempts us all to believe that experience can be boiled down into pixels on a screen. Superior technology does not equate to superior output, a statement supported by the research of Stefan Thomke. In a rigorous comparative study of Japanese, U.S., and European automobile companies, Thomke found that the Japanese outperformed their competition with less sophisticated simulation technology. One of the reasons was that the Japanese avoided creating an intervening layer of specialists to operate and translate the technology for engineers, and therefore had one less link in a chain of tasks and communication.[4]

The fact that so many organizations have backed off in the past several years from overly sanguine expectations of what online education can deliver shows that many educators are aware that even sophisticated technology is limited in its ability to replace traditional modes of education. E-learning is by no means dead; in fact, we continue to learn about the benefits and possibilities of using technology to deliver certain kinds of knowledge. Brown University in Providence, Rhode Island, announced in 2003 a worldwide collaboration of medical schools to create an "International Virtual Medical School" that will allow students to cover much of the science curriculum from afar.[5] Such ventures do not mean that we can capture deep smarts in a bottle—or even in a PowerPoint presentation. Yet trainers and educators remain under strong pressures to deliver complex, experience-based knowledge in simple form—and fast. We hope that this book provides a bit of defensive ammunition for those who appreciate the limits of oversimplification and fast delivery.

Successful Coaching

But while we remain skeptical about the promise of quickly transferring deep smarts, we believe in the power of effective coaching. One of the reasons that we have placed so much emphasis on coaching as an aid to knowledge transfer is that individuals who are sufficiently experienced and motivated to teach can improve the efficiency of knowledge transfer and experiential learning. That is, learning, particularly learning by doing, can be much more effective *and* efficient if an expert knowledge coach is guiding the process, providing the experiences that will fill out an experience repertoire in a strategic, carefully planned manner, encouraging reflection, and supplying helpful feedback. We have focused on knowledge coaches —those who have domain or process knowledge (e.g., the venture and mentor capitalists in our entrepreneuring study), and are motivated to transfer their deep smarts.

In our study of entrepreneuring coaches and their protégés, we had no way of directly assessing the effectiveness of this knowledge coaching. However, we did have a perhaps more important measure of how well these coaches did: the success of the ventures they coached, as perceived by both the entrepreneurs and the coaches. The three variables that correlated most strongly with success were:

- *Alignment.* The strongest predictor of the rated success of the company was the perceived alignment between coach and protégé on strategy and management.[6] (This relationship was briefly discussed in chapter 7.)

- *Experience.* The coach's prior experience, as measured by the number of previous start-ups coached, predicted success, as did the entrepreneur's prior start-up and industry experience.[7]

- *Know-who.* Perceived success was also predicted by how well known the coach was by the other coaches in our sample, and conversely, by the number of other coaches in our study the coach knew.[8]

These findings do *not* suggest that the single most important predictor of a new company's success will be the presence of a knowledge coach. Certainly the quality of the founding team, the availability of money, a market that is friendly to the business model, and a host of other factors will play crucial roles. However, our data do indicate that an innovative undertaking with a coach who is experienced, who has the know-who available to complement his or her own deep smarts, and who can tweak the team into alignment on strategic and managerial issues will have a strong advantage over a coach-less enterprise.

Who Should Be a Knowledge Coach?

The answer would seem to be: almost everyone. Even apprentices can pass along what they know—and they will further cultivate their own deep smarts as they teach. Of course, apprentices need to be mindful of the limits of their own experience. As we saw in the case of incubators, relatively inexperienced coaches with an overweening (and unjustified) opinion of their own smarts can do damage. Consulting company SAIC prefers to link up people with less proximity on the expertise ladder, so as to avoid direct competition for knowledge. The analogy is skipping a generation: grandparents with grandchildren, rather than parents with children. Thus, SAIC matches retirees with managers, and top managers with novices. Other companies are experimenting with a different model: training an intermediary coach to facilitate knowledge transfer between the master and the relative novice.

We argue that knowledge coaching should be part of every manager's job—no matter where on the ladder of expertise that person sits relative to a specific task or role. There are many reasons.

All organizations need bench depth, that is, a clear line of possible successors for key positions. (In academia, we expect associate professors to coach assistant professors and assistant professors to coach doctoral students.) While leaders would emerge from any given employee population even without the attention to succession, it is wasteful to force them to learn by trial and error alone. Moreover, emerging leaders will have more reason to stay with the organization if they have role models they admire in the "tribe." The more that managers create a desirable tribe by linking employees to valued knowledge sources and then facilitating the transfer of that knowledge, the more likely it is that the employees will be motivated to identify with the organization and give their hearts as well as their brains to the endeavor.

How Should Coaches Coach?

Not everyone comes to the coaching role naturally. Nor is mere desire to coach sufficient. As organizations increasingly recognize the role of current leaders in developing the next generation, however, they may need to coach the coaches. As the chapters on experience and expertise suggest, coaches need to learn to calibrate knowledge gaps, recognize when protégés don't have receptors, and figure out how to create them. Then they need to build on those receptors through guided experience. But few experts really know *how* to guide the experience of protégés. Of the four types of guided experience, guided practice is the most familiar, and probably the easiest to institute. Athletic, music, and academic coaches commonly insist on monitoring practice sessions, and most of us have been exposed to this form of guided experience at some time in our lives.

Much less common, guided observation depends for its effectiveness on a coach's willingness not just to model the desired behavior, but to provide other models as well, then to offer feedback to the learner. We suggest that both kinds of guided observation (shadowing and challenging assumptions) as described in chapter 8, are vastly underutilized modes of obtaining deep smarts. Not only do protégés learn domain knowledge and expand their personal networks, but they also sharpen their observational skills.

Guided problem solving requires patience, and willingness to take some risks, for example, failing to arrive at a good solution. However, such highly interactive methods allow protégés to develop their own experience repertoires and know-how.

Guided experimentation is no less important than the other three types of guided experience. More than practice and observation (and in common with guided problem solving) guided experimentation demands an appreciation for the cognitive aspects of learning, the ability to frame hypotheses, and to see the world in terms of possibilities that can be tested. It is a more unusual—and valuable—coach who can provide this kind of direction. Experts trained in the sciences or engineering know how to conduct experiments. However, we have seen rigorous training lead some coaches to rule out "quick and dirty" experiments that can yield a lot of knowledge, or to unconsciously assume that only highly educated people can think in terms of hypotheses. Such assumptions are barriers to guiding experimentation.

So knowledge coaching is a demanding task. It is also highly rewarding, and some individuals near the end of their own careers gravitate naturally toward sharing their dearly bought wisdom. But what organizations can afford to rely solely on such people and such timing to cultivate and share deep smarts? Organizations today have no such option. Managers must not only cultivate deep smarts in those moving up the ladder, they must also develop the skills of the knowledge coaches themselves in the art and science of transferring their own deep smarts. This task requires leadership and foresight, because as we have seen, there are no quick fixes. All managers need to think of themselves as knowledge coaches, to identify employees with deep smarts that are indispensable to current and future operations, to plan programs of knowledge transfer, and to raise the general organizational level of sophistication about how deep smarts develop. One first step is to design projects to deliver dual outcomes.

Designing Projects for Dual Purpose

In the mid 1980s, when costs were being cut elsewhere in the company, GE's CEO, Jack Welch, spent $45 million on new buildings and improvements at what was destined to become one of the most admired and imitated corporate education centers in the world at Crotonville, New York. Tichy and Sherman noted that he "saw Crotonville as a laboratory to create a new kind of management, and a place to produce new ideas. He wanted 'action learning' based on solving real, pending business problems." They also wrote about how the education was designed:

> *Adults learn best in conditions of moderate stress, so conflict and discomfort are essential parts of the process. . . . The trick is putting participants to work on real business issues, with measurable results. . . . The teamwork aspect of this training is not just fun and games: Participants feel that if their team's proposals stink, the career of every member might be hurt. So people learn to work together—some for the first time in their lives. . . . Properly run, such workshops can serve usefully as miniature corporate think tanks.[9]*

As we discussed in chapter 2 on experience and again in chapters 7 and 8 on the transfer of knowledge, managers can design organizational projects for learning, and educational programs for output. The two objectives—learn and produce a useful innovation in the same project—are not incompatible.[10] If we are to develop deep smarts within our organizations, we will need explicit dual objectives for almost every one of our projects—and dual performance criteria for our experienced managers: perform your job well and guide the experience of others. If we think of coaching as a separate activity, conducted in lengthy individual meetings without near-term output, we will never find the time or develop the incentives to support it adequately. In contrast, if we build coaching into every activity jointly undertaken by novices and people higher up the ladder of expertise, it need take only a bit more attention for the project to contribute to the deep smarts of all involved.

Deep Smarts: Implications for Your Career Planning

We turn now to consider how we as individuals can build deep smarts in our careers. At many points in our lives, we are confronted with our own knowledge gaps. Some occur early enough in our lives or are sufficiently noncritical that we can afford the inefficient mode of trial and error learning. Others can be bridged with formal education. The ones that interest us here are gaps in complex, practice-based knowledge—usually with tacit dimensions and especially in management. Generic examples include leadership, entrepreneuring, intrapreneuring, and selling. But of course there are also much more specialized gaps when we take over a new position, move to a new location, or are asked by our organization to absorb as much as we can from someone about to retire.

Acknowledging the Gap

The first step to filling a knowledge gap is to recognize that there is one. Recently in a large company, the senior vice president for strategy, John K., invited a young man who wanted to join his staff in for a talk.

"So, Kent," he asked after the new hire was seated comfortably, "what is your ultimate goal? What kind of job are you preparing for?"

"I want to run a company," Kent replied. John thought a moment about Kent's experience to date: two years at an investment bank; an M.B.A. from a top business school; a year as a controller in a start-up; a year at a large retail and consumer goods company, working as a financial analyst.

"What do you think you need in the way of experience to prepare you for that?" he asked.

"I'm ready now," said Kent.

The names are disguised, but the conversation took place as re
ported. Many thoughts flew through John's head as he considered
how to respond to this simultaneously arrogant and ignorant statement. Kent clearly had no idea how much he did not know—about
sales and marketing, about manufacturing, about working with
customers, about creating alliances . . . the list was almost endless.
His work experience was entirely within finance and in staff positions. Kent was smart; he could learn quickly; he was clearly ambitious. But what experience would be best for him—and how could
John persuade Kent to work in a line position? Working on strategy
would not be the best experience, John was sure. He needed to convince Kent to work in sales or operations, where he would have
some profit and loss responsibility. Persuading Kent would likely be
difficult, as a position in strategy would be closer to the top of the
organization and would involve more of the kind of analysis with
which he was comfortable. A line position would take Kent out of
his comfort zone—which is where he would learn the most.

John delayed further conversation until he could reflect on Kent's
response and then decided to set a small test: suggest a position in
line operations and explain why that experience would be valuable.
If Kent were willing to gain necessary experience through such an
intermediate step, John would take him on as a protégé. If Kent
refused, John would not take the time. Kent flunked the test—and
unwittingly missed a tremendous opportunity.

We may fall into the trap of not acknowledging our need and
willingness to learn more out of insecurity than arrogance. One of
the entrepreneurs in our study, asked what he would do differently
if he could go back and start over, said that he would do a better job
of communicating with his board. "I was very focused on trying
to build a company from scratch and have something to show, versus really working with them. I think I probably should have approached them more from 'help me' rather than 'here's what I'm
doing,' which is a mistake that a lot of first-time CEOs probably
make. You're trying to impress the board and show them that you
can accomplish things."

What these examples show is the need to acknowledge one's ignorance, then to be an active learner, receptive to new opportunities and to feedback—even if it isn't what you would like to hear.

Creating Receptors

One of the perils of living in a world measured in thirty-second intervals is that we may be too impatient or feel unable to take the time to do our homework, that is, to create receptors in preparation for knowledge transfer. A software engineering manager we know volunteered for a job originally assigned to another when he first joined the firm in order to get a quick overview of the highly complex proprietary software system that comprised the company's product. Although he would not be responsible for hardware, he hooked up the dozens of new computers that were set up as a test array, because working through the multitude of physical connections gave him a speaking acquaintance with the component parts, including hardware, software, and firmware modules. This knowledge certainly didn't create deep smarts, but it provided him with the vocabulary to ask intelligent questions as he dove into the intricacies of the software.

When we go into a new situation, we can benefit enormously by investing in learning some vocabulary, a framework, a perspective from which to build. The same holds true for meeting with someone who could advance our career. Doing our homework before we meet with someone (it's easy today to "Google" the person) not only allows us to gain more from the interaction but also motivates the expert to take us seriously.

But building receptors goes beyond creating knowledge frameworks. As the term suggests, an important part of building receptors is being open—receptive—to new knowledge. Too often we have seen colleagues approach new learning situations with an "attitude"—that there is nothing *this* guy can teach them. But when receptivity becomes a proactive *search* for new learning opportunities, or when we use our know-who to build our experience repertoires, then we are truly in a position to develop deep smarts.

Designing an Experience Repertoire

Personal capabilities dictate whether one prefers to build a deep and narrow experience base or a broad one. Many of us will "morph" our way through life on a crooked path to deep smarts. Obviously, we do not want to flit from job to job, or to invest in such a wide range of experiences that we never develop deep smarts of any kind, but remain forever a dilettante. However, as the old model of working at one organization for most of your life gives way to multiple jobs and even a couple of different careers, you have to take charge of your own experience building. If your aim is to be a general manager, you need exposure to different functions within the organization and usually international experience as well. For example, a manager in product development was offered the choice of a promotion within the development function or a lateral move into product management. The latter position, she knew, would force her to learn much more about marketing and customer relations. Although the switch would mean an intensive first few months as she learned, she knew the investment was likely to pay off in a better position later. Similarly, we know an individual who left a good job in a pharmaceutical company to get training and experience with software in another industry. She was then able to return to pharmaceuticals managing an information technology group.

Building Know-who

Know-who, as we have seen, is an element of deep smarts, and for those who need to access the deep smarts of others, know-who provides a path to that knowledge. We all know the value of being "well-connected," but that is not really what we mean by building know-who. The people in your network who have knowledge and enjoy building and sharing it are rich resources to you—and you to them. Being less knowledgeable on a given topic than someone with deep smarts does not mean that you have nothing to contribute in a different domain. Most deeply smart people understand that sharing knowledge, unlike spending money, does not impoverish their own knowledge bank account. In fact, sharing usually results in receiving a knowledge deposit—often unexpectedly.

PROVIDE VALUE. Accomplished networkers work hard to develop their social capital by providing value to acquaintances. If you build relationships with the expectation of reciprocity, that is, to deliver as well as receive knowledge, creating know-who is a win for both sides. One of the best networkers we know interacts with acquaintances an average of a dozen times a day—using multiple media. Most of his e-mails have pointers to information he believes they would find interesting. He keeps the missives short, so that they don't constitute a drain on the receiver's system, but tries always to provide value. As a consequence, he has an extremely wide range of know-who. Nor is he shy about approaching authors and speakers whom he does not know personally—but if he requests information, the request is very specific so that it can be readily answered.

Heidi Roizen understands the importance of providing value—but also of receiving value in return: "There has to be a balance in every relationship. . . . So you have to make sure that your request is really important to you *and* that it has some opportunity to carry a payback with it—either in the request itself or in the promise of a future exchange."[11]

BURN NO BRIDGES. Usually some of the closest linkages are those forged in working together. A middle manager we know was treated oddly at his company. On Friday, his boss gave him a bonus and a handshake, complimenting him on his superb work on a new product release. On the following Monday, he was called into the boss's office and fired. He was told that the job requirements had changed and he was no longer needed; he had two hours to leave. In apparent concern about the manager's potential reaction to this treatment, the boss had invited the vice president of human resources to be present at the firing. Both were nonplussed when the manager took the news calmly and without visible rancor. The vice president of HR later commented on his professionalism and the manager replied, "You only work with a few people in your life; there is no reason to leave in anger." The manager explained that he did not believe in burning bridges with coworkers, no matter how he felt about his treatment by the company. This personal policy has stood him in good stead. He has always been able to reach back into prior workplaces for knowledge.

Alumni networks from prior jobs can be very helpful. In our study, we were struck by how many times entrepreneurs and investors tapped into their working past to locate talent and knowledge. Some companies appear better than others at encouraging this. (One doubts that the company just described has loyal alumni!) In our entrepreneurship study, for example, Hewlett-Packard in particular kept appearing in the job histories of our respondents who had strong know-who—including individuals interviewed in Asia.

Understanding the Influence of Reference Groups

As we saw in chapter 6, social influences are very powerful in shaping what we know and how we evaluate that knowledge. Compliance with superior power or conformity to the herd certainly influences our behavior and sometimes our more superficial beliefs. But our tribes are a major source of influence, affecting how we view our selves, our work, our relationships. What sets this type of influence apart from compliance and conformity is that we are often unaware of how profoundly and unconsciously we accept as our own the beliefs of those we like and admire. When that influence goads us to achieve, to innovate, to succeed, we speak of role models. When it distorts our central beliefs and moves us to behave immorally or unethically, we cry brainwashing. In either case, it pays to acknowledge the power of the influence. We may want to believe that we are independent thinkers, uninfluenced by people we admire. Dream away! A few revolutionaries throughout history have challenged the beliefs of those around them, but the Martin Luther King Jrs and Gandhis of the world are rare. The act of building our experience base will invariably expose us to different reference groups, and we can pause to consider how their influence can drive our beliefs and behavior.

Examining Assumptions and Belief Systems

Our beliefs, as we saw in chapter 5, can blind us to options. A vice president of sales in a software development company was called to task by the engineering group for continually promising customers more than engineering could deliver. His defense was that the company was small and they could not afford to say no to any customer's request. He believed, in short, that his choices were limited to yes or no, and he acted in accordance with that belief. He never considered that there were alternatives, such as spacing out responses to customer requests, bundling them into feature sets for sequential releases, or evaluating them for their potential profitability and/or fit with the product line strategy. The consequence was an engineering group constantly in a state of crisis.

For the health of the organization, it is important that individuals be able to challenge each other's assumptions and beliefs. Impersonal debate is healthy. We see dysfunctional groups and whole organizations whose members do not know how to challenge each other and do not value questioning assumptions. Promoting varied perspectives and encouraging dissent in groups rests with the leaders of those groups, who must first recognize the value of creative abrasion, model it themselves, and reward group members who display it. The resulting smarts will be deepened, not just reinforced.

Choosing Coaches

As noted in chapter 7 on knowledge transfer, the best relationships are born of mutual selection. While coaches are looking for protégés who are "teachable," those being coached look for someone with the ability and motivation to teach as well as a strong knowledge network. The history of *appointed* coaches is not promising. A new college graduate joining a large consulting firm was assigned a mentor—who never spent any time with her. Lacking any direct incentive to do so, the "mentor" apparently saw no benefit in coaching. In contrast, consider the experience of Charlene Begley, who joined GE in 1988 and became the first female CEO of a major GE unit in 2003. Her coach and champion, David L. Calhoun, recognized her talent early when she worked for him on the audit staff. "She looked like a person with massive potential who just needed the right assignments," Calhoun said. He proceeded to give her "stretch" assignments that involved a lot of personal sacrifice (including moving her family twenty times). But as she succeeded time after time, she moved up the ranks—even when she often did not feel ready for the next promotion.[12] It is not clear how much personal coaching Calhoun gave her, but he clearly understood the value of building an experience repertoire.

COVER THE NECESSARY EXPERIENCE REPERTOIRE. When you are trying to learn a skill that involves judgment, a knowledge coach with an extensive experience repertoire will be most helpful. The reason is that, as we discussed in chapters 2 and 3, experience builds pattern recognition, and therefore limited experience results in a smaller set of known options for responding to a situation. However, it is unlikely that any one coach can cover all the situations and perspectives that you may need to fill a given knowledge gap. In our study of start-ups, a small number of the entrepreneurs recognized very early that they needed coaches with complementary deep smarts.

In one company, for example, the entrepreneur went to one coach for tricky personnel issues and day-to-day operations, and to another for issues dealing with strategy and the business. As she characterized the two coaches:

> [D] is highly oriented to production, sourcing, inventory management controls, just old school. I mean, you could just see him in a factory in the sixties where he used to be with inventory cards in his back pocket . . . so different from [E]. . . . [E]'s much more oriented towards the capitalization of the company, where we're going, building shareholder value and managing the board . . .

much more oriented at the front end of the value chain and [D]
very much on the back. So that's why it works so well for us.

SEEK RICH LEARNING EXPERIENCES. As discussed in chapters 7 and 8, there is a huge difference in trying to learn from directives from a coach and being guided through experiences. Coaches are not always aware themselves of that difference—so you may have to push for learning beyond that gained in chats. For example, you have a good argument for sitting in on critical meetings if you can make the guided observation serve a second purpose (perhaps a written report on what transpired in a meeting) or at least not reduce your performance in another area. Small projects are an ideal way to learn through guided experience—but you may have to ask not only for the experience but also for the feedback. Moreover, coaches may not always understand the difference between a guided experiment (where the outcome is not determined) and a demonstration (where it is)—but we trust that you do. Be sure you set the right expectations for any experiment you undertake—that it is an opportunity for learning, and that the outcome may not necessarily be expected or even welcomed!

Morphing

We are best able to develop deep smarts when there is a good match between our own skills and attitudes, and the demands of our jobs or professions. In such cases, we have receptors; we are motivated to add to our experience repertoires; we are open to coaching. However, we work in environments that are constantly, sometimes radically, changing. Individuals, like organizations, adapt to new realities by morphing—taking on different identities at different times. One of the most personal elements of deep smarts (as we pointed out in a different context in chapter 5) is the knowledge that forms our identity, our conception of self. Individual identity is built up over time along with our deep smarts as we gain experience-based knowledge. Some individuals know from early childhood who they wish to be, and with single-minded devotion go straight for the target. (Of course, the path may seem clear at first, until greater maturity or changed circumstances prove the original plans to be flawed.)

But for individuals blessed with many talents, extensive networks, and abundant resources, there are so many possible selves that they need to plunge deeply into one persona or profession to find out if there is a match. If there is a mismatch with a particular position, they move on to try another and perhaps yet another. With each foray, they test the match between the demands and rewards of the job and their own skills, preferences, and beliefs. With each experience, they further deepen their own experience base, growing and changing—morphing—who they are. If as a result of this growth and change process, they still do not mesh well with their new situation, they move on to the next one. We know a former bank vice president who left that position to be a professional golfer for a year before moving on to yet a different (and much more satisfying) position coaching in an executive search firm. He was unhappy with the bank job, found he was not sufficiently skilled to make a career on the pro golf tour, but discovered he had coaching talents, which he developed teaching novice golfers; then he found a match in a position that utilized those talents.

Herminia Ibarra, who has studied people making major work changes in their lives, writes that successful career changers all used what she calls this "test and learn" model: "[T]he only way to create change is by putting our possible identities into practice, working and crafting them until they are sufficiently grounded in experience to guide more decisive steps."[13] Some find out that a given identity is uncomfortable and voluntarily leave it to resume the search; some get fired or are otherwise shocked out of a poor fit. Morphing is inefficient, for sure, but it is unavoidable in conditions of extreme uncertainty. One has to dive into the chosen identity and learn enough to move on to the next trial, but if this focused commitment of resources turns out to be ill spent, one can only move on to another commitment of time and effort to explore another possibility. Sofia Coppola, who at thirty-two became a highly successful film director with *Lost in Translation*, recalls of her mid-twenties that she was trying to run a T-shirt business while doing photography on the side. "I was frustrated that I wasn't great at one thing. It was the typical thing of trying to figure out what kind of person I was going to be." [14] As Ibarra's research shows, this "crooked path" to a new identity, which appears to be "a mysterious, road-to-Damascus process," is actually learning-by-doing through sequential experimental forays to test different possible selves. And one hopes to deepen one's smarts with each foray—Ms. Coppola doubtless learned much about filmmaking in her photography work, if not in the T-shirt business.

Unsuccessful career changers tend instead to endlessly diagnose, analyze, and reflect in order to figure out the next move. But they lack the knowledge to make an informed choice. Ibarra writes, "We learn who we are—in practice, not in theory—by testing reality . . . by *doing*. . . ."[15] Even the diagnostic tests developed for people looking for the right match can't tell them if they will really like a particular job and identity. For an individual undergoing morphing, the feedback that determines when there is a fit with an identity and when it is time to try something new may come from others, but it most likely comes from their own experience during the morphing.

Coaches can similarly help individuals through their career morphing, although Ibarra cautions would-be career shifters against those coaches who look at a person's track record to determine the future. Headhunters, for example, have trouble seeing radically new applications for a person's skills set; even friends and family may not be good coaches if they have a fixed idea of a person's abilities. Such lack of imagination is one reason that individuals are urged to action rather than just reflection—to gain some experience by assuming the desired identity for a while as an experiment.

Conclusion

What we know is a marvelous, complex aggregation of our formal training, what we have learned on the streets of life, combined with less formal mentoring and coaching, and tempered by more subjective elements—our beliefs and social influences. Our education and professional training give us our credentials, our legitimacy, and a good chunk of our smarts. For most of us, however, what we learn when we don't realize we are learning is at least as critical. The activities and decisions—large and small, planned and serendipitous—of an entire life build deep smarts. Some of those decisions are obviously important: where we go to school, our choice of career, moving our family to take a new position. But seemingly incidental or even trivial decisions can aggregate to make large differences in whether and how we progress up the ladder of expertise: the way we approach a project, the e-mail to a colleague to strengthen a weak tie, what we choose to observe on a trip. We develop much of who we are and what we are able to do outside of the formal choices—in how we think about daily routines, in how actively we learn, in how we tap into the expertise of those higher on the ladder.

Mentors help. But knowledge *coaches* can help even more. More than giving moral support, explaining the organizational "ropes," or even assigning select positions, knowledge coaches help their protégés recreate—through guided experience—the deep smarts (including tacit knowledge) that have bestowed on the coaches their right to teach. Why recreate rather than just transfer knowledge? Because today is not exactly like yesterday, and the current situation is inevitably a bit different from the one the coach experienced. Some of the coach's deep smarts apply directly. Some need to be adapted. In the act of recreation, protégés sift through these options and figure out for themselves what applies. They will make some mistakes—reject wisdom in favor of expediency. But a wise knowledge coach will prepare for that and allow some room for learning through experimentation.

We are all bombarded constantly by what others think. We cannot wholly escape the sculpting of our own knowledge by the currents around us any more than a rock can avoid being shaped by the river it lies in. But we are sentient, purposeful creatures. With effort, we can recognize the influences when we are being swept up in a herd and make the decision to resist. We can choose our role models and carefully assess what knowledge is needed, what parts are transferable, and which are not. We can, in short, decide for ourselves what we accept as part of our own deep smarts.

So learning—developing smarts—is not entirely a formal or always a deliberate process. We might wish it were, because our lives are so complex, so hurried, so filled with social connections that it would be easier if we could gain all we need through formal instruction in classrooms or in online courses. These are tremendously valuable, of course. But what we suggest in this volume is that our deep smarts develop continuously—at work, in leisure, at cocktail hours, and in morning meetings. We can be more mindful of how experience repertoires build, of assumptions and beliefs posing as unquestioned truth, of the power of apprenticeships. The more consciously we design our own experience and that of those individuals we can help move up the ladder of expertise, the deeper the resulting smarts.

The Entrepreneurship Study

IN 2000, we began a study of start-up companies in Silicon Valley. We were particularly interested in how knowledge was transmitted to founders of new companies from experienced coaches: venture capitalists; "mentor capitalists," or cashed-out entrepreneurs who invested time and money working with start-ups; and managers of incubators. Eventually, the study expanded to Boston (where many of the incubators were found), India, and East Asia (Singapore and Hong Kong). After the collapse of the dot-com boom, we decided to reinterview each of our respondents. These interviews took place mostly in 2001; a few were conducted in early 2002. We thus have a sort of naturally occurring experiment, a "before-and-after" investigation of entrepreneuring and coaching during and after an extraordinary time in U.S.—and world—business.

The Companies

Our sample of companies included nine that were mentored by venture capitalists (six in the United States, one in India, one in Singapore, and one in Hong Kong); eighteen by mentor capitalists (ten in the United States, seven in India, one in Singapore); and eight by incubators (six in the United States and two in Hong Kong).

Of the thirty-five companies, four were given extra attention. Collabrys (coached by two venture capitalists) and ActivePhoto (coached by two mentor capitalists) were studied longitudinally. We conducted multiple interviews over a two-year period and sat in on numerous board meetings. In both cases, we were literally in at the beginning, as the two companies had only recently begun their entrepreneurial journeys. Two other companies, Zaplet (mentored by a venture capitalist) and XMarksTheSpot (coached by a mentor capitalist) were subjects of Harvard Business School cases. A final company, incubator Garage.com, though not included in our sample of thirty-five companies, was also the subject of an HBS case in order to give us some deeper insight into the incubator phenomenon.

Finally, thirty-four "informants" were interviewed. Most of these were senior venture capitalists and entrepreneurs who could provide particular insights and perspectives on entrepreneurial activity in the United States and abroad.

Procedure

The two of us conducted most of the interviews in person, although a number of the follow-up interviews took place by telephone. The Boston incubator interviews were all conducted by our research associate, Brian DeLacey (assisted by Mimi Shields, Allison Nicolle, and Michael Restivo). In some companies, a single founder and a single coach were interviewed. In others, we interviewed multiple founders and/or multiple coaches. Most interviews lasted between forty-five minutes and an hour and a half. All were recorded, with the permission of the interviewee. Most were transcribed; the rest were typed up as detailed notes. Transcriptions and notes were coded and entered into a database, from which reports were subsequently drawn.

In the follow-up interviews, we solicited résumés and included a number of standardized questions to assess experience, success, and alignment between coach and protégé. We subsequently performed a number of statistical analyses, such as examining the relationship between perceived success and alignment.

Coaches answered six questions:

1. What percentage of the companies you have ever mentored would fall into the following categories: ("Failure," "Somewhat successful," "Moderately successful," "Extremely successful")

2. Compared to your expectations for the company a year ago, how well has it done? (7-point scale ranging from "Fell far below expectations" to "Far exceeded expectations")

3. Compared to all the other companies you have ever coached, how well has the company done? (7-point scale ranging from "Very unsuccessful" to "Very successful")

4. Compared to other Silicon Valley [or Asian] start-ups over the past three years, how successful would you say the company has been? (7-point scale ranging from "Very unsuccessful" to "Very successful")

5. How would you characterize the degree of alignment between your view and that of [the protégé] regarding business strategy? (7-point scale ranging from "Very misaligned" to "Perfect alignment")

6. How would you characterize the degree of alignment between your view and that of [the protégé] regarding company management? (same 7-point scale as #5)

Entrepreneurs answered six questions:

1. Compared to your expectations for your company a year ago, how well has it done? (7-point scale ranging from "Fell far below expectations" to "Far exceeded expectations")

2. Compared to other Silicon Valley [Asian] start-ups over the past three years, how successful would you say your company

has been? (7-point scale ranging from "Fell far below expectations" to "Far exceeded expectations")

3. Same as #5 in the preceding list.

4. Same as #6 in the preceding list.

5. Indicate on an arrow with labels "Novice (Beginner)," "Apprentice (Intermediate)," "Journeyman (Advanced)," and "Master (Virtuoso)" where you would have put yourself a year ago and now.

6. Rate the percentage of the entrepreneuring knowledge you relied on to lead and run the company (not industry or technical knowledge) that came from various sources: "My own knowledge, experience, and education," "The contributions of the primary coach," "The contributions of other coaches," "The contributions of others in the company," "The contributions of peers, friends, etc., outside the company," and "Other." The respondent was asked to distribute the 100 percent among these sources for two different points in time—when the company was started and at present.

Chapter 1

1. Peter F. Drucker, *Managing for Results: Economic Tasks and Risk-Taking Decisions* (New York: Harper & Row, 1964), 5.

2. We thus focus on a *subset* of the topic of knowledge; in our personal library alone, several bookshelves are lined with excellent works on knowledge. We have not the space to list all those authors here, and for that we beg pardon of them, and of our readers.

3. Malik Om, "Why Vinod Khosla May Be the Best Venture Capitalist on the Planet," *Red Herring*, 13 February 2001, 43.

4. Moreover, we recognize that experts function in a social milieu and that their expertise is usually grounded in real-world practice. Therefore, while we draw heavily upon the research of cognitive scientists in defining expertise and distinguishing experts from novices, our concept of expertise is also grounded in the work of social scientists who have written about social practice and the knowledge that accumulates in workplaces. See, for example, Jean Lave and Etienne Wenger, *Situated Learning—Legitimate Peripheral Participation* (Cambridge, UK: Cambridge University Press, 1991) and John Seely Brown and Paul Duguid, *The Social Life of Information* (Boston: Harvard Business School Press, 2002).

5. Dorothy Leonard and Walter Swap, "Gurus in the Garage," *Harvard Business Review*, November–December 2000, 71–82.

Chapter 2

1. In medicine, as in many other fields, experience is generally associated positively with performance. However, recent research has demonstrated the significant variance in the learning curve slopes of different individuals and teams—that is, that different teams learn a new procedure at different rates. See Gary Pisano, Richard Bohmer, and Amy Edmondson, "Organizational Differences in Rates of Learning:

Evidence from the Adoption of Minimally Invasive Cardiac Surgery," *Management Science* 47, no. 6 (2001): 752–768.

2. David DeLong, *Lost Knowledge: Confronting the Threat of an Aging Workforce* (New York: Oxford University Press, 2004).

3. All quotes are from Dorothy Leonard and Melissa Dailey, "Retirement at JPL," Video Case 603-082 (Boston: Harvard Business School, 2002).

4. Corey Dade, "The Experience of Loss: City Offer Thins Ranks," *Boston Globe*, 24 June 2003, B1, B8.

5. For an explanation of how personal experience builds episodic memory and then may be abstracted into procedural memory and used in performance, see Robert J. Sternberg et al., *Practical Intelligence in Everyday Life* (Cambridge, UK: Cambridge University Press, 2000).

6. Unless otherwise indicated, direct quotations are taken from interviews conducted by the authors and/or research assistants and are published with permission from those quoted.

7. Not all experience repertoires are bell shaped, with rare events lying at the two tails. Some distributions are unidimensional—for example, if the experience variable for a pilot is "air turbulence," the most common occurrences would be "little or no turbulence," and "catastrophic turbulence" would be at the one tail. The resulting experience distribution would be half of a bell curve.

8. Some specialists avoid the tails deliberately—for example, the hospital that specializes in routine hernia operations and avoids any unusual cases.

9. Atul Gawande, "The Learning Curve," *The New Yorker*, 28 January 2002, 55–56.

10. John Strege, *Tiger: A Biography of Tiger Woods* (New York: Broadway Books, 1997), 14.

11. John D. Bransford, Ann L. Brown, and Rodney R. Cocking, eds., *How People Learn: Brain, Mind, Experience, and School* (Washington, DC: National Academy Press, National Research Council Commission on Behavioral and Social Sciences and Education, 2000), 125.

12. As we will discuss in subsequent chapters, the slope of the much-researched learning curve differs among individuals, groups, and organizations, depending in large part upon the dedication to learning from repetition—and the strategy for doing so. See Pisano, Bohmer, and Edmondson, "Organizational Differences in Rates of Learning," for an in-depth example of different learning curve slopes among medical teams all implementing the same surgical innovation.

13. Bransford et al., *How People Learn*, 126.

14. Walter Swap et al., "Using Mentoring and Storytelling to Transfer Knowledge in the Workplace," *Journal of Management Information Systems* 18, no. 1 (2001), 95–114.

15. Extensive research in education has demonstrated that how well and how quickly people learn depends on what they already know. See Bransford et al., *How People Learn*.

16. Isabel Gauthier et al., "Activation of the Middle Fusiform 'Face Area' Increases with Expertise in Recognizing Novel Objects," *Nature Neuroscience* 2, no. 6 (1999): 568–573.

17. A rather formal definition of a simulation is Thomke's: "the representation of selected characteristics of the behavior of one physical or abstract system by another system." Stefan Thomke, *Experimentation Matters: Unlocking the Potential of New Technologies for Innovation* (Boston: Harvard Business School Press, 2002), 58.

18. Dorothy Leonard, Brian DeLacey, and Melissa Dailey, "Best Buy Co. Inc. (A): An Innovator's Journey," Case 604-043 (Boston: Harvard Business School, 2003).

19. Beth Greenberg, "War Games: Hollywood Helps with Training," *Boston Globe*, 22 April 2003, F13.

20. Ibid.

21. Tamara Chuang, "Virtual War Turns Real: Quicksilver Software Develops War Game Exclusively for U.S. Army Use," *Orange County Register*, 7 May 2003.

22. James J. L'Allier, "The Value of Performance Simulations," *Chief Learning Officer*, May 2003. Available on the Web at <http://www.clomedia.com/content/templates/ clo_feature.asp?articleid=163&zoneid=29> (accessed 14 December, 2003).

23. Sandra Ervin, "Urban Warfare Simulation Helps Train Company Commanders," *National Defense Magazine*, February 2003.

24. Jim Dwyer, "With the 101st Airborne, in Central Iraq, March 27," *New York Times*, 28 March 2003, 1.

25. C. Shawn Green and Daphne Bavelier, "Action Video Game Modifies Visual Selective Attention," *Nature* 423 (29 May 2003): 534–537.

26. Mary E. Ballard and J. Rose Wiest, "Mortal Kombat™: The Effects of Violent Video Game Play on Males' Hostility and Cardiovascular Responding," *Journal of Applied Social Psychology* 26 (1996), 717–730.

27. Arlene Dohm, "Gauging the Labor Force Effects of Retiring Baby-Boomers," *Monthly Labor Review*, July 2000, 24: "Among the broad occupational groups, the executive, administrative and managerial occupations will experience the greatest turnover. Those 45 and older make up 41 percent of this group, and 42 percent of these older workers are expected to leave by 2008. That is equal to nearly 3 million job openings in this field due to retirements, resulting in a significant loss of managerial skills and experience."

Chapter 3

1. K. Anders Ericsson, "The Acquisition of Expert Performance: An Introduction to Some of the Issues," in K. Anders Ericsson, ed., *The Road to Excellence: The Acquisition of Expert Performance in the Arts and Sciences, Sports, and Games* (Mahwah, NJ: Lawrence Erlbaum, 1996).

2. Herbert A. Simon and W. G. Chase, "Skill in Chess," *American Scientist* 61 (1973): 394–403.

3. For example, Scott Rozic's short-lived company, Verge, provided a central registration service where an Internet user could register for a variety of business-to-consumer Web sites, avoiding the hassle of having to sign in each time and remember multiple usernames or passwords. Verge compensated users financially each time they registered for a new site, and marketers paid the company for access to these new customers. But in the dot-com carnage of 2000, the Web sites disappeared faster than Verge could sign up consumers. Another start-up, Ziptran, funded and nurtured by

the Reach incubator in Boston, suffered a similar fate. Ziptran serviced business-to-business Internet companies by providing an electronic credit management system. When the Internet companies foundered, the market disappeared for these services and Ziptran shut its doors.

4. Not all of the entrepreneurs starting businesses at the turn of the century were as inexperienced as managers or entrepreneurs as our trio from Stanford, nor were all the coaches as expert as Gibbons and Krause. Two of the founders and both coaches had technical backgrounds, but the two founders were more expert in wireless technology. This is typical in many such relationships—the coach is more expert in one domain (entrepreneurship), while the protégé also has something to teach the teacher (although this is usually of secondary importance). In our study of entrepreneurship there was a wide distribution along the ladder of expertise (see chapter 1) for both entrepreneurs and coaches and, consequently, greater or lesser "spreads" between their levels of expertise. In our study, ten of the forty-two entrepreneurs (some of the thirty-five companies we interviewed had multiple founders) had founded at least one company before, one had started three, and the most experienced had been a founder of four companies. A number of the entrepreneurs were actively involved in coaching founders even less expert than themselves. Similarly, not all of the coaches in our sample could be considered experts. While some had spent their entire professional lives as entrepreneurs and coaches, others could claim little more expertise in entrepreneurship than those they were coaching.

5. Ericsson, "The Acquisition of Expert Performance," 17.

6. Ericsson, "The Acquisition of Expert Performance," 14.

7. Gary Klein, *Sources of Power* (Cambridge, MA: MIT Press, 1998), 17.

8. Kim J. Vicente and JoAnne H. Want, "An Ecological Theory of Expertise Effects in Memory Recall," *Psychological Review* 105, no. 1 (1998): 48.

9. The ability of experts to extrapolate is bounded, however. Research on the ability of experienced scientists and their ability to create research designs showed that they could do so only in relatively familiar areas. See Jan Maarten Schraagen, "How Experts Solve a Novel Problem in Experimental Design," *Cognitive Science* 17 (1993): 285–309.

10. Judy Foreman, "A Conversation with Paul Ekman: The 43 Facial Muscles That Reveal Even the Most Fleeting Emotions," *New York Times*, 5 August 2003, D5.

11. Hubert L. Dreyfus and Stuart E. Dreyfus, *Mind over Machine* (New York: The Free Press, 1986), 35–36.

12. Simon and Chase, "Skill in Chess," 394–403.

13. H. B. Richman et al., "Perceptual and Memory Processes in the Acquisition of Expert Performance: The EPAM Model," in Ericsson, "The Acquisition of Expert Performance."

14. Dreyfus and Dreyfus, *Mind over Machine*, 35–36.

15. Dorothy Leonard and Walter Swap, "The Value of 'Been There, Done That,' " in *Leading for Innovation and Organizing for Results*, eds. Frances Hesselbein, Marshall Goldsmith, and Iain Somerville (San Francisco: Jossey-Bass, 2001), 169.

16. Allan D. Rosenblatt and James T. Thickstun, "Intuition and Consciousness," *Psychoanalytic Quarterly* 63 (1994), 696–714.

17. Researchers have also found that people organize information into "chunks," in order to retain the information in short term memory. Chunks are "familiar patterns" that through experience come to be understood as a unit, and as learning continues, these units become increasingly larger and more interrelated. When new stimuli are related to this stored information and recognition of a pattern occurs, ideas and actions appropriate to the situation are elicited from memory. A related theory suggests that cognitive elements in working memory, long-term memory, and short-term memory are represented as nodes in a network. As a person gains more knowledge in an area and begins to make connections between abstract principles and actual events, links between nodes are created and strengthened. Experts' networks may be more efficient as a result of increased speed through network links. See Debra Hampton, "Expertise: The True Essence of Nursing Art," *Advances in Nursing Science*, 17, no. 1 (1994): 15–24.

18. Rosenblatt and Thickstun, "Intuition and Consciousness," 705.

19. Dorothy Leonard, *Wellsprings of Knowledge: Building and Sustaining the Sources of Innovation* (Boston: Harvard Business School Press, 1998).

20. Klein, *Sources of Power*, 32.

21. Klein, *Sources of Power*, 32–33.

22. Arthur S. Reber, "Implicit Learning and Tacit Knowledge," *Journal of Experimental Psychology* 118 (1989): 229.

23. Much depends, apparently, on whether the underlying structure is in fact readily accessible, as participants in the experiments deduced incorrect rules from their implicitly learned skills. "Looking for rules will not work if you cannot find them," Reber notes. Furthermore, explicit instructions apparently aid learning only insofar as they match the person's idiosyncratic implicit learning structure. Reber, "Implicit Learning and Tacit Knowledge," 223.

24. Richard E. Nisbett and Timothy DeCamp Wilson, "Telling More Than We Can Know: Verbal Reports on Mental Processes," *Psychological Review* 84 (1977): 231–259.

25. This and the following two brief quotes are from Sharon Begley, "Science's Big Query: What Can We Know, and What Can't We?" *The Wall Street Journal*, 30 May 2003, B1.

26. Tom Kelley, with Jonathan Littman, *The Art of Innovation* (New York: Random House, 2001), 181.

27. Susan Gilbert, "For Depression, the Family Doctor May Be the First Choice but Not the Best," *New York Times*, 24 June 2003, D5.

28. See, for example, Pete Yost, "Senate Report: Enron Board Ignored Evidence," Associated Press, 7 July 2002, <http://dukeemployees.com/deregulation1902.shtml#board> (accessed 19 December 2003).

29. The classic studies were conducted by Abraham S. Luchins, "Mechanization in Problem Solving," *Psychological Monographs* 54, whole no. 248 (1942). Luchins's subjects were given a series of problems requiring them to measure out a specific quantity of water using three jugs of different capacities. The first few problems all had to be solved in the same moderately complex way (e.g., fill Jug A twice and fill Jug C once and pour them into Jug B). After working on several such problems and developing a

"set," Luchins's subjects stayed with the complex formula even for problems that could be solved far more simply (e.g., by simply dipping a smaller jug from a filled larger jug).

30. Columbia Accident Investigation Board, *Final Report* (Washington, DC: Government Printing Office, 2003): 122.

31. Ibid., 130.

32. Ibid., 196.

Chapter 4

1. Rosabeth Moss Kanter, *When Giants Learn to Dance: Mastering the Challenges of Strategy, Management, and Careers in the 1990s* (New York: Simon & Schuster, 1989).

2. This extended in many cases to replacing the founder as CEO. See our discussion in chapter 7.

3. Dean Foust et al., "The Best Performers—Ouch," *BusinessWeek*, 24 March 2003.

4. See Andrew Hargadon, *How Breakthroughs Happen: The Surprising Truth About How Companies Innovate* (Boston: Harvard Business School Press, 2003), for a fascinating discussion of "technology brokering" by Edison and numerous more-modern examples.

5. Tom Kelley, with Jonathan Littman, *The Art of Innovation* (New York: Random House, 2001).

6. Dorothy Leonard and Walter Swap, *When Sparks Fly: Igniting Creativity in Groups* (Boston: Harvard Business School Press, 1999).

7. I. William Zartman, ed., *International Multilateral Negotiation: Approaches to the Management of Complexity* (San Francisco: Jossey-Bass, 1994).

8. Naomi Aoki, "The Crusader," *Boston Globe Sunday Magazine*, 25 May 2003.

9. See Leonard and Swap, *When Sparks Fly*, for a discussion of this example.

10. Christopher A. Bartlett and Afroze Mohammed, "3M Optical Systems: Managing Corporate Entrepreneurship," Case 395-017 (Boston: Harvard Business School, 1994).

11. Dorothy Leonard, Brian DeLacey, and Melissa Dailey, "Best Buy Co. Inc. (A): An Innovator's Journey," Case 604-043 (Boston: Harvard Business School, 2003).

12. Don Cohen and Laurence Prusak, *In Good Company: How Social Capital Makes Organizations Work* (Boston: Harvard Business School Press, 2001), 4.

13. Dorothy Leonard-Barton and Gary Pisano, "Monsanto's March into Biotechnology (A)," Case 690-009 (Boston: Harvard Business School, 1990, revised 27 January 1992), 3.

14. Dorothy Leonard and Walter Swap, "Gurus in the Garage," *Harvard Business Review*, November–December 2000, 71–82.

15. As we have written elsewhere (Leonard and Swap, "Gurus in the Garage"), a commons does not require direct reciprocity. Rather, members of the commons will

do favors for one another in the expectation that "bread cast upon the waters" will return in some form, from some member, at a future time.

16. Cohen and Prusak, *In Good Company*, 9.

17. Cohen and Prusak, *In Good Company*, 4.

18. Herminia Ibarra, "Homophily and Differential Returns: Sex Differences in Network Structure and Access in an Advertising Firm," *Administrative Science Quarterly* 37, no. 3 (1992): 422–447; and Herminia Ibarra, "Personal Networks of Women and Minorities in Management: A Conceptual Framework," *Academy of Management Review* 18, no. 1 (1993): 56–87.

19. Rob Cross, Wayne Baker, and Andrew Parker, "What Creates Energy in Organizations?" *MIT Sloan Management Review* 44, no. 4 (2003): 53.

Chapter 5

1. Amy Waldman, "Guilty or Not, U.S. Is Blamed in Mosque Blast," *New York Times*, 2 July 2003, A10.

2. In fact, of course, many for-profit and nonprofit organizations have proven that they can work together collaboratively for the benefit of both. James E. Austin, *The Collaboration Challenge: How Nonprofits and Businesses Succeed Through Strategic Alliances* (San Francisco: Jossey-Bass, 2000).

3. Stefan Thomke, *Experimentation Matters: Unlocking the Potential of New Technologies for Innovation* (Boston: Harvard Business School Press, 2003), 194. See also Stefan Thomke and Ashok Nimgade, "BMW AG: The Digital Car Project (A)," Case 699-044 (Boston: Harvard Business School, 2001).

4. The following illustration draws heavily upon the work of Professor Mary Tripsas. Mary Tripsas and Giovanni Gavetti, "Capabilities, Cognition, and Inertia: Evidence from Digital Imaging," *Strategic Management Journal* 21 (2000): 1147–1161.

5. Ibid., 1150.

6. Ibid., 1151.

7. Ibid., 1155.

8. Clayton Christensen, *The Innovator's Dilemma: When New Technologies Cause Great Firms to Fail* (Boston: Harvard Business School Press, 2003).

9. Joseph E. Stiglitz, *Globalization and Its Discontents* (New York: Norton, 2002).

10. Tarun Khanna and Krishna Palepu, "Why Focused Strategies May Be Wrong for Emerging Markets," *Harvard Business Review*, July–August 1997, 41.

11. In her comparative analysis of Silicon Valley and Boston's Route 128, AnnaLee Saxenian proposed that the spirit of creativity and entrepreneurship in Silicon Valley traces its roots to Lewis Terman's efforts to encourage cooperation between Stanford University and area businesses. Then Fairchild Semiconductor began incubating high-level entrepreneurs such as Andrew Grove, Gordon Moore, and Robert Noyce, who, along with their direct descendents of "Fairchildren," seeded many of the new high-tech start-ups in the 1960s and 1970s. AnnaLee Saxenian, *Regional Advantage: Culture and Competition in Silicon Valley and Route 128* (Cambridge, MA: Harvard University Press, 1994).

12. Paul A. Gompers and Josh Lerner, *The Money of Invention: How Venture Capital Creates New Wealth* (Boston: Harvard Business School Press, 2001), 73.

13. John Hechinger, "Stay in Your Dorm and Score 'Dough for your Dotcom,'" *The Wall Street Journal*, 20 April 2000, A1.

14. Dorothy Leonard and George Thill, "Hewlett-Packard: Singapore (A)," Case 694-035 (Boston: Harvard Business School, 1993), 4.

15. Peter Landers and Yumiko Ono, "A Japanese Web Star Takes a Wild Tumble; Can He Rise Again?" *The Wall Street Journal*, 28 April 2000, A1.

16. Bob Parks, "25,000 Minds Are Better Than One: Executives at Stagnating Appliance-Maker Whirlpool Turned to Employees to Find Entirely New Market," *Business 2.0 Media Inc.*, 20 May 2003.

17. Amy C. Edmondson, "Framing for Learning: Lessons in Successful Technology Implementation," working paper 02-094, Harvard Business School, Boston, 2002.

18. Philip Gourevitch, "Alone in the Dark," *The New Yorker*, 8 September 2003, 62.

19. Recounted in Dorothy Leonard, *Wellsprings of Knowledge: Building and Sustaining the Sources of Innovation* (Boston: Harvard Business School Press, 1998), 53.

20. William Langewiesche, "Columbia's Last Flight," *The Atlantic Monthly*, November 2003, 77. Emphasis added.

21. Ibid., 73.

22. Ibid., 77.

23. Richard E. Nisbett, *The Geography of Thought: How Asians and Westerners Think Differently . . . and Why* (New York: The Free Press, 2003).

24. For a discussion of the power of minority opinion, see Charlan Nemeth and Pamela Owens, "Making Work Groups More Effective: The Value of Minority Dissent," in *Handbook of Work Group Psychology*, ed. M. A. West (New York: John Wiley, 1996).

25. Langewiesche, "Columbia's Last Flight," 82.

Chapter 6

1. Peter Waldman, "Resigning in Protest, a Career Diplomat Turns Peace Envoy," *The Wall Street Journal*, 1 April 2003, A1.

2. Sometimes the severing of ties is involuntary. William Niskanen was chief economist at Ford Motor Co. at a time (1980) when Ford was seeking protectionist legislation. Niskanen's person beliefs held free trade in high esteem. He was unceremoniously fired. The company's CFO told him "the people who do well wait until they hear their superiors express their views. Then they add something in support of those views." David Halberstam, *The Reckoning* (New York: William Morrow, 1986), 610.

3. Solomon Asch, "Effects of Group Pressure upon the Modification and Distortion of Judgments," in *Groups, Leadership and Men*, ed. H. Guetzkow (Pittsburgh, PA: Carnegie Press, 1951).

4. Teresa M. Amabile, *Creativity in Context* (Boulder, CO: Westview, 1996).

5. Maggie Mahar, *Bull! A History of the Boom, 1982–1999* (New York: Harper Business, 2003), 225.

6. Irving Janis, *Groupthink*, 2d ed. (Boston: Houghton Mifflin, 1982).

7. Po Bronson, "Instant Company," *New York Times Magazine*, 11 July 1999.

8. Romesh Ratnesar and Joel Stein, "Silicon Valley: The Second Wave," *Time*, 27 September 1999.

9. Warren Bennis and Patricia Biederman, *Organizing Genius: The Secrets of Creative Collaboration* (Reading, MA: Addison-Wesley, 1997), 83.

10. Dorothy Leonard and Walter Swap, *When Sparks Fly: Igniting Creativity in Groups* (Boston: Harvard Business School Press, 1999), 182–183.

11. Associated Press, "NASA Promises to Break Culture of Silence," <http://cnn.com/2003/TECHspace/07/27/sprj.colu.nasa.culture.ap/index.html> (accessed 17 December 2003).

12. Etienne Wenger, Richard McDermott, and William M. Snyder, *Cultivating Communities of Practice* (Boston: Harvard Business School Press, 2002).

13. This quotation and the details that follow about the World Bank Thematic Groups are taken from William Fulmer, "The World Bank and Knowledge Management: The Case of the Urban Services Thematic Group," Case 801-157 (Boston: Harvard Business School, 2001).

14. John Seely Brown and Paul Duguid, *The Social Life of Information* (Boston: Harvard Business School Press, 2002).

15. Ratnesar and Stein, "Silicon Valley: The Second Wave."

16. Dorothy Leonard and Liz Kind, "Garage.com," Case 601-064 (Boston: Harvard Business School, 2001).

17. Mark McDonald, "E-mania Spreads to India," *San Jose Mercury News*, 7 February 2000, 4E.

18. Dorothy Leonard, *Wellsprings of Knowledge: Building and Sustaining the Sources of Innovation* (Boston: Harvard Business School Press, 1998), 7.

19. Spear notes that an ABI Informs keyword search turned up 1,428 articles referencing just-in-time from 1983 to 1997. Steven Spear, "The Essence of Just-in-Time: Embedding Diagnostic Tests in Work-Systems to Achieve Operational Excellence," *Production, Planning and Control* 13, no. 8 (2002): 754–767.

20. Steven Spear and H. Kent Bowen, "Decoding the DNA of the Toyota Production System," *Harvard Business Review*, September–October 1999, 97.

21. Ibid.

22. Ibid., 98.

23. Ibid., 103.

24. TiE Web site, <http://www.tie.org> (accessed 15 December 2003).

Chapter 7

1. Jack Welch, interview by Chris Bartlett, Harvard Business School, 1999.

2. Joann S. Lublin, "Even Top Executives Could Use Mentors to Benefit Careers," *The Wall Street Journal*, 1 July 2003, B1.

3. "Market Value," Exodus Communications, March 20, 1998–June 24, 2002, Thomson Financial Datastream, <http://www.thomson.com/financial/financial.jsp> (accessed 11 August 2003).

4. Melanie Warner, "The Indians of Silicon Valley," *Fortune*, 15 May 2000, 368.

5. Belle Rose Ragins and John L. Cotton, "Mentor Functions and Outcomes: A Comparison of Men and Women in Formal and Informal Mentoring Relationships," *Journal of Applied Psychology* 84, no. 4 (1999): 529–550.

6. However, since people tend to select individuals who are similar to themselves, formal mentoring programs are sometimes necessary in order to provide mentors to minority populations in the organization. Ragins and Cotton, "Mentor Functions and Outcomes," 529–550.

7. In our small sample of 35 companies, of the 25 still standing in 2001 (4 had been acquired, 6 had folded), 15 of the founders who started with the title of CEO continued to hold that position, and 10 had been replaced. Five of 8 VC-backed companies were no longer led by the founder we had interviewed a year earlier; 10 of the 15 companies coached by mentor capitalists still had an original founder at the helm. The 2 surviving companies that had worked with incubators were still headed by their original CEO-founders. It would be going well beyond our data to make too much of the apparent differences, but the trend toward CEO succession in the VC-backed companies is noteworthy. Are mentor capitalists more "caring" or protective of their charges? Are the VCs more protective of the *company* and the firm's investment? Or is it really a question of experience? The venture capitalists in our sample tended to have somewhat more industry and start-up experience than the mentor capitalists, and far more than the incubator coaches. Perhaps they realized sooner that for a company to grow, it would have to outgrow its inexperienced founders.

8. For further reading on barriers to knowledge transfer, see Thomas H. Davenport and Laurence Prusak, *Working Knowledge: How Organizations Manage What They Know* (Boston: Harvard Business School Press, 1998).

9. The variation across the companies we studied in terms of location, size, stage of development, and so forth precluded any "objective" measure of success.

10. The correlations averaged about .40, significant at $p < .05$.

11. For an in-depth examination of the difficulty of managing innovative ventures within a large corporation, see Michael L. Tushman and Charles O'Reilly III, *Winning Through Innovation: A Practical Guide to Leading Organizational Change and Renewal* (Boston: Harvard Business School Press, 1997).

12. Dorothy Leonard and David Kiron, "Knowledge Management and Learning at NASA and the Jet Propulsion Laboratory," Case 603-062 (Boston: Harvard Business School, 2002), 12.

13. See, for example, Walter Swap et al., "Using Mentoring and Storytelling to Transfer Knowledge in the Workplace," *Journal of Management Information Systems* 18, no. 1 (2001), 95–114. Storytelling as a knowledge transfer device is becoming increasingly popular in organizations.

14. Johanna M. Hurstak and Oscar Hauptman, "E-L Products (A,B,C)," Cases 691-013, 014, 015 (Boston: Harvard Business School, 1992).

15. John D. Bransford, Ann L. Brown, and Rodney R. Cocking, eds. *How People Learn: Brain, Mind, Experience and School* (Washington, DC: National Academy Press, National Research Council Commission on Behavioral and Social Sciences and Education, 2000), 11.

16. Gabriel Szulanski, "Exploring Internal Stickiness: Impediments to the Transfer of Best Practice Within the Firm," *Strategic Management Journal* 17 (Winter Special Issue, 1996): 27–43.

17. Dorothy Leonard and Susaan Straus, "Putting Your Company's Whole Brain to Work," *Harvard Business Review*, July–August 1997, 110–122.

18. These techniques are derived from our field research. Some of them are more specific examples of the four mechanisms first identified by Ikujiro Nonaka and Hirotaka Takeuchi in *The Knowledge-Creating Company* (New York: Oxford University Press, 1995): Socialization (creating tacit knowledge, such as shared mental models, through experience); Internalization (creating tacit knowledge through practice); Externalization (making tacit knowledge explicit through dialogue and reflection); and Combination (structuring and making explicit knowledge systematic). The model was later elaborated by Ikujiro Nonaka, Ryoko Toyama, and Noboru Konno, "SECI, Ba and Leadership: A Unified Model of Dynamic Knowledge Creation," in *Managing Industrial Knowledge*, eds. Ikujiro Nonaka and David Teece (London: Sage Publications, 2001).

19. Pamela M. Auble, Jeffrey J. Franks, and Salvatore A. Soraci, "Effort Toward Comprehension: Elaboration or 'Aha'?" *Memory and Cognition* 7 (1978): 426–434.

20. The patterns are often heavily contextualized, that is, they represent what some have called "situated" knowledge that draws upon local cues for meaning. John Seely Brown and Paul Duguid, *The Social Life of Information* (Boston: Harvard Business School Press, 2002).

21. Shelley E. Taylor, "The Interface of Cognitive and Social Psychology," in *Cognition, Social Behavior, and the Environment*, ed. J. Harvey (Hillsdale, NJ: Lawrence Erlbaum, 1981), 189–211.

22. Swap et al., "Using Mentoring and Storytelling to Transfer Knowledge in the Workplace," 106–107.

23. Ibid., 95–114.

24. Dorothy Leonard and Walter Swap, "Gurus in the Garage," *Harvard Business Review*, November–December 2000, 78.

25. Larry W. Brooks and Donald F. Dansereau, "Transfer of Information: An Instructional Perspective," in *Transfer of Learning: Contemporary Research and Applications*, eds. Stephen M. Cormier and Joseph D. Hagman (New York: Academic Press, 1987), 129.

Chapter 8

1. The authors gratefully acknowledge Brian DeLacey, who coined this useful term.

2. David A. Garvin, *Learning in Action: A Guide to Putting the Learning Organization to Work* (Boston: Harvard Business School Press, 2000). See also Daniel A. Levinthal and James G. March, "The Myopia of Learning," *Strategic Management Journal* 14 (1993): 105, who discuss exploration as the alternative strategy to exploitation. In this book we are not dealing with exploitation. Experimentation is a form of exploration: "the pursuit of new knowledge, of things that might come to be known."

3. Academic researchers characterize the more modest aims of such experimentation as "local search," that is, a search for solutions that is limited to fairly well understood parameters.

4. The ability of potential users to guide development through traditional market research is limited when the product or service being investigated is without precedent. See Dorothy Leonard and Jeffrey F. Rayport, "Spark Innovation Through Empathic Design," *Harvard Business Review*, November–December 1997, 103–113.

5. Gerald Zaltman, *How Customers Think: Essential Insights into the Mind of the Market* (Boston: Harvard Business School Press, 2003), 53.

6. See Stefan Thomke, *Experimentation Matters: Unlocking the Potential of New Technologies for Innovation* (Boston: Harvard Business School Press, 2003), for examples of how early experimentation using simulation has saved companies such as Toyota much in downstream costs.

7. Alan MacCormack, Roberto Verganti, and Marco Iansiti, "Developing Products on 'Internet Time': The Anatomy of a Flexible Development Process," *Management Science* 47, no. 1 (2001): 146.

8. Steven Spear, "The Essence of Just-in-Time: Embedding Diagnostic Tests in Work-Systems to Achieve Operational Excellence," *Production, Planning and Control* 13, no. 8 (2002): 754–767. In this paper, Spear demonstrates with paired case studies the superior performance that results from the application of the active learning techniques.

9. Tom Kelley, with Jonathan Littman, *The Art of Innovation* (New York: Random House, 2001).

10. See, for example, Michael Schrage, *Serious Play: How the World's Best Companies Simulate to Innovate* (Boston: Harvard Business School Press, 1999); and Dorothy Leonard, *Wellsprings of Knowledge: Building and Sustaining the Sources of Innovation* (Boston: Harvard Business School Press, 1998).

11. See Stefan Thomke, "Bank of America (A)," Case 9-603-022 (Boston: Harvard Business School, 2002), for a full discussion of these experiments.

12. Stefan Thomke, *Experimentation Matters: Unlocking the Potential of New Technologies for Innovation* (Boston: Harvard Business School Press, 2003), 34–35.

13. Research consistently shows that learning is enhanced more by positive reinforcers than by negative. See, for example, the classic work by B. F. Skinner, *The Behavior of Organisms* (New York: Appleton-Century-Croft, 1938).

14. 3M, for example, eked out an existence for twelve years, lurching from one possible value proposition to another, before becoming profitable. And see Dorothy Leonard and Brian DeLacey, "Collabrys, Inc.: The Evolution of a Startup," Case 603-064 (Boston: Harvard Business School, 2002), for an up-close description of a modern-day company morphing its way to security.

Chapter 9

1. The critical incident technique has been used to measure competencies and to identify tacit dimensions of knowledge acquired in solving real-world problems. See Robert Sternberg et al., *Practical Intelligence in Everyday Life* (Cambridge, UK: Cambridge University Press, 2000).

2. See Eric von Hippel, "Sticky Information and the Locus of Problem-Solving: Implications for Innovation," *Management Science* 4 (1994); and Eric von Hippel and Marcie Tyre, "How Learning Is Done: Problem Identification in Novel Process Equipment," *Research Policy* 24 (1995): 1–12.

3. We observed this particularly in those companies hatched in incubators.

4. See Stefan Thomke, *Experimentation Matters: Unlocking the Potential of New Technologies for Innovation* (Boston: Harvard Business School Press, 2003), 149–150, 157.

5. Marcella Bombardieri, "E-School Would Teach Medicine from Afar," *Boston Globe*, 30 July 2003, A1, A12.

6. For example, the correlation between the coach and entrepreneur's combined ratings of the company's success compared to expectations and overall alignment, as judged by both parties, was .41 ($p < .05$).

7. For example, the correlation between the amount of prior experience coaching start-ups and the combined ratings of the company's success by both coach and entrepreneur was .45 ($p < .05$).

8. Correlations of .45 and .48, respectively. Because of a reduced sample size (it was unrealistic to ask coaches in India or Hong Kong about coaches in Silicon Valley or Boston, and vice versa), these correlations, while substantial, did not reach conventional levels of statistical significance ($p < .13$ and .10, respectively).

9. Noel M. Tichy and Stratford Sherman, *Control Your Destiny or Someone Else Will: How Jack Welch Is Making General Electric the World's Most Competitive Corporation* (New York: Currency Doubleday, 1993), 130.

10. Thomas A. Stewart, *The Wealth of Knowledge* (New York: Currency Doubleday, 2001). Chapter 8 makes a very similar point about what he terms "knowledge projects."

11. Kathleen Valley, "Heidi Roizen," Case 9-800-228 (Boston: Harvard Business School, 2000), 8.

12. Diane Brady, "Crashing GE's Glass Ceiling," *BusinessWeek*, 28 July 2003, 77.

13. Herminia Ibarra, *Working Identity: Unconventional Strategies for Reinventing Your Career* (Boston: Harvard Business School Press, 2003), xii.

14. Sharon Waxman, "Quiet Off the Set Too," *Washington Post*, 10 September 2003, C10 ff.

15. Ibarra, *Working Identity*, xii.

BIBLIOGRAPHY

Amabile, Teresa M. 1996. *Creativity in Context*. Boulder, CO: Westview.

Aoki, Naomi. 2003. "The crusader." *Boston Globe Sunday Magazine*, 25 May.

Asch, Solomon. 1951. "Effects of group pressure upon the modification and distortion of judgments." In H. Guetzkow, ed. *Groups, Leadership and Men*. Pittsburgh, PA: Carnegie Press.

Associated Press. 2003. "NASA promises to break culture of silence." <http://cnn.com/2003/TECHspace/07/27/sprj.colu.nasa.culture.ap/index.html> (accessed 13 March 2004).

Auble, Pamela M., Jeffrey J. Franks, and Salvatore A. Soraci. 1978. "Effort toward comprehension: Elaboration or 'aha'?" *Memory and Cognition* 7, 426–434.

Austin, James E. 2000. *The Collaboration Challenge: How Nonprofits and Businesses Succeed Through Strategic Alliances*. San Francisco: Jossey-Bass.

Austin, James. 2001. "Timberland and community involvement." Case 796–156. Boston: Harvard Business School.

Ballard, Mary E., and J. Rose Wiest. 1996. "Mortal Kombat™: The effects of violent video game play on males' hostility and cardiovascular responding." *Journal of Applied Social Psychology* 26, 717–730.

Bartlett, Christopher A., and Afroze Mohammed. 1994. "3M Optical Systems: Managing corporate entrepreneurship." Case 395-017. Boston: Harvard Business School.

Begley, Sharon. 2003. "Science's big query: What can we know, and what can't we?" *The Wall Street Journal*, 30 May.

Bennis, Warren, and Patricia Biederman. 1997. *Organizing Genius: The Secrets of Creative Collaboration*. Reading, MA: Addison-Wesley.

Bombardieri, Marcella. 2003. "E-school would teach medicine from afar." *Boston Globe*, 30 July, A1, A12.

Brady, Diane. 2003. "Crashing GE's glass ceiling." *BusinessWeek*, 28 July, 76–77.

Bransford, John D., Ann L. Brown, and Rodney R. Cocking, eds. 2000. *How People Learn: Brain, Mind, Experience and School.* Washington, DC: National Academy Press, National Research Council Commission on Behavioral and Social Sciences and Education, 125.

Bronson, Po. 1999. "Instant company." *New York Times Magazine,* 11 July.

Brooks, Larry W., and Donald F. Dansereau. 1987. "Transfer of information: An instructional perspective." In Stephen M. Cormier and Joseph D. Hagman, *Transfer of Learning: Contemporary Research and Applications.* New York: Academic Press.

Brown, John Seely, and Paul Duguid. 2002. *The Social Life of Information.* Boston: Harvard Business School Press.

Christensen, Clayton. 2003. *The Innovator's Dilemma: When New Technologies Cause Great Firms to Fail.* Boston: Harvard Business School Press.

Chuang, Tamara. 2003. "Virtual war turns real: Quicksilver Software develops war game exclusively for U.S. Army use." *Orange County Register,* 7 May.

Cialdini, Robert. 2001. *Influence: Science and Practice,* 4th ed. Boston: Allyn and Bacon.

Cohen, Don, and Laurence Prusak. 2001. *In Good Company: How Social Capital Makes Organizations Work.* Boston: Harvard Business School Press.

Columbia Accident Investigation Board. 2003. *Final Report.* Washington, DC: Government Printing Office.

Cross, Rob, Wayne Baker, and Andrew Parker. 2003. "What creates energy in organizations?" *MIT Sloan Management Review* 44, no. 4: 51–57.

Dade, Corey. 2003. "The experience of loss: City offer thins ranks." *Boston Globe,* 24 June, B1, B8.

Davenport, Thomas H., and Laurence Prusak. 1998. *Working Knowledge: How Organizations Manage What They Know.* Boston: Harvard Business School Press.

DeLong, David. 2004. *Lost Knowledge: Confronting the Threat of an Aging Workforce.* New York: Oxford University Press.

Dohm, Arlene. 2000. "Gauging the labor force effects of retiring baby-boomers." *Monthly Labor Review,* 24 July.

Dreyfus, Hubert L., and Stuart E. Dreyfus. 1986. *Mind over Machine.* New York: The Free Press.

Drucker, Peter. 1964. *Managing for Results: Economic Tasks and Risk-Taking Decisions.* New York: Harper & Row.

Dwyer, Jim. 2003. "With the 101st Airborne, in central Iraq, March 27." *New York Times,* 28 March, 1, C5.

Edmondson, Amy C. 2002. "Framing for learning: Lessons in successful technology implementation." Working paper 02-094. Boston: Harvard Business School.

Ericsson, K. Anders. 1996. "The acquisition of expert performance: An introduction to some of the issues." In K. A. Ericsson, *The Road to Excellence: The Acquisition of Expert Performance in the Arts and Sciences, Sports, and Games.* Mahwah, NJ: Lawrence Erlbaum.

Ervin, Sandra. 2003. "Urban warfare simulation helps train company commanders." *National Defense Magazine,* February.

Foreman, Judy. 2003. "A conversation with Paul Ekman: The 43 facial muscles that reveal even the most fleeting emotions." *New York Times*, 5 August.

Foust, Dean, Frederick F. Jespersen, Fred Katzenberg, Amy Barrett, and Roger O. Crockett. 2003. "The best performers—Ouch." *BusinessWeek*, 24 March.

Fulmer, William. 2001. "The World Bank and knowledge management: The case of the Urban Services Thematic Group." Case 801-157. Boston: Harvard Business School.

Garvin, David A. 2000. *Learning in Action: A Guide to Putting the Learning Organization to Work*. Boston: Harvard Business School Press.

Gauthier, Isabel, Michael J. Tarr, Adam W. Anderson, Pawel Skudlarshi, and John C. Gore. 1999. "Activation of the middle fusiform 'face area' increases with expertise in recognizing novel objects." *Nature Neuroscience* 2, no. 6 (June): 568–573.

Gawande, Atul. 2002. "The learning curve." *The New Yorker*, 28 January, 52–61.

Gilbert, Susan. 2003. "For depression, the family doctor may be the first choice but not the best." *New York Times*, 24 June.

Gompers, Paul A., and Josh Lerner. 2001. *The Money of Invention: How Venture Capital Creates New Wealth*. Boston: Harvard Business School Press.

Gourevitch, Philip. 2003. "Alone in the dark." *The New Yorker*, 8 September.

Green, C. Shawn, and Daphne Bavelier. 2003. "Action video game modifies visual selective attention." *Nature* 423 (29 May): 534–537.

Greenberg, Beth. 2003. "War games: Hollywood helps with training." *Boston Globe*, 22 April, F13.

Halberstam, David. 1986. *The Reckoning*. New York: William Morrow.

Hampton, Debra. 1994, "Expertise: The true essence of nursing art." *Advances in Nursing Science* 17, no. 1: 15–24.

Hargadon, Andrew. 2003. *How Breakthroughs Happen: The Surprising Truth About How Companies Innovate*. Boston: Harvard Business School Press.

Hechinger, John. 2000. "Stay in your dorm and score 'dough for your dot-com' " *The Wall Street Journal*, 20 April, A1, A8.

Hurstak, Johanna M., and Oscar Hauptman. 1992. "E-L Products (A,B,C)." Cases 691-013, 014, 015. Boston: Harvard Business School.

Ibarra, Herminia. 1992. "Homophily and differential returns: Sex differences in network structure and access in an advertising firm." *Administrative Science Quarterly* 37, no. 3: 422–447.

Ibarra, Herminia. 1993. "Personal networks of women and minorities in management: A conceptual framework." *Academy of Management Review* 18, no. 1: 56–87.

Ibarra, Herminia. 2002. "How to stay stuck in the wrong career." *Harvard Business Review*, December, 40–47.

Ibarra, Herminia. 2003. *Working Identity: Unconventional Strategies for Reinventing Your Career*. Boston: Harvard Business School Press.

Janis, Irving. 1982. *Groupthink*. 2d ed. Boston: Houghton Mifflin.

Kanter, Rosabeth Moss. 1989. *When Giants Learn to Dance: Mastering the Challenges of Strategy, Management, and Careers in the 1990s*. New York: Simon and Schuster.

Kelley, Tom, with Jonathan Littman. 2001. *The Art of Innovation*. New York: Random House.

Khanna, Tarun, and Krishna Palepu. 1997. "Why focused strategies may be wrong for emerging markets." *Harvard Business Review*, July–August, 41–54.

Klein, Gary. 1998. *Sources of Power*. Cambridge, MA: MIT Press.

L'Allier, James J. 2003. "The value of performance simulations." *Chief Learning Officer*, May. Accessed from the Web at <http://www.clomedia.com/content/tem plates/clo_feature.asp?articleid=163&zoneid=29> (accessed 14 December 2003).

Landers, Peter, and Yumiko Ono. 2000. "A Japanese Web star takes a wild tumble; can he rise again?" *The Wall Street Journal*, 28 April, A1.

Langewiesche, William. 2003. "Columbia's last flight." *The Atlantic Monthly*, November, 58–87.

Lave, Jean, and Etienne Wenger. 1991. *Situated Learning—Legitimate Peripheral Participation*. Cambridge, UK: Cambridge University Press.

Leonard, Dorothy. 1998. *Wellsprings of Knowledge: Building and Sustaining the Sources of Innovation*. Boston: Harvard Business School Press.

Leonard, Dorothy, and Melissa Dailey. 2002. "Retirement at JPL." Video Case 603-082. Boston: Harvard Business School.

Leonard, Dorothy, and Brian DeLacey. 2002. "Collabrys, Inc.: The evolution of a startup." Case 603-064. Boston: Harvard Business School.

Leonard, Dorothy, and Liz Kind. 2001. "Garage.com." Case 601-064. Boston: Harvard Business School.

Leonard, Dorothy, and David Kiron. 2002. "Knowledge management and learning at NASA and the Jet Propulsion Laboratory." Case 603-062. Boston: Harvard Business School.

Leonard, Dorothy, and Jeffrey F. Rayport. 1997. "Spark innovation through empathic design." *Harvard Business Review*, November–December, 103–113.

Leonard, Dorothy, and Susaan Straus. 1997. "Putting your company's whole brain to work." *Harvard Business Review*, July–August, 110–122.

Leonard, Dorothy, and Walter Swap. 1999. *When Sparks Fly: Igniting Creativity in Groups*. Boston: Harvard Business School Press.

Leonard, Dorothy, and Walter Swap. 2000. "Gurus in the garage." *Harvard Business Review*, November–December, 71–82.

Leonard, Dorothy, and Walter C. Swap. 2001. "The value of 'been there, done that.'" In Frances Hesselbein, Marshall Goldsmith, and Iain Somerville, eds. *Leading for Innovation and Organizing for Results*. San Francisco: Jossey-Bass, 165–176.

Leonard, Dorothy, and George Thill. 1993. "Hewlett-Packard: Singapore (A)." Case 694-035. Boston: Harvard Business School.

Leonard, Dorothy, Brian DeLacey, and Melissa Dailey. 2003. "Best Buy Co. Inc. (A): An innovator's journey." Case 604-043. Boston: Harvard Business School.

Leonard-Barton, Dorothy, and Gary Pisano. 1990. "Monsanto's march into biotechnology (A)." Case 690-009, Rev. 1/27/92. Boston: Harvard Business School.

Leonard-Barton, Dorothy, and Deepak K. Sinha. 1993. "Developer-user interaction and user satisfaction in internal technology transfer." *Academy of Management Journal* 36, no. 5 (October): 1125–1139.

Levinthal, Daniel A., and James G. March. 1993. "The myopia of learning." *Strategic Management Journal* 14: 95–112.

Lublin, Joann S. 2003. "Even top executives could use mentors to benefit careers." *The Wall Street Journal*, 1 July.

Luchins, Abraham S. 1942. "Mechanization in problem solving." *Psychological Monographs* 54, no. 248.

MacCormack, Alan, Roberto Verganti, and Marco Iansiti. 2001. "Developing products on 'Internet time': The anatomy of a flexible development process." *Management Science* 47, no. 1 (January): 133–150.

Mahar, Maggie. 2003. *Bull! A History of the Boom, 1982–1999*. New York: Harper Business.

"Market value," Exodus Communications, March 20, 1998–June 24, 2002, Thomson Financial Datastream, <http://www.thomson.com/financial/financial.jsp> (accessed 11 August 2003).

Matthews, Robert. 2000. "Six degrees of separation." *World Link*, January/February.

McDonald, Mark. 2000. "E-mania spreads to India." *San Jose Mercury News*, 7 February.

Nemeth, Charlan, and Pamela Owens. 1996. "Making work groups more effective: The value of minority dissent." In M. A. West, ed. *Handbook of Work Group Psychology*. New York: John Wiley.

Nisbett, Richard E. 2003. *The Geography of Thought: How Asians and Westerners Think Differently . . . and Why*. New York: Free Press.

Nisbett, Richard E., and Timothy DeCamp Wilson. 1977. "Telling more than we can know: Verbal reports on mental processes." *Psychological Review*, 84, no. 3, 231–259.

Nonaka, Ikujiro, and Hirotaka Takeuchi 1995. *The Knowledge-Creating Company*. New York: Oxford University Press.

Nonaka, Ikujiro, Ryoko Toyama, and Noboru Konno. 2001. "SECI, Ba and leadership: A unified model of dynamic knowledge creation." In Ikujiro Nonaka and David Teece, eds. *Managing Industrial Knowledge*. London, UK: Sage Publications.

Om, Malik. 2001. "Why Vinod Khosla may be the best venture capitalist on the planet." *Red Herring*, 13 February, 43–47.

Osherow, Neal. 1999. "Making sense of the nonsensical: An analysis of Jonestown." In Elliot Aronson, ed. *Readings About the Social Animal*. 8th ed. New York: Worth.

Parks, Bob. 2003. "25,000 minds are better than one: Executives at stagnating appliance-maker Whirlpool turned to employees to find entirely new market." *Business 2.0 Media Inc.*, 20 May.

Pisano, Gary P., Richard M. J. Bohmer, and Amy C. Edmondson. 2001. "Organizational differences in rates of learning: Evidence from the adoption of minimally invasive cardiac surgery." *Management Science* 47, no. 6: 752–768.

Pulliam, Susan. 2003. "Over the line: A staffer ordered to commit fraud balked, then caved." The Wall Street Journal, 23 June, A1.

Ragins, Belle Rose, and John L. Cotton. 1991. "Easier said than done: Gender differences in perceived barriers to gaining a mentor." *Academy of Management Journal* 34, no. 4: 939–951.

Ragins, Belle Rose, and John L. Cotton. 1999. "Mentor functions and outcomes: A comparison of men and women in formal and informal mentoring relationships." *Journal of Applied Psychology* 84, no. 4: 529–550.

Ratnesar, Romesh, and Joel Stein. 1999. "Silicon Valley: The second wave." *Time*, 27 September.

Reber, Arthur S. 1989. "Implicit learning and tacit knowledge," *Journal of Experimental Psychology* 118: 219–235.

Richman, H. B., F. Gobet, J. J. Staszewski, and H. A. Simon. 1996. "Perceptual and memory processes in the acquisition of expert performance: The EPAM model." In K. A. Ericsson, *The Road to Excellence: The Acquisition of Expert Performance in the Arts and Sciences, Sports, and Games.* Mahwah, NJ: Lawrence Erlbaum.

Rokeach, Milton. 1970. *Beliefs, Attitudes and Values.* San Francisco: Jossey-Bass.

Rosenblatt, Allan D., and James T. Thickstun. 1994. "Intuition and consciousness." *Psychoanalytic Quarterly* 63: 696–714.

Saxenian, AnnaLee. 1994. *Regional Advantage: Culture and Competition in Silicon Valley and Route 128.* Cambridge, MA: Harvard University Press.

Schraagen, Jan Maarten. 1993. "How experts solve a novel problem in experimental design." *Cognitive Science* 17: 285–309.

Schrage, Michael. 1999. *Serious Play: How the World's Best Companies Simulate to Innovate.* Boston: Harvard Business School Press.

Shih, Margaret, Todd Pittinsky, and Nalini Ambady. 1999. "Shifts in women's quantitative performance in response to implicit sociocultural identification." *Psychological Science* 10: 80–83.

Simon, Herbert A., and W. G. Chase. 1973. "Skill in chess." *American Scientist* 61: 394–403.

Skinner, Burris F. 1938. *The Behavior of Organisms.* New York: Appleton-Century-Croft.

Spear, Steven. 2002. "The essence of just-in-time: Embedding diagnostic tests in work-systems to achieve operational excellence." *Production, Planning and Control* 13, no. 8: 754-767.

Spear, Steven, and H. Kent Bowen. 1999. "Decoding the DNA of the Toyota production system," *Harvard Business Review*, September–October, 96–108.

Sternberg, Robert J., George B. Forsythe, Jennifer Hedlund, Joseph A. Horvath, Richard K. Wagner, Wendy M. Williams, Scott A. Snook, and Elene Grigorenko. 2000. *Practical Intelligence in Everyday Life.* Cambridge, UK: Cambridge University Press.

Stewart, Thomas A. 2001. *The Wealth of Knowledge.* New York: Currency Doubleday.

Stiglitz, Joseph E. 2002. *Globalization and Its Discontents.* New York: Norton.

Strege, John. 1997. *Tiger: A Biography of Tiger Woods.* New York: Broadway Books.

Swap, Walter, Dorothy Leonard, Mimi Shields, and Lisa Abrams. 2001. "Using mentoring and storytelling to transfer knowledge in the workplace." *Journal of Management Information Systems* 18, no. 1 (Summer): 95–114.

Szulanski, Gabriel. 1996. "Exploring internal stickiness: Impediments to the transfer of best practice within the firm." *Strategic Management Journal* 17 (Winter Special Issue): 27–43.

Taylor, Shelley E. 1981. "The interface of cognitive and social psychology." In J. Harvey, ed. *Cognition, Social Behavior, and the Environment*. Hillsdale, NJ: Lawrence Erlbaum. 189–211.

Thomke, Stefan. 2002. "Bank of America (A)." Case 9-603-022. Boston: Harvard Business School.

Thomke, Stefan. 2003. *Experimentation Matters: Unlocking the Potential of New Technologies for Innovation*. Boston: Harvard Business School Press.

Thomke, Stefan, and Ashok Nimgade. 2001. "BMW AG: The Digital Car Project (A)." Case 699-044. Boston: Harvard Business School.

Tichy, Noel M., and Stratford Sherman. 1993. *Control Your Destiny or Someone Else Will: How Jack Welch Is Making General Electric the World's Most Competitive Corporation*. New York: Currency Doubleday.

Tripsas, Mary, and Giovanni Gavetti. 2000. "Capabilities, cognition, and inertia: Evidence from digital imaging." *Strategic Management Journal* 21: 1147–1161.

Tushman, Michael L., and Charles O'Reilly III. 1997. *Winning Through Innovation: A Practical Guide to Leading Organizational Change and Renewal*. Boston: Harvard Business School Press.

Valley, Kathleen. 2000. "Heidi Roizen." Case 9-800-228. Boston: Harvard Business School.

Veverka, Mark. 2002. "Pied piper of the 'Net: How John Doerr sparked the Internet boom and brought home big profits." *Barron's* 82, no. 23: 19–22.

Vicente, Kim J., and JoAnne H. Want. 1998. "An ecological theory of expertise effects in memory recall." *Psychological Review* 105, no. 1: 33–57.

von Hippel, Eric. 1994. "Sticky information and the locus of problem-solving: Implications for innovation." *Management Science* 4.

von Hippel, Eric, and Marcie Tyre. 1995. "How learning is done: Problem identification in novel process equipment." *Research Policy* 24: 1–12.

Waldman, Amy. 2003. "Guilty or not, U.S. is blamed in mosque blast" *New York Times*, 2 July, A1, A10.

Waldman, Peter. 2003. "Resigning in protest, a career diplomat turns peace envoy." *The Wall Street Journal*, 1 April.

Warner, Melanie. 2000. "The Indians of Silicon Valley." *Fortune*, 15 May.

Watts, Duncan, and Steven Strogatz. 1998. "Collective dynamics of small-world networks." *Nature* 393: 440–442.

Waxman, Sharon. 2003. "Quiet off the set too." *Washington Post*, 10 September, C10 ff.

Wenger, Etienne, Richard McDermott, and William M. Snyder. 2002. *Cultivating Communities of Practice*. Boston: Harvard Business School Press.

Yost, Pete. 2002. "Senate report: Enron board ignored evidence." Associated Press, 7 July. <http://dukeemployees.com/deregulation1902.shtml#board> (accessed 19 December 2003).

Zaltman, Gerald. 2003. *How Customers Think: Essential Insights into the Mind of the Market*. Boston: Harvard Business School Press.

Zartman, I. William, ed. 1994. *International Multilateral Negotiation: Approaches to the Management of Complexity*. San Francisco: Jossey-Bass.

INDEX

ABOUT THE AUTHORS

DOROTHY LEONARD is the William J. Abernathy Professor of Business Administration emerita at Harvard Business School. She served on the Harvard faculty for twenty years and before that taught at the Sloan School of Management, Massachusetts Institute of Technology, for three years. Her teaching, research, and consulting for major governments and corporations have focused on innovation, creativity, new product development, and knowledge transfer. At Harvard Business School, she was a Director of Research and Director of Research and Knowledge Programs for Harvard Business School's nonprofit venture, HBS Interactive. She served on the corporate board of directors for American Management Systems for over a decade and for Guy Gannett Communications until its sale. She has also worked on the advisory boards of small companies and for Daimler-Chrysler.

Her more than one hundred publications appear in academic and practitioner journals and in books about innovation, knowledge assets, and human resource management.* In addition, Professor Leonard has written more than fifty field-based text, video, and multimedia cases used in business school classrooms around the world. She is on several editorial boards and was a senior editor of *Organization Science*. Her book *Wellsprings of Knowledge: Building and Sustaining the Sources of Innovation* was published in 1995 and 1998 by Harvard Business School Press. Harvard Business School Press also published *When Sparks Fly: Igniting Creativity in Groups* (coauthored with husband Walter Swap in 1999). Before obtaining her Ph.D. from Stanford University, she worked in Southeast Asia for ten years as a teacher, journalist, and artist.

WALTER SWAP is Professor of Psychology emeritus and former Chairman of the Psychology Department at Tufts University. He was also a Professor in the Gordon Institute at Tufts, which offers a degree in engineering management to practicing engineers and scientists. Dr. Swap served for nine years as the Dean of the colleges, responsible for all aspects of undergraduate academic life at Tufts. He earned his bachelor's degree at Harvard and his Ph.D. in social psychology at the University of Michigan.

Dr. Swap's professional life has been divided among teaching, research, and administration. He has received two awards for teaching excellence. He was a founding member of the university's innovative Center for Decision Making, where he introduced undergraduates to the complexities of choice and group dynamics, and conducted workshops for midlevel managers from a variety of industries. As dean, he developed centers and programs promoting excellence in teaching, undergraduate advising, critical thinking, and interdisciplinary education.

Dr. Swap is the coauthor, with wife Dorothy Leonard, of *When Sparks Fly: Igniting Creativity in Groups* (1999). Among Dr. Swap's other publications are *Group Decision Making* (1984), numerous book chapters, and articles in professional journals, including *The Journal of Personality and Social Psychology* and *Personality and Social Psychology Bulletin*, on topics including group dynamics, attitude change, personality theory, altruism, and aggression. Dr. Swap is also a runner, gardener, pianist, singer, and amateur composer.

*Some works published under Dorothy Leonard-Barton.